The *Father* NOBODY KNOWS

Other Books by Catherine Fendig

Linking Up

Strangers and Synchronicity

Becoming a Well Woman

Way of the Well Woman

Miracle Breakthrough

The Father Nobody Knows

A True Story of Deception,
DNA, and Redeeming Love

CATHERINE FENDIG

Copyright © 2024 by Catherine Fendig
First Sales Edition: September 2025

All rights reserved. Except as permitted under the U.S. Copyright Act of 1976, no part of this publication may be reproduced, distributed, or transmitted in any form or by any means, stored in a database or retrieval system, without the prior written permission of the publisher.

Cover and interior design by Frame25 Productions
Edited by John Nelson, Bookworks Ltd.
Cover art by Midjourney and Jonathan Friedman

Linkpoint Publishing
P.O. Box 20211
Saint Simons Island, Georgia 31522
catherine@catherinefendig.com

Visit the author at www.catherinefendig.com

Paperback ISBN: 978-09967372-1-0
eBook ISBN: 978-0-9967372-2-7

Library of Congress Control Number: 2025919212

10 9 8 7 6 5 4 3 2 1

Printed in the United States of America

The Father Nobody Knows
is dedicated to

My Father . . .

Author's Note

This book is based on a true story. I have changed some names and identifying details of individuals to protect their privacy; however, every person in this book is aware of this written account. Any similarity to real persons is purely coincidental. I have refrained from writing about my adult children to honor their privacy, and I have compressed some time frames to maintain the integrity of storytelling. The title of this book is inspired by my brother's Tony Award-winning play, *The Me Nobody Knows,* and this variation will become apparent to the reader as the story unfolds.

Acknowledgments

I want to express thanks to the following people for their contributions to *The Father Nobody Knows*:

I will begin with the family I found through DNA testing. Your kindness and care enabled me to persevere on this journey and helped heal my heart. Thank you for the family memories we have made, reunions, dinners, barbeques, weddings, events, and visits. I will be forever grateful for the warmth and welcome you extended to me on this journey of discovery. I am proud to call you family!

To Cap Fendig, my loving husband and friend, whose care, support, and wisdom have contributed significantly to my life. Thank you for being there as I chartered unknown territory, and especially for our early morning talks.

To my children and grandchildren: Christina, Tyler, Mary Ellyse, Brett, David Fendig, Chandler, Kayla, Lulu, David, and Amelia. The joy and inspiration I receive from being a mother and grandmother to you cannot be measured. Thank you for your love and this privilege.

To my parents, Frances and Charles, who taught me so much and did the best they could with what they had. To Irving, my father, I will always think of you and wear your ring. Thank you for being a guiding light and leaving me a wonderful group of relatives to meet and get to know you through them.

And to my brother Steve for your loving care and for filling in some important missing pieces in my life.

To all the Fendigs: our many aunts, uncles, sisters-in-laws, and brothers, nieces, nephews, cousins, second cousins, and family for showing me what it's like to be part of a large family.

To my friend and editor, John Nelson, for his exceptional editing talents, expertise, insights, and keen eye for detail. To Jonathan Friedman for his excellent cover and interior design.

To Ruth, who is actually two of my revered mentors, I offer my deepest gratitude, and to my many teachers near and far, who have shown me another way to think, live, and love.

To my many recovery friends. I'd be lost without you. And thank you to my dog, Abby, for being such a faithful companion during the time it took to write this book. I miss you terribly. You will always have a special place in my heart. Until we meet again.

*"I am not what happened to me,
I am what I choose to become."*
—Carl Jung

*"What lies behind us and what lies before us are
tiny matters compared to what lies within us."*
—Ralph Waldo Emerson

Table of Contents

Prologue   xv

PART ONE: Adopted Identity
1. Once Upon a Time   3
2. Childhood Messages   15
3. Following the Flow   23
4. Parting with the Past   35
5. Traveling on Trust   45
6. Making Connections   63
7. Down and Out in Beverly Hills   77
8. Relationship Nightmare   91
9. Gift of Desperation   103
10. Breakdown and PTSD   111
11. Breakthrough and Recovery   117
12. Love and Self Worth   133
13. Provision and Safety   141
14. Tragedy and Troubles   151
15. Gratitude   165
16. The Art of Surrender   173
17. Overcoming Trials   181
18. Passing the Test   195
19. Wailing Wall Prayer   205
20. Heaven's Gate   215

PART TWO: Genetic Identity

21. Date with Destiny   227
22. Staying True   239
23. A New Life   247
24. The DNA Test   257
25. Who's Your Daddy?   265
26. The Davidic Dynasty   273
27. Cousins or Siblings   287
28. Finding my Father   297
29. Brothers and Sisters   305
30. My Father's Ring   315
31. Rabbi Rachel   323
32. A Shiksa Reunites the Family   331
33. The Closest Link   341
34. Somewhere in Time   347
35. DNA and Memoir Writing   355
36. The Cousin's Table   363
37. No More Secrets   371

PART THREE: Spiritual Identity

38. Finding Me   381
39. Going Deeper   389
40. The Haunted Cabin   397
41. Entertaining Angels Unaware   405
42. The Secret Place   413
43. The Summit   419

Epilogue   447

Prologue

It was time to meet the family I never knew I had, whom I never knew existed until recently, yet we shared the same DNA. My "new" Jewish family was made up of highly educated professional New Yorkers. I took one more anxious look at myself in the hotel mirror before I left my room. Was I dressed right? What would they think of me? Would they dispossess me like my Greek father had? Would I be good enough to be accepted in their eyes? I tried to calm my nerves.

I was a local politician's wife from a sleepy island off South Coastal Georgia, part of the Bible Belt. There were churches on every corner there. I had married into a large "old Island family," Christians who had been part of the area's first settlers. On the Island, I had created a different life that had nothing to do with my past—a life where no one knew my whole story. It was worlds apart from where I was born and how I grew up in a one-bedroom apartment in the Bronx and "dirt poor," as the folks would say in Georgia.

When I first moved to the Island, I discovered road etiquette. On St. Simons Island, you only honk your horn for a life-and-death reason. Otherwise, honking was considered rude. Other Island drivers reminded me immediately if I did that. If someone waited after a red light turned green, you were to wait, too. At most, lightly tap your horn. Do not honk like a New Yorker or as a Yankee!

I stepped out of the hotel and onto Times Square, where bright lights and billboards lit up the evening sky. It reminded me of the familiar sounds of my childhood—incessant honking, a siren off in the distance, the commuter buses with their diesel engines running, and their air brakes pumping as they pulled up to the next bus stop. Then, there was the rhythmic sound of cars clanking over the metal grates, where the underground steam became thicker when it hit the cold air. It was raining, and I could smell the wet asphalt, too. I passed a food cart with the smell of onions and peppers grilling, reminding me that I had been so anxious I forgot to eat lunch. As I walked down the sidewalk, I tried to pick up the New York pace. I needed to hail a cab. I had thirty minutes.

Standing on the sidewalk's edge, I hailed a cab quickly. I was relieved to get out of the rain. When I told the driver the address, he said I had to find another cab since it was near his shift change. I got out and stood again on the sidewalk's edge. After a little while, I flagged down another taxi. I got in the back seat and told him the address. "Sorry, I can't take you. It will run past my shift change," I heard once again.

Now, I was starting to panic. I stood back on the sidewalk, and within a few minutes, I hailed a third cab. I got in and gave the driver the address. "Please don't tell me you are near shift change," I pleaded.

"I am! Sorry, lady," he said apologetically.

I had to wonder if all these turn-downs were a sign. Maybe God didn't want me to connect to this family.

"I must get to this address now. You have to help me," I informed him. He explained that he had to turn in his taxi and could not drive me there. However, he offered to take me to Penn Station on 34th Street, where he promised to find a cab to get me to my destination.

At Penn Station, he pulled up to a cab at the front of a line. He signaled the driver and told me to get into the taxi. He did not charge me, and I was grateful and relieved.

"Greetings!" I recognized the Jamaican accent. He was the fourth cab driver I met in thirty minutes. He was personable and friendly. I exhaled and put my hand to my forehead, shaking my head. Then I smiled back at him.

"Are you troubled?" he asked in a slight Jamaican accent. It was nice to hear his voice after being alone in my thoughts all day and then playing musical chairs with taxis.

"I'm nervous! I am about to meet my biological family for the first time." I didn't tell him that I found them after an exhaustive DNA search or that I feared they might not like me. I had a father who didn't want me and made my childhood hellish. I figured the worst that could happen is I would feel like I didn't belong again. It would hurt, but I have always felt that way. "So I want to be on time."

"Everything is gonna be okay," he reassured me. Then, he shared how he missed Jamaica and had a close relationship with his family. The ride passed quickly, and I felt slightly calmer when it ended.

We pulled up to a beautiful new building on the waterfront with lights from the New York City Skyline in full view. There was valet parking. I handed the driver a big tip, although I don't think you could put a price tag on the comfort he gave me. "Go along. Go discover your family. They are going to love you," he said as I left the cab.

The doorman escorted me into the lobby, where there was a security check and ID clearance. I stepped off the elevator onto the eleventh floor. My family would be on the other side of the next door I walked through. Would I be facing another rejection like how my father treated me my entire life, or would they accept me as family? What if they asked me about my childhood? I didn't want them to know the truth. I took a step forward and opened the door.

PART ONE

Adopted Identity

1

Once Upon a Time

I had locked my grandmother, Bessie, out of the house during a snowstorm, and I did it on purpose. I was about four years old. I was afraid of her. She had a temper. She could be very mean and unpredictable at times. When she left through the front door to get the mail, I pulled a chair over, climbed up, and connected the chain latch. When she returned and found the door locked, she looked through the window and told me to open it. I stood there frozen. "You better let me in, girl! When you do, I'm gonna tan your hide," she commanded in an angry Southern drawl. Then she started kicking the door and yelling at me. The snow was coming down, and it was cold. The more she yelled and threatened me through the door, the less I wanted to open it.

Even at four, I knew I was in a bad spot. I also knew I had to let her inside. So, I climbed back on the chair and unlocked the chain. I prepared for a whipping. Instead, she walked right by me and marched to her room. I could hear her open her tin container of snuff. After she dipped some snuff, she opened a can of her favorite soda, Cherry Coke. Then, she retaliated by not looking at or talking to me for days. I cried and apologized, but there was no mercy. It felt worse than a "tanned hide."

Bessie was born and raised in the Deep South and liked nothing about New York. I felt like that included me. When my parents would talk her into coming for a few weeks to watch me each year, the deal included ordering her soda and snuff. Neither of my parents was lucky in love. Maybe it had all started with their parents, passing their karma on to them and then to me. Bessie, my grandmother, grew up in a small town in Alabama. They lived in poverty. She never went to school, so she could not read or write. When she was a teenager, her older sister responded to an ad on Bessie's behalf. It was in a national magazine for mail-order brides, placed by a Michigan farmer 13 years her senior. The farmer chose Bessie and sent her the train fare to move to Michigan and become his wife. Sight unseen.

My grandmother married Clyde in 1923 and joined his life on the farm in the north. Clyde was a laid-back man from a good, solid family. His family had migrated here from England in the 1600s. Clyde preferred a simple life and was a gentleman. He was getting on in years and was eager to have children. Bessie and Clyde did not waste any time starting a family; in December of 1923, my mother, Frances, was born. Three more siblings followed her shortly after.

From family history, I learned that the winters were harsh on the farm. Bessie was miserable and missed living in a warm climate and resented being away from Alabama and running the house. Frances adored her father, Clyde, and resonated with his calm and tender demeanor. When she was eight years old, Clyde fell ill with pneumonia. Eight days later, he passed away in his sleep at their farmhouse. It was dark outside and snowing. Bessie walked to the neighbor's farmhouse for help. When she returned with the doctor, there was nothing anyone could do to revive him. My mother, at such a young age, was brokenhearted at the loss of her father. He had been her world. Clyde's extended family tried to rally around

Bessie and the children for support. Bessie rejected their efforts and immediately packed up the kids and took a train back to Alabama.

With very little money and no potential income, Bessie moved into a two-room shack on the same dirt road as her brother, Willie. Bessie could not drive, read, or write, and had four children to raise by herself with no income. They lived in extreme poverty. The kids walked to school. My mother took a job handpicking cotton in the fields after school, returning home each day with bleeding fingers. Frances was committed to succeeding at school and leaving the poverty and abuse she experienced in the South behind when she came of age. Despite the challenges growing up, she was elected class president during her senior year in high school.

When she graduated, she joined the Navy and never looked back, hoping to create a new life. It was the beginning of World War II. She was sent to New York for boot camp. While there, she buried her Southern identity and worked on losing her accent. Frances fell in love with New York. To her dismay, after training, she was sent right back to Alabama where she was assigned to work in the PX (post-exchange) in Seibert, Alabama. Camp Sibert was a training base for women in the Navy and a training base for chemical warfare soldiers in the Army. Unlike in her childhood, Frances got a lot of attention from young, attractive single servicemen and army soldiers in training. She blossomed into a beautiful young woman with many admirers.

As my mother told me, a handsome man came into the PX one day, picked up a few items, and approached Frances at the counter. He was trim and muscular, with an olive complexion, bright blue eyes, and dark brown hair. She was impressed with his good looks and gentle demeanor. He introduced himself, "I'm Charles."

He quickly looked at her nametag. "Hi, Frances," he said. They locked eyes for a moment. That was all it took.

"Nice to meet you," Frances replied.

Then Charles awkwardly grabbed his few items. "Hope to see you again," he said, turning around and bumping into the young man behind him. Frances thought Charles was different from the other young soldiers who flooded the PX each day. He was older and more mature. He had a slight accent as if he were from another country. She was attracted to him and curious, maybe even intrigued. Charles was also instantly drawn to Frances. She was young, beautiful, and had a big smile. He was surprised to feel his heart flutter when he looked into her green eyes. Charles wanted to shake off the feeling. He was thirteen years older than the average enlistee, but he joined the Army anyway to leave behind his past, too. Charles had apparently sworn off women. Still, Frances had an innocence or naivety that appealed to him.

As I later learned, my father was a 100% full-blooded Greek. His parents were born in Nehoria, Greece, and all his relatives and ancestors were also born there. His parents met through an arranged marriage when his mother was fifteen and his father was sixteen. They went on to have ten children. In 1908, they immigrated to the United States, hoping for a better life. They settled in Biddeford, Maine, where they opened a little store importing Greek food items and olive oil. Charles was born shortly afterward, in 1910, as the firstborn immigrant in their family lineage. His parents fought incessantly. When Charles was eight years old, his father had an affair, and then he left his mother for his mistress, moving to New York City, where he opened another store that imported Greek delicacies.

With his father gone, Charles became the man of the house and dropped out of school in the third grade. He had to stay home and help with chores, including shoveling coal daily to heat the home. He worked to help pay for household expenses. His mother became bitter and took out her resentment on Charles, beating him regularly. When he was fifteen, Charles left home and moved to New York City, where his father had settled and remarried. Charles made peace with his father and formed a good relationship with his stepmother.

Charles worked in his father's store selling Greek specialty food items. Before the army, Charles met a beautiful young Greek woman named Lillian and married her. By his account, Charles thought they were happy. They had been married for ten years when he learned of his wife's infidelity. Their marriage ended, and Charles was devastated. He was thirty-six years old. To escape from his heartache, he joined the Army. Charles was sent to Camp Sibert for chemical warfare training.

Frances and Charles started dating right after they met at the PX. Eight weeks later, he was posted to Cebu in the Philippines to serve on the front lines and oversee the mortar shell inventory. Charles knew there was a good chance he might not make it back alive. Even though their relationship was in the early stages, he offered to marry Frances so that if he did not return, she could have his military benefits as a widow. But he hoped they could continue building their relationship if he made it back. Frances accepted. They married immediately in Gadsden, Alabama, and enjoyed a short honeymoon on the base.

For months after Charles was stationed in the Philippines, he exchanged passionate letters with Frances. When the war ended,

THE FATHER NOBODY KNOWS

Charles returned home to find his wife waiting for him, and they began their new life outside the military. They decided to move back to New York and took a one-bedroom apartment in the Bronx. Charles got a job in a luncheonette near Fifth Avenue, and Frances became pregnant. Nine months later, the couple welcomed a baby boy, naming him Steve, following a Greek tradition of the firstborn boy being named after the paternal grandfather. When Steve was old enough to start school, my mother got a job as a secretary. This seemed to be a happy time for them.

Frances started her job at the Damon Runyon Fund in Manhattan. Part of her duties included selling Broadway tickets to donors for the company to raise money for cancer research. After work, some of her coworkers met for a cocktail. On occasion, Frances would join them. She enjoyed her new friends at work and dressed with style and elegance. Frances was realizing her dream of living in New York. She had come a long way from picking cotton and living in that two-room shack on the dirt road in Alabama. There were no traces left of her Southern identity or accent.

Nine years passed, and Charles began to complain of extreme pain in his knee, making it almost impossible to walk. After the doctor ran tests, he was diagnosed with a rare and deadly cancer, given a grim prognosis, and had his leg amputated. Through France's connection at work and with her new friends, Charles saw one of the leading cancer doctors in the country. Further treatments were continued, and after an extended stay in the hospital, Charles was sent home to recover.

As Charles, now 50, began his recovery, Frances discovered she was pregnant. They lived in a small one-bedroom with paper-thin walls. Steve slept in the small living room on a pullout ottoman that converted into a twin bed. When Steve went to bed at night and

Frances and Charles retired to their bedroom, he could hear them arguing through the walls. This continued night after night. Then, after a few months, the arguing stopped.

I was born on July 20, 1957. We were a family of four living in a small one-bedroom apartment in the Bronx. As the baby, I slept in the bedroom with my parents, and Steve continued to sleep on the pull-out ottoman in the living room. My mother returned to work as a secretary and Broadway ticket agent, and my father finally got a part-time job as a counterperson in a small luncheonette. Charles struggled to adjust to his new wooden leg and was stressed out because he barely made enough money for them to get by, with little thought of how to get ahead. Desperate for childcare, Frances convinced her mother, Bessie, to stay in the tiny apartment with them for six weeks. Tension ran high. Then, just when it felt like they were all reaching a breaking point, a down payment was made on a new modest three-bedroom home in an affluent, suburban area predominantly Jewish, on Long Island. Shortly after that, our family of five moved into this house. Despite the better circumstances, my mother's drinking increased, and Charles started raging when they were at home, as told to me by my brother Steve, many years later.

When I was almost three years old, my parents worked in Manhattan and commuted by train from Long Island. They were gone from the house for 12-14 hours a day. They hired an attractive young woman named Queenie from the Bronx to live with us and care for me during the week. Since my parents already had a volatile relationship and were away from home all the time, they were oblivious to what the babysitter did during the day while watching me. We lived near a college. Queenie would lock me in a closet for hours while she prostituted a clientele of local college boys out of our house. On Thursdays, her Pimp would come from the Bronx and spend the day in our home with her and me. He was a rough man.

My brother Steve was a teenager at the time. He would come home after school and often find me sad and very still. He described Queenie as beautiful, and all his friends had a crush on her. Steve described her Pimp as a big, scary guy. My brother feared for my safety, being left alone with these two all day. He tried to warn my parents, but they didn't believe him. I suffered abuse from Queenie and her Pimp for six months until one day the cesspool caved in. When the plumbing company pumped it out, they discovered hundreds of condoms. Since my parents had bought the house new and had never used condoms, this was proof of what my brother had been telling them, and they fired her. Many years later, I had a daughter of my own, and I did not let her out of my sight when she was this age.

After Queenie left, I remember crying a lot, especially when my mother came home from work. No one knew why I cried so much. One night, my mother brought me a gift from her friend in the city. His name was Mr. L . . . It was a small box of gold and silver coins. I had never received a surprise gift. It made me happy, and I kept the coins in a special place. My mother told me not to talk to anyone about them. Over time, my mother continued to bring me coin gifts from Mr. L. I kept the coins in a shoebox under my bed and stopped crying as much.

My parents needed another babysitter for me. One day, an older black woman entered the Manhattan luncheonette, where my father worked as a counter server. She lived by herself in a tenement in Harlem. She was looking for work, and my father offered her a job looking after me and living at our house on Long Island, five days a week. Maude took the job. They moved me into the small room and gave her my bedroom. I was very withdrawn and still cried a lot. No one knew what to do with me.

Maude was in her early seventies and very laid back. She wore an apron over a muumuu and shoes more like slippers. For breakfast, we would walk across the street to the diner. I can still see the melted butter forming pools in the toasted English muffin. Then, she would spread grape jelly over the top. Maude explained to me that there was a Heaven, and when we got there, we would eat English muffins with butter and honey. After eating at the diner, we walked over and sat on the steps of an old, abandoned church across the street. She would sing the song, "He's got the whole world in His hands." I would sing with her, and she told me we couldn't see God, but he was there and loved each of us. It was the first time I heard of Him.

Maude would give me life lessons like don't steal or tell a lie, which my father also drummed into me, but his words were much harsher than Maude's. She did everything I thought a mother would do, like brushing my hair, telling me to brush my teeth, reading to me, and teaching me how to use the phone. I snuggled up to her when we watched soap operas on TV, and she gave me big hugs that comforted me. I felt safe with her and grew to love Maude more than anyone in my world. It felt like she was my real mom.

Then, one Monday, when I was six years old, I came home from school, and Maude was not there. My mother was home and told me Maude got sick and was in the hospital. She didn't tell me my nanny had a near-fatal stroke and was paralyzed and couldn't speak. I cried and insisted we go to see her. It took more crying and pleading, but my mother took me to Maude's Harlem hospital.

The room felt sterile and cold. Maude was hooked up to lots of wires and tubes. I put my hands through the guardrails of her hospital bed. She took her good hand and stroked my head. "You're coming home, right?" I asked, terrified of the answer. She nodded. I didn't want to leave her.

I came home from school two days later, and my father was in the kitchen. "When is Maude coming home?" I asked.

"She's not. She died this morning," my father said and continued chopping the soup vegetables.

I ran to the phone and dialed my mother at work. When she answered, I blurted out, "Is it true? Maude's dead? I'm not going to see her again."

My mother said it was true and assured me she would be home soon, and we could talk. I hung up the phone and went into Maude's room. She had a little orange book kept by her bed. It was one of her few worldly possessions, and she treasured it. I picked it up and held it to my chest. It was her God book, and was all I had left of Maude. I cried so hard I thought I would throw up. What would I do without her? It felt like my world had caved in.

I missed Maude with all my heart and wanted to see her again so badly. I pictured her in Heaven eating English muffins with butter and honey. She used to say to me that Heaven was up in the stars. So, I became fascinated with looking at the stars in my backyard at night. They were so peaceful, and I was so drawn to them. I wanted a telescope to see them better, but couldn't afford one. My older brother pointed out an ad in a magazine that offered the prize of a telescope if you sold a certain number of greeting cards. He helped me sign up. It was winter, and when the box of greeting cards was delivered, I waited until we had a blizzard and then went door to door selling them. People were moved to see a six-year-old by herself selling cards in the middle of a blizzard, and I sold them all. I was determined to get to Maude. I sent in the money and received my telescope a month later. I looked for Maude in the starry Heaven and found a star grouping that resembled eyes looking back at me. I wanted to be there with her because it felt like I belonged somewhere else to someone else. I started to wonder if I was adopted.

When I was six, I was left home alone. I looked in my father's nightstand drawer out of boredom and curiosity. I carefully combed through various items and saw a picture of my father embracing another woman. I didn't know he had been married before, so I thought I had found the proof that I must be adopted. I was sure my mom and dad were not my real parents, and they had hidden this fact from me. When they came home and found me crying, I told them I knew I was adopted. They insisted I was not, and I showed them the picture of my dad and this woman. My mother said she was my mother. My father stormed out of the room, and another huge fight erupted between them. I stayed in my bedroom for hours. Then, an uncomfortable silence fell in the house. Where was my real home? Maybe it was in the stars where Maude lived now. Wherever my natural home was, it was more comforting to imagine it somewhere else than to accept the harsh reality that my parents were not happy to have me.

Shortly after Maude died, my mother stopped working in Manhattan, and her drinking escalated. Then the coins stopped coming, too. By then, I had a shoebox full of them and hoped to meet Mr. L one day.

I remember Maude's death in every detail, but I hardly remember my mother sober. My mother was not well, either. She became a "functioning alcoholic" and was never sober at night. Instead of protecting me from my father, she medicated her repressed feelings with alcohol and spiraled down with the dysfunction that they both created in the household. I grew up seeing my mother put up with total disrespect and abuse from her husband; I did not see her defend me or herself from his rages and criticisms. Instead, I saw her pretending it wasn't happening.

2

Childhood Messages

One Saturday, when I was eight, I went into a dog grooming shop in a neighbor's garage two blocks from mine. The owner was a single woman in her late fifties named June. The garage had been converted into a room filled with dog cages, a linoleum floor, and a raised tub to bathe the dogs. Dryers were aimed at dogs in cages that had been bathed, and the floor was covered with hair clipped off the poodles. I asked if I could vacuum and watch. A few hours later, she gave me a nickel and offered to pay me a nickel if I wanted to come after school to vacuum and learn how to groom dogs.

June was a workaholic who did not like children, but she loved money. I was paid meager wages for working hard every day after school and on Saturdays. June was demanding, rude, and critical of me. I felt right at home and immediately served her every wish. I was desperate for a pat on the back and was driven to get a compliment from her. I thought June's approval would counter my feelings of being defective, dirty, stupid, and selfish. Despite my hard work, June never complimented me or paid me much money. She repeatedly told me, "If you become spoiled, you'll become lazy. You don't need to waste your life having fun like every other no-good kid."

I was nine and barely beginning puberty. One day, I had a stomachache and couldn't go to school. June let me stay at her house so that neither of my parents would have to take a day off from work to watch me. While she worked out in the garage, I watched television in the den, lying on the couch. I had been alone for a few hours when a man entered the room. He said he was a doctor and had come to examine me. He had gray hair, was in his sixties, and was dressed in a shirt and tie. I thought June must have called a doctor to check on me. So, when he told me to lift my dress and pull my tights down, I thought it was okay. Instead, he violated the private parts of my body, warning me that if I told anyone, I would never see June again.

I froze. I couldn't speak or even move. Why was this man doing this to me while I was sick? Before he got too far, the clickety-clack of June's high heels on the tile floor warned of her approach. The man stopped and quickly fixed my clothes before June entered the room. Then we all had lunch together in her kitchen at the table. The man insisted I sit on his lap. I made it through the day, thinking I might throw up the whole time.

I never said a word to anyone, not even to my mother, because I didn't want to risk losing June. I was sure I could avoid that man if he ever came again, but I was terrified.

When I woke up the following day, a strange thing had happened: I couldn't remember the man's face. Whenever a man with gray hair, a shirt, and a tie came into June's house, I hid. I would go into the laundry room to fold towels, or the kitchen to cut up chicken for the dog food, or just go to the bathroom and disappear until he left. When June worked, she kept her male friends from staying long.

Three years later, when I was twelve, June received a call from Shirley, who owned a large dog grooming shop and had taught June the business years ago. June felt indebted to her. Shirley asked if her young girl could come over to help since she had overbooked the day. June hesitated, but I jumped at the opportunity. This could be my big chance to prove myself.

I went to Shirley's and worked harder and faster than ever. When the day ended, Shirley said she was confused about what to pay me. June had told her not to pay me more than my current slim wages, or I could become "spoiled." Shirley told me she was very impressed with my work and felt I should be paid much more, considering what I had accomplished. She also invited me to work for her whenever I was available.

I felt betrayed by June, yet there was nothing I could do or say. I remained loyal to June for the next three years, but I grabbed any opportunity to work for Shirley. It wasn't just the money but Shirley's acknowledgment that I craved.

For the seven years I worked for June, she repeatedly said, "Cathy, I don't need you to get my workload done." I always showed up, though. Then, when I was 15, I opted to go with a friend to the beach one day instead of working at June's. When I called June and told her, she asked me to stop by her house before going out. When I got there and knocked, she opened the door and handed me a bag with a few possessions I had left there over the years. "You really did turn out to be a no-good bum like the rest of the kids I know. We're finished," she said with an icy look. She shut the door before I could say anything. I was stunned. Just like that, June had deleted me entirely from her life.

I walked away. I felt shaky inside. I had devoted so much of my time and energy working for June throughout my childhood. After seven years, didn't she care about me at all? Was I that disposable? I couldn't win with June, just like my father. The difference was that June fired me from her life and her employment. I could become an employee for someone else, but I couldn't quit being my father's daughter. What was wrong with me that he couldn't love me?

My earliest memories of my father are of him raging at me. He got agitated whenever I entered the room for reasons I never understood. He would explode over the littlest things I did, like ripping a paper towel the wrong way or not evenly skimming the top of the cream cheese. One time, I didn't put the milk back in the refrigerator in its designated spot on the top shelf to the right, and my father flew into such a terrible rage that I thought he would kill me.

He would scold me about everything. I would shake inside but stand obediently and listen to his tirade for fear of prolonging it. These encounters happened all the time, no matter what I did. I was always trying to make sense of his response to me. I figured that something was deeply wrong with me. It was not my behavior; it was me. This is where the disparaging feeling of shame began in my life. If I did something wrong or my conduct was improper, instead of 'I made a mistake,' I learned 'I was the mistake.' If you are the mistake, the only way you can fix it is to take yourself out of the equation. I did that by withdrawing from who I was with others. I tried to be who I thought others wanted me to be until I could figure out what was wrong with me. If I experienced even the slightest rejection, I could feel shame and a sense of panic. Maybe they saw the fatal flaw in me that I had yet to identify.

One Sunday morning, I was having breakfast with my parents. When we finished, I got up to clear my dishes. Dad asked why I hadn't finished my orange juice. He pointed to a little bit left in the glass. I told him I had had enough. He flew into a rage about how stupid and selfish I was for not finishing the orange juice. There was no calming him. He finally left the table, went to his room, and slammed the door. I ran out of the house. I was shaking the way

CHILDHOOD MESSAGES

I did as a child when he did this to me. I walked down the street and sat on the curb until I could get centered. I was overwhelmed. I wanted to become invisible. A young woman walking her poodle smiled at me as they passed. I was plagued with the same questions again. Why did he hate me so much? Sometimes, in a rage, he would tell me I was stupid, didn't know anything, and would never amount to anything. I was always left deeply confused, as my actions never warranted so hateful a response. I gathered the courage to return to their house. He met me at the door. "I don't know why I get so mad at you, but I promise I will just leave the room when it happens again," he told me. It was the nicest thing he had ever said to me, and I was grateful. I set my standards of being loved by my father very low.

I understood that I was the common denominator in all my father's rages, so, obviously, I was the problem. I lived very vigilantly, hoping to predict how my father would respond to anything I said or did. I became terrified of saying or doing anything at all.

I came to believe, down to the very core of my being, that I was stupid, unlovable, and a pain in the neck. I learned to deny any emotional needs I had, and I developed a very low self-esteem. How can you build confidence when someone is constantly asking, "What's wrong with you?"

Dinnertime was the only time I saw my parents, but I had to keep quiet because Dad listened to the television while he ate. For thirty minutes each night, I sat at the dinner table amidst the dogs and the smell, and the only voice I heard was Walter Cronkite's from the evening news. The other sound came from the ice clanging against the sides of my mother's glass of bourbon.

After dinner, I would retreat to my room and fantasize about a day in the future when I could move away. Then, I would play music or talk on the phone to drown out my parents' incessant arguing until they went to bed.

Since I was a little girl, my mother had a puzzling story she told me repeatedly regarding my birth. Each night, my mother would come home from work, drink a few strong drinks, and sit on the edge of my bed to tuck me in before I went to sleep. I still hear the ice cubes clinking in her glass as she drank and spoke.

"When your father's relatives found out I was pregnant, each one of them came to me and pleaded with me to get an abortion. Abortions were illegal at that time," she explained, and would add, "the only reason you are alive is because I wouldn't listen to them. You need to be thankful because you wouldn't be here if it weren't for my courage. But I am so glad I had you, and always remember you are a miracle child and can do anything you set your mind to."

It was a strange story to say to a child. It never painted a picture of being warmly wanted and welcomed into the world. When I was young, I thought she was my hero and was glad she had saved my life. As a teenager, I was glad I no longer had to hear about my potential demise as a baby.

My childhood had taught me:

I did not belong;
The world is not safe;
There is no one to protect me;
There is something very wrong with me;
and that I had something of value that men wanted.

I wanted to escape the life I had with my parents. Since I was a small child, I fantasized about living in a beautiful, clean house and having a happy family one day. I would have a good life, whatever it took, and find out what was wrong with me and fix it. I continued to work hard and save my money. I would need a car and a bank account to do that. Was my happiness, freedom, and love now finally within my reach?

3

Following the Flow

I graduated from high school at seventeen, accepted a partnership in Shirley's dog grooming business, and bought my first brand-new car for cash. I hoped to create a new life for myself, and Shirley had become the light in my life. She was a real go-getter and embraced life with such zest, not allowing anything to stop her. Even though she had polio at a young age and lost the use of both her legs, it didn't stop her from owning and riding a horse for ten years, sailing her sailboat, canoeing down white rapids, traveling extensively, and working a thriving business. During the years I worked with Shirley, we traveled together every winter. She would pick some remote location and, in return for helping her get around in her wheelchair, she would pay my expenses. Over the years, we visited Bermuda, St. Thomas, Barbados, Costa Rica, Bogota, Colombia, and the Yucatan in Mexico. Traveling opened a world of new possibilities and pathways.

An experience on our trip to the ruins in Yucatan, Mexico, dramatically affected me. We had spent the day at *Chichen Itza* exploring the Mayan ruins, and I climbed the Pyramid of Kukulcan, built by the pre-Columbian Maya civilization. It is aligned with the sun during the spring and the fall equinoxes and has 91 steps on all four sides. The temple at the summit was the 365th step, the number of days in the Mayan solar year. The steps were steep, but I felt compelled to climb them and reach their summit. Later in the afternoon, when there were no more tourists on the pyramid steps, I took a picture of it with my Polaroid Instamatic camera. The picture revealed a ghostly image of a man on the pyramid steps close to the top. It was puzzling because no one was there, but at the time, we just thought it was a defect in the film.

That night, we stayed at a luxury hotel, Villas Arqueologicas Chichen Itza, which was nestled on the edge of the archeological site and only a three-minute walk away. In the morning, I shared my troubling dream with Shirley. It felt so real. I dreamed of seeing her in an empty white room, and she seemed sad. I asked her what was wrong. She said that her close friend Peter had passed away unexpectedly. Shirley agreed it was an odd dream since Peter was in his fifties and in excellent health.

Shirley was the president of the Cocker Spaniel A.K.C. Club and had been a judge at the Westminster Dog Show at Madison Square Garden. Peter was known for sponsoring the hunting field trials for the Spaniels on his old Long Island estate. I had never met him, but I knew he had been close friends with Shirley for most of her life. They shared a great love and passion for the breed.

We thought about the dream again when we arrived home two days later, and she heard that Peter had died the day before. I was stunned. Somehow, I had dreamed about the death of someone I had never met. Did it have something to do with sleeping by the Chichen Itza Pyramid? Could the image of the man in the picture I took there be related to Peter's passing? This felt like a spiritual invitation of some kind, and it made me think about my own life and my future. It was the first time I thought about what I wanted to do rather than just surviving day to day. I was honest with myself and admitted I wanted to do something more than dog grooming.

I no longer needed this occupation to save me from harm as I did as an eight-year-old child.

Through the years, Shirley has been my lifeline. She had opened a whole new world for me and gave me a way to survive mine. I owed her a lot. Finally, I shared with her my desire to plan a future beyond dog grooming. "You're important, too! Find out what you want and go for it," she advised. So, I began taking courses at a local college.

Shirley comforted me when I became overwhelmed by my uncertain future. Sometimes, I froze in fear and wondered how to face the unknown. What if I'd always be alone? What if I never found what I wanted to do? What if I made a mistake? In her wisdom, Shirley would encourage me to take life one day at a time. My first decision was to create space away from my parents. I had longed to get away from them since I was a child. As I contemplated how I would pay for college and cover my living expenses, Shirley offered to let me fix up and live in the upstairs loft at her home, making college more affordable.

So, with plans to attend college, I moved into Shirley's loft—two small rooms and an upstairs bathroom she had used for storage. I cleared it out and organized a garage sale to unload things she didn't want or never used. I laid down wall-to-wall carpeting upstairs so she wouldn't hear me walking on the wooden boards. I was not tall, but I learned to navigate the angled roof by walking in the middle of the room. I got a hot plate and a mini refrigerator to give Shirley some privacy in her home. The living situation was a win-win for both of us, and I could stay there until I finished college.

I worked hard at the dog grooming shop and in college. I managed to keep straight A's. I had no more psychic dreams until my last year at school. One night, I dreamed a friend's father had a heart attack, but he survived. The following day, she called to tell me what I already knew from my dream. Another night, I dreamed that an older student in one of my classes had become pregnant, and then the next day in school, she told me the good news. On my birthday, a friend wanted to surprise me and take me to a restaurant in New York City. The night before, I clearly saw the restaurant's name in my mind's eye. When I told her, she was stunned because there are 23,000 restaurants in New York City, so it could not have been a lucky guess.

A few nights later, I woke up at four a.m. with a strong feeling that something was wrong with another friend. I finally gave in to the intuitive prompting and called her. She answered and was out of breath. She had been throwing up for hours, and her roommate was helping her. I stayed awake the rest of the night until I heard she was better. I remember sensing things as a child that would come true. My mind started to race with questions. How did this knowing happen? Why did it happen when I was a child? Why was it happening now? Could I control it and make it happen?

There were more incidents of premonitions throughout the semester. Then I had a short dream about Shirley not having long to live. I didn't want to even think about it for fear that it would help it come to pass. I asked her repeatedly, and she said she felt fine. I prayed it was not one of "those" dreams.

With one more semester left and no idea what I wanted to do with my life, I researched psychic phenomena at the local library. I was surprised to find only a few books on the shelf and none that answered my questions. A young librarian must've sensed my frustration and came over to me. I told him I wanted to learn about psychic phenomena and how and why they happen. He suggested that I read about Edgar Cayce, a famous psychic who passed away in 1945. He was able to go into a trance and tell sick people what they needed to get well. I found the book *Edgar Cayce - The Sleeping Prophet* by Jess Stearn. I learned that Cayce had given psychic readings to thousands of people, providing them with incredible information about their lives.

What I read only made me want to find out more about Cayce. I discovered that the Association for Research and Enlightenment (the A.R.E.) in Virginia Beach, Virginia, was formed to preserve and provide access to the information recorded during Cayce's readings. I immediately called them and found they still had a few openings to attend a five-day conference called "Psychical Research Experience," conducted by a research staff of psychologists. The conference offered one the opportunity to become a researcher for a week. You could explore different ways of obtaining personal direction from higher sources about relationships, finances, career goals, or anything else you have questions about. During the five days, you would also be given two psychic readings anonymously by two of the six psychics selected for the conference based on their extraordinarily high accuracy rate—neither the participant nor the reader would know each other's identities.

I was excited about attending this psychic conference. I wanted to take a chance and explore my psychic potential. It felt right. In the meantime, I graduated from Adelphi University on Long Island with honors and a marketing degree. I was excited as I boarded the plane bound for Virginia Beach. It was the first venture I took after earning my degree.

The first few days, we attended lectures on meditation, dreams, and psychic impressions and readings. The meals were wonderful, and I had many interesting conversations with people about their spiritual journeys. Then, we were given our recorded readings. The first reading addressed my tendencies toward self-criticism and self-judgment and said that it would be helpful for me to seek things that bring me joy and to be honest with myself about them. There were suggestions for dealing with this tendency, so that I could bring myself more peace and joy. There was also a reference to my fears of feeling limited in my life, along with suggestions on creating and attaining goals. Then, regarding them, the reader explained that I should choose goals that were attainable, do what I could toward accomplishing the goal, and then "watch the creative forces bring it to you." Everything fit and made sense, but I wondered what "the creative forces" were. Then the reading closed with, *"The pursuit of one's joyful purposes opens the bond of oneness with God and binds His will, His work, His purposes into those joyful pursuits. Each soul has its pathway of choice upon which it seeks to return into full consciousness of its own nature and its oneness with God."*

The second reading referenced a separation I would soon have from a dear friend, and that this would be a sad time for me. I was stunned because I had not talked with anyone about my dream, yet it weighed heavily on my heart. How did the psychic reader pick that up? I thought about how I kept having the strangest feeling that Shirley would die soon. She seemed relatively healthy, but I couldn't shake the feeling. A perfect stranger who knew nothing about my life was picking up on my distressed feelings. How did the psychic reader pick that up? Was I being prepared for her passing by some unseen force? Then, the psychic said that other people and opportunities would present themselves to fill the void I would feel.

Next, she addressed the subject of a job. She saw me exploring choices and making many decisions. I would move around April or May. She saw an opportunity for me out of state in Virginia or Vermont. A job offer would materialize, but it would not happen for a few months because the position had yet to be vacated. I'd be working around a big school or an institution. It would be administrative work in a big building. I would attend a lot of conferences with many people, some of them the heads of different departments.

After listening to both readings, I had this profound feeling that I was not alone and that God exists. Even though we seem separate in our lives and bodies, we may be connected spiritually in some unseen, intangible way. I was struck by a powerful "knowing" that there really was life beyond the physical world, and we are more than just our bodies. This would explain how we can be aware of each other regardless of how far apart we may be physically. How else could these readings feel so prophetic? How else could I have had dreams, premonitions, intuitive insights, and a sixth sense of things to come? We are all innately born with this ability and can tune into it if we choose, just as we can use our five senses. I decided to become more mindful of my sixth sense in my everyday life by listening to and following it.

After graduation, I started sending resumes to different businesses the following week. I wanted a job with an organization promoting self-help in some way. Yet every job I applied for was either a dead-end lead or a misfire. I decided to follow my feelings and take temporary jobs until April or May to see what happens. One job working for a mail-order catalog business lasted a month and paid well. Working temporary jobs while waiting for a mysterious job somewhere to be vacated was not something most people would understand. I had no idea where this job was, what it was, or how I'd find it. It all just felt right.

I wondered how this would all come about. How was I to be offered a job in another state? One night, I broke down and cried tears of confusion and despair until I escaped into sleep. The following day, I awoke, knowing in my heart that I was going to Virginia Beach. I didn't question how I knew. But I recalled last night's dream as I lay there thinking about this strange knowing.

I was walking down an unfamiliar street, feeling as though I had lost my way in the night. Most houses were dark and lifeless, except one that was bustling with activity. There were colored lights and happy people talking and singing. There were beautiful, mysterious strains of music wafting through the night. I went to the door to ask for directions and was invited to join the festivities. I glanced around the room at the strangely familiar faces. They explained that they were working with the Cayce Foundation and that I was welcome to help. I said sure and made myself at home.

When I awoke, I thought *I'd love to work for the A.R.E.* in Virginia Beach, which is such a beautiful place. The ocean has a certain magic, the climate is mild, and the pollution is almost nonexistent. The A.R.E. has the world's most extensive library on parapsychology, which could keep me busy for a lifetime. It was certainly worth considering.

A second "invitation" happened to lead me to my mystery job. That weekend, I was dog-sitting overnight. In the middle of the night, the dog woke me up by barking and running to the living room. How odd! When I got up to investigate the problem, I noticed the TV was on, although I hadn't watched it that night. It was 3:00 a.m.

As I reached to turn it off, a documentary on Edgar Cayce began. Despite my groggy state, I sat down and watched it. The dog settled down at my feet and went to sleep. When it ended at four o'clock, I went back to bed. The first thing the following day, I knew where I needed to look for the mystery job. It couldn't have happened more perfectly if I had planned to watch that show. How did that dog know to wake me up at that time? Who turned the TV on? How did I end up in front of the TV in the middle of the night at the precise moment an Edgar Cayce documentary was playing? Why did all this happen when I was debating whether to go to Virginia Beach?

The following weekend, I visited the A.R.E. The personnel manager was on vacation, so I left a resume. I overheard a woman commenting on a vacancy in a duplex where she lived, and I made an inquiry about it. She suggested I grab it fast if interested, so I went there immediately. The apartment was lovely. It was two blocks from the ocean, close to the A.R.E. and to a beautiful state park. The rent was half of what I would pay in New York, so on blind faith, I left a deposit and the first month's rent. I had just enough money saved to move and survive for a month.

I had two weeks to prepare for the move to Virginia Beach. In the meantime, Shirley mentioned that she had finally seen a doctor about the increasing pains in her leg and stomach. I had never told her what the psychic had said in my reading because I didn't want to give energy to that prediction, yet it nagged me, and I had tried to encourage her to seek medical help. When her tests came back, her doctor called her for a consultation, suggesting she bring a family member. We went together to hear the results. He gently broke the news that she had cancer of the pancreas. He told us she might have three to six months to live. She refused chemotherapy and said she would stay home and live normally until she couldn't.

I felt numb. It was like dreaming or watching a movie where I knew the ending. Shirley was a trouper even in the face of death. I pushed her wheelchair back to the car. I never saw her as handicapped and always thought of her as being immortal. She had such inner strength, determination, and compassion for others. I never thought anything could ever stop her. We drove to the beach and parked the car in the sun. Then I broke down. I wanted to be strong for her, but I buckled under the thought of losing her. "I don't want you to die," I cried out as I hugged her tightly.

"Catherine, we all must die sometime. It wouldn't be happening if it weren't my time. And it's your time, too. It's time for you to start a beautiful new life for yourself in Virginia."

"No, I'm not going to go. I'll change my plans after all you've done for me. Since I was twelve years old, you've been my guardian. You took me into your business, under your wing, and encouraged and supported me. You've been there through some of my hardest times. You taught me so many things. Shirley, I can't leave you now."

"Catherine, if I've taught you anything, it's to *respect the flow of life and grasp the opportunities when they present themselves. The essence of life is change.* You must respect that. Part of what's held me here this long is my desire to see you make it. You're beginning to take hold of your life now. That brings me such joy. You don't owe me anything. I've never done anything for you that I haven't wanted to do. Use the time while I'm still here to build a new nest. I know you love me. Show me that love by choosing life for yourself right now so I can see my little fledgling fly to it."

She was right. I should have known better. She was among the few people I knew who were delighted to see others happy. We had always been honest with one another, no matter how painful. Then I remembered how I hid from her what the psychic said about losing a dear friend. I felt tremendous guilt, thinking that this was maybe my fault, that I could somehow have prevented this from happening.

"Shirley, I must tell you the truth about the psychic readings. One of them warned me that I could lose a friend. I sensed it but didn't tell you because I didn't want it to come true. Maybe this is all my fault."

"Nonsense. I've had this tumor way before your prediction occurred. This was already set into motion. Who do you think sets my fate into motion anyway, you?"

"No," I answered, realizing my guilt was unfounded.

"I've sensed my time was short for a while." Shirley took my hand and continued, "Let's be thankful we have this time together to adjust. I'm not the one who needs to be told ahead of time. You were."

It was true that I would've now been a basket case without that forewarning. Instead, I was just reacting to what I already sensed and had privately shed many tears. I began to collect myself and contain my feelings.

"Shirley, are you afraid?" I asked.

"Of death? No, pain, yes. I don't believe death is the end of us, so I'm looking forward to the journey that comes next. My belief offers me comfort as I face death. If I had been afraid of death all these years, I would never have been able to live such a full life and do the things I've done. *You've got to choose the beliefs that give you the greatest freedom to enjoy life while you're here.* "

Since I was twelve years old, Shirley had talked to me about reincarnation. I used to debate its validity as I tried to understand her views. I hadn't ever considered life after death until I met Shirley. I thought that when you died, you died. She said, "We're free to choose what we want to be from lifetime to lifetime, depending on what we need to learn. This time around, I'm learning patience. That's why I have polio in both legs and a curvature of the spine. Try moving around with this body, and you'll learn patience. Next time, I'll be a dancer with a beautiful, healthy body that fluidly expresses movement. Dance is such an art."

"I have trouble believing what you say without proof," I would respond at such times.

"Well, let's agree to give each other proof should either of us die," Shirley once suggested.

"Okay. Whoever goes first must try to signal the other if there really is life after death."

"Agreed," she said.

I paused to recall our past conversations and looked at Shirley. "Remember how we used to settle our death debates by agreeing on our deal to help one another solve the mystery of life after death?" I asked.

"Sure do. Do you want me to still honor that agreement?"

"Yes. If someone's going to let me know, I'd rather it be you," I answered. "I love you, Shirley."

"I love you, too, Catherine."

We both wept at the bittersweetness of life.

4

Parting with the Past

Before I left for Virginia Beach, I told Shirley I was planning to come back to check on her every weekend, and if she needed extra help, I would move back in a heartbeat. The last few weeks in New York moved like a slow funeral as I witnessed the death of my old life. I thought of this as I drove for eight hours with my home at my back. It was eerie, almost as though I was in between lives.

The day after I arrived, I went straight to the A.R.E. personnel office. This time, I found the manager. She greeted me, "I was just reviewing your resume, and a position has opened up this week that seems to match your qualifications and goals. It's in our marketing department. The manager is retiring, and her assistant will move into her position. The assistant's job will now be vacated. Would you like to schedule an interview tomorrow?" Of course, I agreed.

A strange feeling came over me. I felt like I was dreaming again. Was this the job the psychic said I would be offered out of state when someone vacated it? Was this the brick building, the institution she saw where conferences were held? It had to be possible for me.

The job description looked promising. I would search for, review, and select the best and most helpful books and tapes following the Edgar Cayce philosophy. I would also design fliers, letters, and catalogs, maintain sales and inventory, and implement procedures and policies for the bookstore.

Before I left, she handed me two books. She asked me to write reviews on each of them in preparation for the interview. Things were happening fast. I turned in my reviews in a couple of days. When I was called in for an interview, the manager said she was impressed with the reviews I wrote.

The interviews went well. I was completely myself, and by the end of the day, I had the job. I would begin on Monday. I was on cloud nine. Everything had worked out as foretold. I had recreated a new life for myself! Within one week, I had laid the foundation for living in Virginia Beach and doing precisely what I wanted. I was grateful that one of my temp jobs taught me the mechanics of the mail-order business, an important outreach at the A.R.E. Other temporary jobs filling in at retail stores helped me enormously in operating the bookstore. Accidents? Coincidences? I seriously began to wonder!

I was guided to my new job and home without ever scanning the employment or rental ads in the newspaper. I just did what felt right to do at each step along the way. If this is what using my intuition could achieve, I decided that from now on, my intuition would have free rein in my life and decision-making. Maybe these were the creative forces at work.

The second day I worked at the A.R.E., I was covering the bookstore alone at lunchtime when a man walked in. I had noticed him sitting in one of the lobby chairs most of the morning. He had gotten into one conversation after another with people as they passed by where he sat. I remember feeling suspicious of his open friendliness. Growing up in New York, I had an inborn reserve and distrust of friendly strangers.

Ray was in his early sixties with thinning blonde/gray hair, kind eyes, and a warm smile. He then strolled up to me and introduced himself. "I'd like to welcome you to town," he said, offering me a handshake. Ray told me he lived in a log cabin in the Blue Ridge Mountains and traveled where and when he was guided. He said he had seen me in his dreams and wanted to talk with me sometime over lunch.

I was reluctant, but something told me to agree.

I spent the rest of my day at work, occasionally checking up on Ray. I found that he was sincere, and he really did live in an authentic log cabin in the mountains. Indeed, he was a true free spirit and had countless friends and acquaintances living in the beach area. What was even more unique about this man was his presence. I felt an aura of warmth around him. As he later told me, he was a real believer in miracles, and many miracles occurred around him and the people he touched.

I was disappointed when he didn't show up the following day. I would learn he had followed an inner message to go to Chapel Hill, North Carolina. Finally, after two weeks, Ray returned. This time, I gave him a warm greeting. He felt like a long-lost family member to me, even if I didn't know why.

We went out for lunch, and I learned more about his life story. He had been a traveling salesman for a national company. In those days, he said he was only concerned with sales and dollars, smoking, drinking, and avoiding his wife of twenty-five years. He had two grown children. Back then, he was unhappy, and his life lacked meaning and purpose.

Then he said he got tired of being sick and tired, went to A.A., sobered up, quit smoking, got divorced, left his job, read the Bible, and moved into a 350-year-old log cabin where he lives rent-free. He told me that now he works for God.

I was fascinated by his story. "What does God have you do?" I asked.

"Assisting Him with His miracles," he answered. "It's tricky business. I have to stay in the moment and be flexible."

I wanted to know more. I didn't even feel like eating. I somehow knew this was exactly how I wanted to live one day. I heard miracles provide hope. Living a hopeful life is what could save me. "How do you live in the moment when everything in our society revolves around yesterdays or tomorrows, and planning goals, making commitments, and honoring obligations?" I asked.

"By using your inner clock! We've become so dependent on outside forces telling us how to think, how to feel, and when to act that we've lost touch with our own inner knowingness. *If you were to become still and just listen, you would hear all those answers just as you need them. Your body would tell you when to go to sleep and when it was hungry. Your inner sense would tell you when to wake up, whom to call, and which direction to go in.*"

"Your timing always seems perfect. How do you do it?"

"I started gradually," he answered. "I wasn't that clear on my first inner directives and intuitions. I began playing with listening to and acting on my gut feelings to see where they led me. I called them Adventure Days. There were days when I got up in the morning with no pre-planned structure for the day. I'd leave the cabin and drive or walk in whatever direction I felt like going. If I felt like stopping, I would stop. If people were there and I felt like talking to them, I would talk. Before long, I would be on my way to a destination, whether it was from a conversation with a person or a sign I read, a brochure I saw, or a hunch I followed. Inevitably, there would be some unknown adventure awaiting me, some miracle ready to unfold!"

"Is this how miracles happen?" I asked.

"There's no ready formula to miracle-making. Miracles are not logical or scientific. They usually defy all the laws of possibility. That's why they're called miracles. They're of God. I don't make them happen. That's my Boss's job. He's got a much better vantage point. I just assist Him in executing them."

"And how do you do that?" I asked.

"I follow my inner directives to be in the right place at the right time and just go where I'm told. I have to stay clear to hear and be mindful to watch for signs. Most of the miracles I assist with only require me to introduce people to one another. You would be amazed at the magical creations of putting two or more suited people together with complementary needs and resources."

Before Ray left that evening, he placed something round, metal, and cold in my hand. "This is your profession," he said. "Take pride in it. Keep this with you as a reminder of your connectedness to all life." I looked down at my hand and saw a metal link from a chain.

Ray took my hand in his. "You have an important purpose for being here. You are a link in the chain of the human experience. Understanding you're a link is one of the keys to creating miracles."

I wanted to believe that my link in the chain was purposeful and interconnected. I was starting to envision a new identity for myself.

Over the next few months, I got to know Ray better. We got together whenever he was in town, and he became my mentor. He inspired me to explore the connection between what I did at work and how I could serve others. Ray helped me learn how to serve God, which I was doing at my job. I was exposed to more self-help philosophy and books on parapsychology than I ever dreamed existed—every book published on man's experience. "Understanding you're a link is one of the keys to creating miracles," was a quote that passed over my desk. I read and read and read! Most of the day, I wrote book reviews and copy for their promotional material, and at times, I would operate the bookstore. I discovered my innate ability to connect people, groups, and energies there. I would get into a conversation with someone with a need, and then the next day, someone else would walk in who could fulfill that need. When my intuition nudged me, I went ahead and introduced them.

It became an exciting pastime for me. I used it as an exercise to strengthen my intuitive faculties, like putting a jigsaw puzzle together. Whenever I introduced people, and their meeting benefited each of them, I called it a hit. That meant I heard and acted on my intuitive directive clearly and accurately. I scored. The more I played the connecting game, the better I became, and everybody benefitted. I made good friends and exciting connections, as did the others. When I introduced people and my directive came from my thinking mind or ego rather than an intuitive feeling, those introductions turned out to be unnecessary and fruitless. I called those misses. No scores! But the misses were also valuable because they taught me to discern between my conscious mind and intuition.

One day, a handsome outgoing man came into the bookstore. He was visiting from New York. I suggested places to go and talked with him about the A.R.E. He invited me to lunch, and I shared how I was working on my intuitive networking abilities. We became good friends. It turned out he was one of the producers of *The Today Show*. One day, he called from work and asked if I knew of a new author I would recommend for a show segment on healing. I had just written a review on a new book that had come across my desk. It was *You Can Heal Your Life* by Louise Hay. He looked her up and booked her on The Today Show. Her book later became a huge bestseller, exploring the connection between physical illness and thoughts and beliefs.

While new and exciting books and people showed up at work, Shirley was always on my mind. Every other week, I drove to New York to visit her. She was failing in health. In those months, I literally watched the life force drain from her. She worked until she couldn't tolerate the pain in a sitting position any longer. By the end of June, she was in constant pain, unable to eat, and bedridden. I phoned her every day. The doctors predicted she would only live for another two to three weeks. On Friday, I was supposed to drive to New York again. I sensed it might be the last time I saw Shirley, so I was anxious to go. But Friday morning, I woke up with an intuitive feeling not to go to New York. Of course, I'm going to visit Shirley, I argued with myself. My friend is dying. I've got to see her.

A few minutes later, Shirley called, sounding a bit out of breath. "Are you still planning to come here today?" she asked.

"Of course, why do you ask?"

"Well, this weekend, I need to be alone to rest, and I wanted to know if we could change your visit to next weekend?"

My intuition was correct, I thought. I was worried about Shirley, but I had to respect her request. I told her I would call her in the morning.

That night, I came home from work and sat on the sofa to read. Later, I went into the bathroom to wash my face and prepare for bed. As I bent over the sink to turn the water on, I heard Shirley's voice in my left ear: "Hello, Catherine!" I felt a presence around me, and the hair stood up on my arms.

I ran into the living room. No one was there. Was it Shirley?

The following morning, at seven o'clock, the phone rang. It was my father. "They just found Shirley. Looks like she died in her sleep last night. The coroner estimated about midnight."

"I know," I said as I started crying. "Shirley was here. She came to see me like she promised. Shirley called my name. I felt her presence. As soon as she died, she let me know. That's why she didn't want me to visit yesterday. Somehow, she knew. Well, she's free now, just like she wanted."

"Catherine, stop talking nonsense. Shirley's dead. Her sister wanted you to know," he said. I started to cry. He hesitated and said, "You'll be all right," and then the phone went dead. He was dutiful in letting me know, and as emotionally harsh as always.

I went to work on Monday and Tuesday. I felt detached from everyone and everything. I needed to say goodbye to Shirley, to see the house empty and know she was no longer there. I needed to be with other people who knew and loved her, and I needed to cry. I knew I had to get to New York right away. My boss understood, so I took the rest of the week off. I grabbed some clothes, drove straight to the airport, boarded a plane, and flew to La Guardia.

I called Shirley's sister from the airport. She said she had just found a note from Shirley addressed to me on her bedside nightstand. Her sister thought Shirley must have written it just before she died.

I took a cab from the airport and had the driver drop me off about a mile from Shirley's home. I needed to walk there and collect myself to say my goodbyes. I walked down the long, dead-end street and up to the door, which her sister had left unlocked. There was no one in sight. I listened to the birds singing and tried to calm myself. My heartbeat was so fast I could hear the rhythm in my ears. What did the note Shirley wrote say? What if I needed to respond to it with her spirit? I couldn't, could I? I ran inside the house and went into her bedroom. By her nightstand, I saw the note on top of a book she had given me years earlier. I grabbed them both and went back outside to the street. I sat on the curb and opened the note.

It said:

Dear Catherine,

Remember this card? We bought it in Bermuda when we traveled there, the first trip we took. It reminds me of our friendship. I wanted to let you know how much it has meant to me. I'm in tremendous pain now. Please excuse the brevity and messiness of this note. I have very little time left. I have to go . . .

We'll stay in touch through love . . .

Shirley

I closed the note. The card was a lovely watercolor of a little cottage nestled on a hillside in the country. Spring flowers bloomed around it, and the sun spread its rays upon the landscape. Then I opened the book *Gift from the Sea* by Anne Morrow Lindbergh. There was the inscription Shirley had written when she gave it to me:

To Catherine,

May this story inspire you to continue the search to know yourself. This is truly the most important journey in life. Know that you always have a friend ·who loves you. Keep that love with you in your heart and use it to help you find happiness and peace wherever life leads you.

Shirley

When the weekend ended, and I had said my goodbyes to Shirley and other friends, I got in the limousine to head back to the airport. We pulled onto the main road and stopped behind a car at the next red light. There was a sign attached to their rear window. It was orange, and it said *Dancer on Board*! I let out a gasp and burst into tears. I knew it was Shirley letting me know she had made it to the next part of her journey as a dancer.

Back in Virginia Beach, everything seemed different. My heart hurt. Losing Shirley reminded me of the pain I felt losing Maude when I was little. I went through the motions of work and living, but I felt an emptiness inside of me every day. I missed talking with her. I missed knowing she was there, only a phone call away.

5

Traveling on Trust

Because of my travels with Shirley, I held on tight to the idea of new possibilities. I loved my job, but I was craving more. I felt a gentle calling but couldn't identify what it was. Shirley lived a full life and had no regrets. She embraced adventures and mysteries and didn't give in to her fears. She often took risks and found great joy in the journey. I wanted to follow in her footsteps. While I believed I was traveling and seeking higher truths, I was also unknowingly escaping my past.

Jacob, a friend I had met through the institute, and some friends from New York called to invite me on a trip to Peru in two months. During the trip, a group of us would go to Cuzco, where we would explore ruins that are closed to the public through Jacob's contact. Then, we would travel to remote villages in the Andes before heading up to Machu Picchu, then back to Cuzco, Lima, and home. We would be hiking at altitudes from 15,000 to 18,000 feet.

Jacob said we'd have a unique opportunity to meet with three Peruvian professors: one who had extensively researched UFOs (Unidentified Flying Objects), another an established archaeologist, and the third a physicist. These men were dedicated, enthusiastic, and open to sharing their findings with us. I wanted to hear what he discovered about UFOs. I wanted to know if life existed beyond our planet in the greater universe, and if we are connected to it. I wondered if I could have a first-hand experience like I had in Chichen Itza.

We'd sleep overnight in Machu Picchu, meditate in hot mineral baths under the open night sky, hike over Incan trails to ancient ruins, and sit in temples built some five hundred years ago to worship the stars.

It was a once-in-a-lifetime adventure. The challenge was that the trip would cost $1500, and I had no extra money. I was accustomed to having small miracles happen more and more in my life. During quiet moments, I learned to ask for the things I needed. Then, lo and behold, a friend would arrive at my door feeling compelled to bring me what I had secretly asked from God. I also learned to make the same prayer request for others.

I kept thinking about this impossible dream and grand desire to travel to Peru. In a leap of faith, I called Jacob in New York and told him that if it were God's will for me, I would travel with them to Peru. He said I would need to send him $1500 in four weeks, and he would send me a list of items to bring on the trip.

So, I decided to be open to a miracle happening with me going to Peru. Numerous times during the day, I focused on the adventure and excitement I felt about traveling there as though it were happening. I couldn't lose either way, feeling the joy of going even if it didn't happen. I always asked God in such cases that if it were His will, all conditions would be met to enable my miracle to occur. I would also let go of my attachment to the outcome and always give thanks. I felt at peace and allowed the natural flow of events to unfold. So, I told Jacob to hold a space for me temporarily. He agreed and told me one more space was available if I had an interested friend.

Two weeks later, I ran into Judith, a woman I had briefly met at a research conference the previous year. We had not spoken more than a few words at the conference, but when she walked into the bookstore, we greeted each other like long-lost friends. We had lunch together, and I shared with her many of the changes that had occurred in my life since that seminar. She had experienced some shifts in her life as well. After lunch, I mentioned my trip to Peru and asked if she wanted to go; one more placement was available. She declined but suggested we keep in touch.

I felt so comforted by Judith's presence. She was in her late fifties, with silver hair and a gentle smile. Judith reminded me of Shirley. Maybe she was one of the people who would step in to fill that void in my life, as the psychic said. She had been married for twenty-five years and raised three children who were grown and out of the nest. Judith was divorced and on her own. I never asked her last name, phone number, or address. I hoped she would show up again so I could find out more about her. She exuded such contentment with life.

Three and a half weeks flew by, and there was no sign of the needed $1500 fee. With three days left, I tried not to feel disappointed. Then, Monday morning, Judith entered my office and placed an envelope on my desk. "I'm not sure why I'm doing this, but all weekend, you were in my thoughts. The number 1500 kept coming to mind, and I knew I needed to give you this money. What is this all about?"

I opened the envelope. Inside were fifteen hundred-dollar bills. My eyes teared up. I told Judith that I was asking God if I could go on this trip to Peru, but I couldn't afford it. Then I told Judith I couldn't accept this money from her.

"It's a gift," she insisted.

I immediately declined again. It just didn't seem right. I barely knew this woman. I thought there were always strings attached to free money. I found the courage to tell her why I couldn't accept such a gift.

"There are no strings attached."

"Why are you giving me this?" I asked, still feeling uncomfortable.

"Because this is not from me, it's from God," she insisted. "If you refuse, you'll deny me the opportunity to serve God. Worse yet, you'd be refusing God's gift."

This was an inspired twist.

"You see," she added, "If we give when God asks us to give, whatever He asks us to give, then we will find our dreams coming true more and more. You need to learn to receive, or you will never be able to walk hand in hand with God in your life. This is a key to living a God-directed life."

She was right. I needed to learn how to receive. "Why is this so hard for me?" I asked.

"I think you believe you're not worth it," she replied. Judith picked up the envelope and put it in my hand again. I still felt very uncomfortable, but this time, I said, "Thank you." I told Judith there was still one more space available if she was interested. Judith was concerned that she was too old for the altitude. I said I would help her adjust if needed, and she decided to come.

She squeezed my hand and walked off. I was beginning to understand her point. Still in amazement, I called Jacob that evening to tell him the money was coming and that my friend Judith would take the last spot.

A week later, I looked out the window of our plane flying over some of the world's most incredible mountains, the Andes. It was a small plane that flew us from Lima to Cuzco. To entertain the passengers, the stewardess passed out bingo game cards. The numbers were called in Spanish, which she translated into English for our group. The prize was a round-trip ticket for two to the Amazon Jungle. Was I really flying over the Andes Mountains playing bingo to win a trip to the Amazon?

Finally, we reached our destination, all twelve of us. The plane bumped down on a runway centered between a group of mountains. We had left Lima at sea level and arrived at Cuzco in a valley at an altitude of 15,000 feet. The cabin doors opened, and I immediately felt lightheaded in the thin air.

I quickly looked at Judith. "Are you okay?"

"Yes, I'm fine."

"Just let me know if you need my help," I reassured her. We then walked across the runway to the terminal. I tried to remain calm as my breathing deepened. It felt as if I couldn't get enough oxygen. My vision blurred, and Judith grabbed my arm.

"Are you okay?" she asked.

I mumbled, "No," and collapsed on the floor.

Judith grabbed my suitcase and carried it along with her own. Some of the others helped me to my feet and walked me to the cab waiting for us. So much for the young helping the old, I thought. I had assumed I would be the strong one because of Judith's age, but instead, she had to help me until I adjusted to the altitude.

The following day, just as Jacob was about to contact the professors, they showed up to greet us at our hotel. We were all quite surprised, and Philip, our translator, asked, "How did you know we would be here today?"

"We were told when you'd arrive," the professor enthusiastically replied. "Professor Jose has spoken with those who visit our planet from the Pleiades star system. They said that a group of American students would be arriving on Tuesday and to share their message with them."

This sounded wild, but we did arrive on Tuesday and called ourselves students.

Philip introduced us. One of the professors said, "We welcome you as our brothers and sisters. Even though you live far away, and our cultures are so different, we know we are all one family."

We were eager to hear about their UFO contacts. They agreed to tell us about their experience with extraterrestrials and took us to a local restaurant near our hotel for lunch. The restaurant had colorful Peruvian décor and was built next to an original 800-year-old Incan wall. They suggested we eat very lightly since we would be hiking in higher altitudes, and when taking in less oxygen, one's digestive system slows or temporarily stops. I ordered a traditional local dish, Sopa de Quinua, or Quinoa Soup, with quinoa that grows in the Andes Mountains. Leeks, onions, garlic, celery, cabbage, sweet potatoes, and seasonings were some of the ingredients that made this a delicious soup.

Professor Jose began to fill us in on the details of their ET contact. "My first physical meeting was very unexpected," he shared. "I thought it was a joke at first. I received a phone call from a male voice identifying himself as the commander of a spacecraft. He said it was the one I had often seen in the sky near my home. He invited me to meet with him and his 'traveling companions.' He told me to meet him in the countryside on a farm outside Cuzco. I didn't know what to think. Getting a phone call like that seemed ridiculous, but I had to find out if it was authentic.

"So, I went to the farm, and there was a male figure in the field. About a hundred feet behind him were two other figures, one a female. They looked human, their skin tone fairly pale, but their eyes were more prominent than ours, and their earlobes were small and blended into the sides of their heads. They wore identical uniforms of a dark gray-black solid color that fit their slim physiques.

"At first, I hesitated as I approached their apparent commander. I could hear the other two in the background laughing, so I stopped walking toward them.

"Why do you stop?" he asked.

"I don't like being laughed at," I replied.

"My friend," he explained, "we are not laughing at you. We are just laughing! You see, we live in a high vibration of joy. It is natural for us to laugh spontaneously. It feels good. We only wish for you to share our joy with us. We do not wish to disturb you."

The professor wiped the tears from his face as they slowly rolled down his cheeks. I was moved and amazed at the same time.

"I still cannot talk about this meeting without tearing up," the professor added and continued. "I was deeply moved by these beings. In their presence, I felt joy, love, and acceptance. It was different from what we're accustomed to experiencing with people here. I asked them why they had come.

"They said they came to remind our race of its unrealized potential. When we learn to believe in ourselves as unlimited spiritual beings, we will know the infinite possibilities that exist for our race. They said to look within ourselves to tap that potential."

The professor continued, "I asked them why they did not make themselves known to the masses. They said that those in power at the moment would not welcome the disclosure of their presence here. However, they are introducing themselves to individuals, and they welcome the opportunity to meet with the citizens of our world eventually.

"They have seen other planets such as ours that have experimented with nuclear energy. They've watched worlds with great potential destroy themselves through their ignorance. They said our nuclear experiments pose potential dangers far beyond our current understanding of physics. The waste byproducts of our current research and use of nuclear power could make our planet uninhabitable for human life within only a few hundred years.

"Even the explosion of a single nuclear war device is not acceptable and has the potential to upset the energies of the universe, far removed from our planet. If they did not believe in the probability that this event exists in our future, they would not be here to offer their assistance.

"They said mankind is fast approaching a crossroads. They of the Pleiades, along with others from outside our galaxy, approach us with open arms as we enter this time of awakening. Only we hold the key to our own door of knowledge and understanding. They said that if we use our creative potential to rebuild our planet in peaceful cooperation, we will be ready to assume our rightful place in the universe. They offer us their love, their encouragement, and their support. They believe in us even when we fail to believe in ourselves.

"Before the end of our meeting, they told me to expect your group on Tuesday. They suggested I tell you about this encounter. They do not wish to be sought out, revered as gods, or to frighten people. They only want to serve as a reminder that the God we seek exists and is within all of us," the professor said, obviously inspired.

It was a thrilling, moving message, and we were indebted to him for sharing it. In many ways, it created a point of reference for future ET encounters I would have. We all took turns embracing them. We really felt no separation between us. The bigger truth was that we were all beings on planet Earth—no separate countries, governments, cultures, or even languages could change this.

We now had to change our focus toward starting our hike and spent the rest of the day exploring ancient ruins, some newly excavated. The professors led us to ruins near the summit of a mountain that rose to about 18,000 feet. It had been a long, slow climb. The mountains were breathtaking, but the air was very thin. The land, the air, and the mountains were void of man's modern technology. They were untouched and beautiful. It was nature in its purest and most natural state. There was a silence, a clarity, and crispness here like I had never experienced. There was an immense serenity, more comforting than I had ever imagined or experienced.

A few days later, we set out for Machu Picchu, traveling forty-six miles southeast of Cuzco by train in the chill of the predawn morning. Leaving Cuzco and the valley, the train traveled along switchback tracks and climbed some 20,000 feet at one point. Then, it descended into the densely forested valley of the Urubamba, following the river westward.

We pulled into the train station at the base of the mountain where the ruins of Machu Picchu lay. We then piled into a small white bus and headed out. The road was narrow and winding, carved into the mountain's edge. It zigzagged back and forth vertically across the face of this steep mountain. It was barely wide enough to fit one bus in one direction, even though it was a two-way road. Every time we met with another bus on our way up, one vehicle had to back up and pull off to the edge of the road to allow the other room to pass. Every time we backed up, someone on our bus shrieked. That didn't help ease my fear of heights. The bus driver, who spent his days driving up and down this mountain road, looked bored. Each time the woman shrieked, he would accelerate the bus faster when we resumed our climb. The woman's shrieks got louder as we climbed higher, and the bus went faster. They seemed to play off one another. I couldn't bear it any longer and went over to the woman and begged her to stop shrieking in front of this crazy driver. When we arrived at the top and deboarded, I told Judith I would find another way down the mountain.

The view was magnificent. The group was excited to be there and unanimously voted to split up and meet back at the hotel the next day for dinner. It was incredible to think we were going to spend the evening here.

I walked around for hours trying to imagine what kind of lives were lived here centuries earlier. I had yet to research the Incas and knew little about their civilization. It felt familiar walking around this ancient village with its roofless stone buildings and structures. I climbed the terraces until I found myself in the oldest part of the ruins, off to the right side. There was a large structure I wanted to investigate. To reach it, I had to walk down a path that was some twenty feet long. It looked perfectly safe, but I stopped dead in my tracks when I got closer. Something terrified me about this little path. I couldn't seem to lift my foot off the ground. There was nothing apparently threatening about this path. I was utterly baffled. Why couldn't I proceed?

I stood there frozen for twenty minutes. A couple came and went along the path without a reaction, but I couldn't move. Yes, I wanted to overcome my fears, but now I didn't even know what I feared. Finally, I threw up my hands in despair, defeated, and walked back.

In a state of bewilderment, I wandered through the ruins. What was that all about? Ten minutes later, I walked right into Judith.

"You look pale as a ghost. Are you all right?" I asked. She was quite shaken. I had never seen her act this way.

"I just had the strangest experience," Judith told me. "I came across a trail that I couldn't walk along. I just felt sick, as if something horrible had happened there. It didn't make any sense to me. It was all I could do to turn around as fast as I could. I'm still agitated by it."

"That was exactly what happened to me."

"Do you think it's the same spot?" she asked.

When we returned, we found we had stumbled upon different ends of the same short pathway. "Why are we reacting to this seemingly innocuous spot like this?" I asked.

"I don't think this spot is so innocent," Judith answered.

It was late afternoon, and I walked around for another hour. I asked a tour guide if he knew anything about the area's history, precisely the spot where Judith and I had the reaction. He said it was the oldest section of the ruins and that a mound of female skeletons had been discovered at the base of the mountain directly below that pathway. He speculated that the preponderance of female skeletons found at Machu Picchu suggests that this was the home of the Mamaconas, or chosen women, whose lifetime obligation was to serve the personal needs of the Inca himself.

I sat on the terrace overlooking the area at the mountain's edge. *Had I been here before? Why did Judith and I react so strongly to the exact location where the Mamaconas had met their death? Were we feeling the energy of that tragedy? Had I died from a fall? Was that why I feared heights? Did my fears stem from a memory not experienced in this life?* Maybe I didn't need to be afraid of heights anymore. Maybe my fears had stemmed from past events I had no conscious memory of but had now acknowledged.

The next day, I climbed a portion of the Inca trail alone. I wanted to overcome not just my fear of heights but my fear of fear. I climbed up the terraces to the upper portion of the mountain, where the Inca trail began. It was a trail that led all the way to Cuzco. If one were to hike the entire length, it would take four or five days. I was going to the top of an adjacent mountain. The trail led to a gateway with a magnificent view of the other side and the Sacred Valley of the Incas.

The trail was hundreds of years old. It was made of stones, now misaligned and out of place. What was once a smooth pathway was now a choppy, inconsistent pattern of rocks. The challenge lay in paying attention and keeping your balance. The path was wide enough here for even me to feel secure—about three feet across. The ascent was rather slow. Throughout history, the land had suffered earthquakes that had moved boulders out of their original places, so occasionally, I had to creep around these obstructions.

As I climbed higher, the trail narrowed and became steeper until I reached about fifty yards from the top where the gateway was. I became paralyzed with fear as I surveyed where I stood. The path had narrowed to about a foot and a half. It was on the top edge of a cliff made of little steps, now very worn and difficult to define. The drop-off was a few thousand feet straight down, with no trees to break a fall. For the next fifty yards, I would have to climb a treacherous, narrow, rocky stairway barely wide enough for one person, nestled on the top half of a steep mountain with a vertical drop-off.

I sat down on my rear and began easing my way up one step at a time. I was so determined that I managed to go about a third of the way. Then I froze completely. The silence was deafening. The wind drew all my attention. I became completely aware of every heartbeat. A moment became an eternity. I couldn't command my legs to push me toward the top, nor would they respond to the signal to pull me back to safer ground.

I don't know how much time passed before I could move again. Which way would I go? If I went up the path and faced my fears once and for all, I suspected these moments would open to a beauty I could not even perceive. On the other hand, if I abandoned the trail now, I could stop feeling this awful fear that consumed me. Nobody would know or care whether I got to the gateway except me. I could come back and try again another time. Another trip to the Andes. Who was I kidding?

I was about to coax myself down in defeat when I heard some pebbles scatter by me. I gasped. I hadn't seen any sign of life since I began this hike. I looked behind me to the top of the path and saw a young man who must have been hiking from the other side of the mountain. "You look stuck. Can I give you a hand?" he asked.

"No. Thank you, I was just leaving," I answered.

"Well, it's a shame not to see the view from here. You've only got a little bit more to go. Admittedly, the last bit is the hardest, but it's worth it. Here, I insist; besides, I could use some company. I haven't seen or spoken to anyone all day."

Then he got behind me and guided me up each step, one by one, until I got to the top. Just as I was about to give up, this stranger appeared. Where had he come from?

The view of the soaring mountains and virgin lands was one of the most spectacular I have ever seen. Having faced my fear and attained my goal left me exhilarated. The elation I felt from seeing a helping human appear as I was about to experience defeat was overwhelming.

To place my hands on the stone gateway, becoming a part of the Sacred Valley's history, and sampling the feeling of self-empowerment from transcending a limitation was worth every bit of the effort.

The following day, Judith and I hiked a few miles to the mineral baths. First, we had to take the bus down the mountain to the railroad tracks. As Judith and I approached the bus, I said, "I'll meet you at the bottom!"

"How are you going to get down?" she asked.

"I'll find the Hiram Bingham Trail and hike down it. I'll do anything rather than go on one of those crazy bus rides again. Jacob told us that in 1912, Hiram Bingham cut through the jungle and overgrowth and created a trail when he climbed this mountain and discovered Machu Picchu. He said it was a steep and difficult vertical climb, but how bad could it be going down?"

"You're still afraid of heights?" Judith asked.

"Yes, and I'm not in the mood to face my fears on a bus right now, thank you," I said.

"Okay, but sometimes when you run away from what you fear, you recreate it somewhere else."

I tried to ignore her last comment, but was pleased she decided to join me, and we began climbing down the Hiram Bingham Trail. It was steep, with shelves of flat-topped rocks that stood perpendicular all the way down the mountain trail. Each shelf layer was three or four feet high. We slid down some of the rock formations, but the farther down the trail we went, the more lost we felt. The forest growth was thick. We thought we had been struggling forever when we finally came to a clearing and realized we had only gone a third of the way down. We didn't have the strength to climb back up, so we continued. I gasped for breath, and we took a momentary break as the trail cleared at the road. "The road," I yelled. "Judith, this is the road where the bus travels. We're safe! Let's catch that glorious bus."

As the bus approached us, I waved my hands and jumped up and down. I was so grateful to get on that creaking bus. I could even appreciate the reckless drivers. We got off the bus at the mountain's base and followed a better trail to the mineral baths. They were nestled farther back in the mountains. The water was green and hot, and a thick steam vapor rose constantly from its surface. We put our clothing and towels in a little hut beside the baths. Nearby, a stream danced over the rocks and provided soothing background music for our meditation.

It smelled of sulfur, and I experienced more invigorating buoyancy than in my past saltwater dips. The combined steam and heated water created the effect of a soothing sauna and jacuzzi. I relaxed and let all my tensions, fears, and anxieties leave my body. Time seemed to stand still. I felt safe, secure, and comforted. We soaked up the healing minerals for a long time. I felt centered. We then dried ourselves and dressed.

Before leaving, I stood at the bath's edge and took a deep breath of fresh air. As I exhaled, a beautiful butterfly flew around me and landed at my feet. I lowered my hand to the ground next to it, and it walked onto my hand. I slowly stood up, and it remained perched in my palm. Five minutes must have passed as Judith and I admired it. "Do you know what butterflies symbolize?" Judith asked.

"No, what?"

"Transformation," Judith answered. "They are a symbol of growth and change. Butterflies begin their life cycle as caterpillars, then spin a silken cocoon where they submerge themselves. After some time, they emerge with magnificently beautiful wings, ready to fly away. And one day, Catherine, you'll fly, too!"

As she spoke, the butterfly gracefully lowered and raised its wings. It was surreal, like an episode from an animated Disney movie.

We walked back down the trail to the base of Machu Picchu. The butterfly never left my hand. When it was time to go, I didn't want to take it on the bus, so I thanked it for coming to us. It lowered and raised its wings gracefully one last time and flew off.

The rest of our trip continued at a fast pace. Between the high-altitude hiking, exploring ancient ruins, soaking in natural mineral baths, sleeping in the Amazon jungle, and climbing Machu Picchu, along with the professor's stories of extraterrestrial encounters, I felt stretched and drained emotionally, physically, mentally, and spiritually. I wondered what the bigger picture and purpose were from this amazing trip to South America.

I felt ready to go home. Living without phones, electricity, television, cars, radios, and refrigerators had been a nice break, but there was something to be said for the comfort of modern conveniences. I longed for a comfortable bed and a bug-free room. Living in these extremes did stimulate a sense of survival and a heightened feeling of aliveness that I was unaccustomed to at home. With so little at hand, you didn't take anything for granted. A more profound sense of appreciation was part of this new feeling of aliveness.

I was grateful to have visited this quaint, high-altitude village, but I was just as eager to leave. When I left the hotel, I breathed a sigh of relief at the thought of never seeing this place again. Some experiences were invaluable to do once, but didn't need repeating. I was not going to miss the snakes, bats, and bugs.

We marched down the two miles of train tracks, dragging our suitcases through the tunnels and back to Machu Picchu. There we waited in line to buy train tickets to Cuzco. We were the only Americans, the only tourists in line. The man in front of us grabbed his ticket and vacated the spot. Philip walked up to purchase our tickets, and the cashier looked at him and shook his head. The cashier was an older man with many wrinkles, especially when he frowned. "Why aren't we being sold the tickets?" Philip asked in Spanish.

"I have no more tickets to sell you today to go on the train." The man replied in Spanish. It didn't make sense. He hadn't sold a trainload of seats by far. Philip stood back, confused.

Then we watched the man continue to sell tickets to the local people behind us in line for the same train ride. This time, Philip went to the window. "You're selling tickets to these people. You have to sell to us," he demanded in an aggravated voice.

The old man replied, "I don't have to do anything for you. If you yell at me again, I won't sell you tickets tomorrow either."

Philip turned to the group and calmly explained our situation, saying we would have to return to the village and spend another night. Most of us were tired, dirty, and frightened. Again, we had to drag our suitcases down the dirty railroad tracks for two miles.

When I asked Judith what she thought, she said, "Sometimes being in the flow means things go differently than planned."

"But we're in a foreign country and refused tickets because of an arbitrary whim of a local cashier. We're left stranded in the jungle where no one knows where we are, and then we must drag ourselves two miles back to the village. Doesn't this seem like we are out of the flow?"

"I think we're not supposed to be on that train, and that man's prejudice of foreigners made that happen. Maybe we'll find out why, maybe we won't. It really isn't important. For whatever reason, we are being directed back to the village. I'm at peace with that," Judith said reassuringly.

We returned to the hotel and were relieved that they had vacancies. At least the front desk clerk was happy to see us. We walked to the restaurant near the train tracks at dinnertime and found the bugs were unusually bad. We suffered a full-force mosquito attack until we stepped inside the restaurant. The owner told Philip in Spanish, "There was a fire in the jungle, and it sent these bugs upwind. You're lucky you didn't leave today. I just heard the train to Cuzco you were supposed to take today broke down a few hours from here, in the middle of nowhere. Those poor people are also being attacked by these bugs on the open-air train. Another train is being sent to rescue and bring them back here."

We successfully bought our train tickets to leave the jungle the following day.

As I rode the train, I reflected on the trip, which I considered to be a gift from God. I wondered how UFOs might fit into His plan. I made a deliberate choice to remain open to the possibilities. Things were happening around me that I couldn't see or understand, but I was willing to accept that.

6

Making Connections

During my first week home from Peru, I found it hard to readjust. I felt different. In those three weeks, I had gotten used to being in the moment and ready for anything. I had learned there was a river, a flow. I knew that following your own life flow means doing what brings you joy. Embracing and allowing joy into your life meant listening to your inner promptings and following your heart.

Returning to a nine-to-five job no longer felt right, even for work I enjoyed. I didn't know what else I wanted to do except to feel free. I had never felt free, especially as a child. All I had known was working hard since I was eight and feeling stifled and oppressed for as long as I can remember. I wanted to leave my job at the A.R.E., not because I was dissatisfied but because of an increasing desire to be free and open to the "flow." I wanted to live like Ray.

During the next week, two opportunities showed up. Judith invited me to visit her in Arizona and meet with the Elders on the Hopi Indian Reservation; then, I had the chance to travel to Egypt. I wanted to do it all, but I needed two more weeks off from work. I talked it over with my supervisor. Of course, I understood she couldn't approve it since I had just taken three weeks off to go to Peru. I decided to do what my heart yearned for, not out of fear but trust. I made my choice and gave her my two weeks' notice.

I felt compelled to see my friend Ray. I shared my decision and concerns with him because other friends told me not to leave my job, saying it was too risky. They didn't understand that I had worked since I was eight years old. I needed to find my passion, joy, adventure, and freedom. Maybe I was running from myself and my wounded past. When I tried to settle down into a conventional life, I felt anxious and needed to get on the move. I wanted to create a life where I did things because "I want to," not because "I have to."

I began experiencing an identity crisis. If I weren't my job, who was I? "Ray, what do I tell people when I'm asked what I do?" I asked him during a visit. "I don't know what I am doing, but it feels right to be footloose now."

"Tell them the truth! You're figuring out who you really are and what you really want."

"That's going to make me look really pretentious," I said sarcastically.

"You can't let what you do determine how successful you are. What you are determines that. If you strive for worldly success, it will always remain outside your grasp," Ray said, speaking intently.

Ray said I needed a support group of like-minded souls. The following evening, he invited me to a hotel across the street from the A.R.E. On the beachside patio was a gathering of eight people. I was introduced to each one of them: There was an elementary school teacher, a photographer, a Russian college professor, a French chef, a waiter, a writer, an artist, and a plumber. Ray said, "Here is the Do-Nothing Club. Everybody here is jobless out of choice, especially through the summer. Everybody here, for one reason or another, is exploring the realms of just being . . . to be in the moment and form a new and less limiting identity not wrapped around what one does for a living. It takes a lot of guts to go without a job and be at ease with that. We live in a country where hard work is revered and doing nothing is frowned upon. These people are pioneers in exploring a state of 'doing nothing.' It's not easy to stay still and be in the moment. I thought you might like to join the club."

Everyone laughed a bit. Ray continued, "I have a background of trying to overachieve and overwork myself to prove my self-worth. I was always striving for success. This club is a random group of people who have come together to learn, relax, and be happy with who we are, not with what we do! We met a few weeks ago when we came here to 'get away from it all.' The goal is not to fear failure or a lack of success and accomplishments. It's just being you without attaching who you are to everything else. It really takes the pressure off and brings us closer to joy."

From then on, I met two nights a week with the Do-Nothing Club down at the hotel by the ocean. We all developed friendships and shared our innermost thoughts, which often gave rise to spirited debates. Other times, we laughed so hard that we would turn the gathering into laughing contests. As I continued my many meetings with the Do-Nothing Club, I shared with them the numerous miracles that had occurred to me so I could continue my experiment of following my heart and letting God direct me to be part of a miracle in someone else's life. What I needed each week and could not afford to buy appeared in different forms from different places, sometimes in money, other times in clothes, food, or household items. I was eternally grateful that I could live a life I was enjoying. It was a time of healing for me to experience a spiritual family, a sense of belonging, and self-acceptance. I never felt judged, and it filled something in my heart that had never been fed.

I sensed a season of change was coming. I learned a lot about focusing on the positive, using affirmations, writing out goals, and imagining the desired goals as already accomplished. I reminded myself I did not have to figure out how the goals would unfold; that I could leave that up to God. I was to listen to my intuition and follow it. I had been focusing on the affirmation: *I allow the creative expression of God to flow through me and take form in my life.*

Then, one of the friendships from the Do-Nothing Club had a profound effect on the trajectory of my life. John Nelson, an author who wrote a bestselling novel, *Starborn*, I had sold through the A.RE. bookstore. He was an excellent writer. In a chance encounter, I told him I was thinking of writing about my following-the-flow experiment but had no experience in that arena. I told him about my ideas for this future book. After another meeting, he suggested that I write a personal story that explored how we draw people into our lives to reach new levels of awareness and form a more conscious connection with God.

He gave me specific ideas about organizing my experiences into book form. Then he went a step further and spoke to his publisher about me. I met with the publisher, and he was interested in my book idea but needed to see a finished manuscript before he could offer me a book contract. For the first time, I had a direction, a goal, and a real and meaningful challenge. I was elated.

The following morning, I woke up overwhelmed with lots of questions about how to write a book. I needed some help. The problem was that I didn't know any other authors, and John had already gone out of his way to help me. So, I did what some women would do when troubled: I got my hair done. Jessie, my beautician, was also a good friend. I couldn't wait to tell her the news. Jessie agreed that I needed more professional advice about writing. Surprisingly, she told me she was good friends with another accomplished author, Jess Stearn, author of *The Sleeping Prophet*. She called him up and introduced us over the phone. He lived in Malibu but often came to Virginia Beach and offered to help me.

Then, only a few days later, I got a call from my producer friend Lewis at the Today Show. I met him years earlier and helped him connect with a few self-help authors. A few months earlier, he invited me to the Phil Donahue Show to meet Shirley MacLaine. When I arrived at the studio, I went looking for Lewis and was mistakenly led to the green room where Shirley MacLaine and Phil Donahue were waiting for his show to begin. I sat with them, and we spoke for a while. I then made my way to a seat in the audience. After the show, I was invited to Shirley's penthouse in Manhattan, where Brian Gumbel would interview her. While that happened, I was seated between a soap opera star and the president of Warner Publishing.

Six months later, my producer friend called me to see if I wanted to work with him, running Shirley MacLaine's *Higher Self Seminar* tours. He said he thought of me because of my natural ability, enjoyment of networking, and spiritual interests and pursuits.

Shirley offered him a short-term position in Los Angeles as her seminar tour manager, and he needed an assistant to help him set up the home office and work with registration. He said her first seminar would be in Virginia Beach, my home territory. It would be a short-term position for me, as well. So, I accepted the job and planned to travel to California. I had been excited to meet Shirley months earlier, and now I would be working for her full-time.

The following week, I boarded a plane for Los Angeles to work for Shirley MacLaine. It turned out Jess Stern lived just down the street from Shirley in Malibu. When I arrived in Los Angeles and called Lewis, he said Shirley wanted us both to come to her home so she could meet with us and we could discuss the upcoming plans for her seminars. Her house was warm and inviting; there were trinkets and artifacts from her worldwide travels, and it had the most beautiful ocean view from the living room.

She asked me to sit on her Persian rug across from her, Indian-style, and have our hands touch. Shirley invited me to be open to perceiving a past life together, so we sat silently in a loving gaze for a few minutes. What came up remained unspoken. It was a unique way to get to know my new employer. Then we discussed the budget and the 10,000 pieces of fan mail that had just been delivered to her suite of offices in Century City. The mail was generated from Shirley's interview on the *Oprah Winfrey Show* earlier in the week, the release of her new book *Out on a Limb*, and her upcoming Higher Self Seminars. We talked until two in the morning and had a great time. It was a wonderful opportunity to see her as a person instead of a famous actress. She's so creative, sharply intelligent, and totally natural.

The following day, I reported to work and found Lewis upstairs in an empty suite of offices. Shirley's offices were next door to Frank Sinatra's. Was I awake and dreaming? He introduced me to the rest of the staff, and then the furniture arrived, and we got to work organizing the offices and preparing for the tour. My days were devoted to making hotel inquiries, booking seminars, ordering stationery, arranging postal service, and answering the never-ending questions from curious well-wishers. Every moment was crammed with frenzied activities and fraught with deadlines. The hectic pace never changed.

Most of my time was spent working twelve to thirteen hours a day. The rest of the day was spent commuting in L.A. traffic, with an hour-and-a-half drive to work and back to my apartment. Every evening, I was exhausted.

MAKING CONNECTIONS

Then, after work one evening, Shirley invited some of us to her home for dinner with Bella Abzug. Bella was a lawyer, social activist, and congresswoman, best known as a leading feminist. She was of Russian-Jewish descent, born in the Bronx like me, and lived in Manhattan. The evening was fun, and the conversations were very lively. On another occasion, I met Midge Costanza, who joined our seminar team. Midge was also a social activist and the first female American Presidential advisor in the Jimmy Carter era. Her office was next to the Oval Office, and Midge became a White House insider. She was also born in New York and is of Italian descent. She grew up in Rochester. I enjoyed meeting people I only knew through television appearances or in news stories. Bella, Midge, and Shirley were larger-than-life personalities for me while growing up and living in New York. The "flow" had certainly given me some unusual opportunities.

On another occasion, Shirley invited me to Ojai with some of her friends for a psychic surgery session. The healer was from the Philippines. I'd met him in Virginia Beach the previous summer. It was nice to be invited, but it was my only day off, and I'd been feeling drained after a hectic week, so I declined. It took some thought, but I've learned I must care for myself first. Two days later, when the healer visited Shirley's home, she invited me back, and this time I went. It reminded me that opportunities are never lost if we are doing what we need for ourselves.

Shirley's first inaugural seminar was in Virginia Beach. There were a lot of details regarding ground coordination for this event. Since I had been living there, Lewis asked me to organize this seminar, including rounding up a large group of volunteers. I jumped at the opportunity. It would give me a chance to connect with lots of people I knew there.

When I arrived, I set up the phone lines in the spare room of a friend's house and went to work. After contacting the media, I called all my key links I knew in the area and within the surrounding states. Each link led me to another contact. The chain kept growing. It was a very heartwarming experience.

While I manned the phones for registration during the week, friends came to help out. Each linkup I had made during the past few years showed up and played an integral part in helping the project succeed. One man stopped in to say he wanted to volunteer his van for anything we might need. It was carpeted and luxurious. He was retired and available as a driver. I thanked him and took his number. I knew he'd showed up for a reason.

Ten minutes after he left, the phone rang. It was Lewis from L.A. "Catherine, can you look into renting a van? We need one with carpeting to pick up the audio equipment from the airport." I just told him that it was already done!

Another friend offered to help me and asked what she could do. I gave her a box of one thousand pencils that needed sharpening for the seminar. "I've been contemplating writing a book, but I think now I've gotten the point," she confessed.

Within one week, the registration went from one hundred to six hundred. The first seminar was an overwhelming success, and I returned to L.A. satisfied that my job had been well done. After I completed working for Shirley's seminar series, I met with Jess Stearn, who took me under his wing for two days and taught me the best of what he had learned about writing. I returned to Virginia Beach to write my first book.

Everything was in place for me to write: my computer, journals, notes, and office supplies. I sat at the computer and wrote one sentence. I looked at it and then deleted it. I wrote another sentence.

My mind was empty. I reread the sentence a few times and then deleted it. I continued to repeat my one sentence and then deleted it. A few hours later, I was looking at a blank screen. I had three months to complete the first draft but couldn't complete one sentence. I was in a panic. The pressure I felt was overwhelming. Was this writer's block?

My friend John Nelson called. I confided in him since he was the writer who helped get me the book publisher's interest. "I can't write," I told him.

"I want you to start writing your story, and this time, don't reread anything you have written until you finish the first draft. I also want you to write as badly as possible," John instructed confidently.

"Why would you want me to write badly?" I was confused by his directions.

"You are your worst critic, and you have put too much pressure on yourself to be perfect. Take the pressure off, write badly, but get the story down, and I'll fix it," John said. I agreed to follow his suggestions.

I got out my outline and notes and started writing. I didn't stop. I didn't look at what I had written. Like Forest Gump, I kept writing day after day. Then, one day, 300 pages later, I finished. I wrote the story. It needed a lot of editing and was terrible, but like sculpting a statue, I now had a rock to chisel on and hope with John editing it.

When I asked John how many pages it should be, he said 300. What he failed to clarify writing it double-spaced, not single-spaced. So, I now had a 600-page double-spaced manuscript. Go figure.

Writing this book was my way of sharing the hope I found at the beginning of my spiritual journey. Little did I know that book had just scratched the surface of the actual healing I needed to undertake.

After finishing my book, I felt compelled to visit my parents. While I was at their house, looking through the window, I saw about twenty birds diving wildly toward the ground and swooping back into the trees. They were trying to protect a stranded younger bird from a cat that had begun to stalk it. Within a few moments, the cat ran for cover. The birds in the trees continued to cry out for their friend. When my father and mother heard all the ruckus, they came out to see what was happening.

As the young bird started to walk toward the street, my father went over and picked it up. It almost seemed able to fly, but might have suffered some shock from falling to the ground.

"I'll take care of it until it can fly on its own," Dad said as he took it into the house.

He found a shoebox and poked a few small holes in it for oxygen and to allow a bit of light to shine through. Placing a towel inside, he put the bird in its temporary home and closed the lid. Then he brought the box outside and set it on the patio.

The other birds' frantic chirps continued for a while until they accepted the departure of their young family member. I sat on the patio, listening to their diminishing cries and the occasional chirp of the baby bird. I was caught up in the drama of it all, and it stirred a lot of emotion in me.

The following morning, I watched my father feed the bird with an eyedropper and put it back in the dark shoe box. I felt my heart ache. Seeing this bird so young and so far away from its home, I imagined how frightened it was and worried it might not see its real family again. I told my father I wanted to try to put it back in its nest. He told me not to touch it. "I'm in charge of this bird," he said abruptly. "I know what's best. I'll let it go when I feel it's strong enough."

His stern reply made me feel like a child trapped in my own dark box. I didn't understand my emotional reaction to freeing that young bird. That evening, I lay in bed reflecting on my exaggerated attachment to the bird's predicament.

Why was I so upset about my father not immediately letting the bird go? Then, an old memory popped into my head. When I was about four years old, I would look up at the night sky and think that I was adopted. I would run into the house crying to my parents that they weren't my real family. I would tell them I was adopted and wanted to go home. I don't know why I felt so strongly about it, but I remember crying myself to sleep over it for nearly a year. My feelings reminded me of a book I had sold at the A.R.E, *Starborn*, about a child who felt his true home was in the stars.

At first, my parents were distraught. It didn't take long, however, before I was praised if I missed a day of crying. Calling me "supersensitive," a child who cried at the drop of a hat, was their way of explaining it away. That's not the way I saw it, however. As far as I was concerned, I had another home and family, which had something to do with the stars in the sky.

Then I remembered how, at age six, I sold greeting cards to buy a telescope so I could search the stars for Maude in Heaven. I would bring out my telescope every night and gaze at the heavens. I was searching for what felt like my real home and my real mother. It was comforting to search the skies.

Eventually, I stopped asking about my real home or looking up at the stars. Now, I wondered what the drama with the bird and my childhood memories had to do with each other. The three didn't seem to be connected, but I felt they had to be. I thought about how the bird couldn't see its family or home in the trees. Was the same thing happening to me? I thought about my father. Why did I resent his treatment of the bird? Was I afraid he would prevent the bird from returning home? Then I realized my father was only a momentary caretaker of the bird, and the shoe box was only its temporary home. I wanted that bird to see its home and family soon. Was my father, for a time, God's chosen caretaker for me? Was the time nearing when I would see this other home and the family I had longed to know? If this were true, where was my real home? I had always felt different from everyone else, as if I were an outsider who didn't belong on Earth. I could never figure out what was behind that longing for my real home and family.

I released my fears about the bird, knowing it would be okay. My questions went unanswered for now. I fell fast asleep, knowing that the answers would come soon. The following morning, I woke up and listened for the little bird's chirps. My bedroom was by the patio where the shoebox was kept, but I couldn't hear anything. I hoped it hadn't died. I grabbed my robe and went outside. I found the shoebox empty. Then I saw my father looking up at the trees near the street.

"Dad, what happened to the bird?" I asked.

"It seemed real chipper this morning, so I decided to let it out," he answered. "After a couple of tries, it flew into that tree."

I was relieved and excited. Like the bird, I hoped I would learn of my real home, too. I asked my father if he knew what kind of bird it was.

"*It's a starling,*" he said.

I thought about the little bird again. I wondered if, while it was in the shoebox, it was thinking that nobody cared, nobody loved it, and it was all alone—thoughts I've often had myself. From my vantage point, I could see trees filled with birds crying out for him. Could that be true for each of us? I told myself that the next time I woke up in the middle of the night thinking I was all alone and that no one cared, I'd think of the starling.

I realized that I was being shown, little by little, who I was as a spiritual being. I needed to learn more. This journey was the only way I would find peace and self-acceptance and truly enjoy my existence here on Earth. I had to trust and follow the clues life gave me.

Over the last few years, I had explored the concept of trust. I now suddenly felt empowered. I had challenged myself daily to trust in the goodness of God and Life. Because I had taken so many risks, I have seen the amazing results of trusting in my Life. Through one experience after another, my connection with God has come alive. I must admit that it would not have meant anything if someone had told me this wisdom. I had to experience it for myself.

7

Down and Out in Beverly Hills

After submitting the manuscript to Hampton Roads, I spent months completing the editing process and selecting the cover art. Finally, the book came out in print. We sent review copies to media outlets and key bookstores, including the popular *Bodhi Tree* in Los Angeles. I did some radio interviews and attended a large booksellers' convention in Seattle. Then, one day, I received a call from a screenplay writer, Deborah, a friend of a friend living in Beverly Hills, who had picked up a copy of my newly published book. She wanted to write a script based on my book to send to film producers. The idea was a long shot, but the phone call triggered a feeling that I would be going west soon, maybe even moving there. The screenplay writer was convinced that the only way this could work was if we could meet regularly, which meant I had to move back to Los Angeles. I decided to relocate.

Then, when speaking to another friend in California, I learned of a soon-to-be-vacated, reasonably priced two-bedroom apartment in Beverly Hills. I contacted the landlord, who agreed to let me move in once the current tenant moves out. With a royalty check coming, I had just enough money to do it. I felt like everything was falling into place.

Still, I couldn't shake the feeling that I may have jumped too soon without thinking this through. Was this blind faith I was acting on? If so, why did I feel unsure? Why was it so easy to let go of my life and run to a promise of another life somewhere else? When I had followed synchronistic coincidences before, they had always been fruitful. So why did I have a questionable feeling in my gut? I ignored my intuitive sense in favor of seeing if things lined up. When knowledgeable friends asked why I didn't have a contract, I assured them I would get one when I got there.

I sorted through all my things. I kept my best clothes and packed them in two boxes in my car. I gave away my furniture since moving it would be too costly. With the car loaded and another chapter of my journey complete, I said goodbye to my friends and left for California.

I drove Route I-40 across the country. It was 2,800 miles, and I planned to do it in five days, driving around 600 miles a day. I was not planning a leisurely sightseeing trip since I needed to resettle and get to work based on my limited finances. The first night, I made it to the border of Tennessee and stayed in Knoxville. On the third night, I stayed in Amarillo, Texas, after spending the day driving through Oklahoma's rolling hills. I listened to the radio, sang songs, and ate lots of granola, nuts, and raisins during the long hours of driving. When I made it to Flagstaff, Arizona, I was only one day away from my destination.

The morning before I arrived in Beverly Hills, I checked out of a motel. When I got to the car, I found it unlocked and partially empty. Someone had broken into it and taken boxes containing all my clothes except two pairs of shorts, a pair of jeans, two T-shirts, and my sneakers. All my favorite shoes, belts, dress clothes, and casual wear were gone. I was very distraught over losing my clothes, but grateful I had taken my computer into the motel room. At least I could still write on it. I arrived in Los Angeles the next afternoon and got the key to the apartment. It was beautiful, with new plush carpeting and freshly painted walls in a lovely neighborhood. The bareness of the rooms drove home the fact that I now owned nothing—no furniture, clothing, or possessions. I felt depressed as I moved into the apartment, which took only about ten minutes. Later, I drove around town and bought a sleeping bag, an inflatable mattress, a sturdy folding table and chair for the computer workstation, and some plastic silverware and plates. I was hoping to find part-time work soon to furnish my apartment. I immediately started searching for ways to make money. Without business clothes or money to buy them, I was limited in my job search. I took temporary jobs where wearing jeans and T-shirts was suitable while I worked on the screenplay with Deborah.

We first met at a coffee shop and talked about how to approach the screenplay. I liked how she wanted to open the story. We then went to her apartment and sat at her dining room table. She pulled a copy of my book that had a lot of Post-it notes on pages where she had underlined passages. Deborah's friend had purchased it at the bookstore and then bought an extra copy for her, knowing she would relate to it. We went over the first scene she had been working on. I liked the episode from the book she had picked out and how the dialogue flowed. I felt we were on the same page. Over the next few weeks, we moved it along, writing the next four scenes. We would talk, Deborah would write the scene, and I would mark it up on paper for the rewrite. It was early in the project, but we were making steady progress. Knowing we were making progress on this project made holding down my temp day jobs easier. It was all positive.

Then, out of the blue, Deborah called to tell me that she had been given a big promotion with her company and had to relocate to San Francisco. She said the added workload meant she had to stop writing our screenplay. She apologized profusely, and I knew she felt terrible about it. Deborah had even tried to get me a weekly radio show through a friend at a local L.A. station. She said it could be another way to break into the business and promote my book. Deborah had arranged a meeting with the station's producer, but I was unprepared and had no talk-radio experience. I appreciated her effort, but I had moved to L.A. to work on the screenplay of my book. I realized too late why people insist on contracts for significant projects.

Had God let me down, or had I mistaken the direction to take in my life? I thought *I would never have come out here if I had known how iffy such film projects were.* I believed everything happens for a good reason, but I couldn't figure out why I had been led into this stagnant and painful situation. Over the next few days, I examined my life. I repeatedly went to work at jobs I didn't want, each day dressed in the few clothes I had to wear over and over again. I came home to an unfurnished apartment that felt barren and empty, with nothing to sit on except the carpet. I felt like a loser.

I wondered if God had forsaken me. Why wasn't I good enough to have even the most basic comforts in life? It was a cruel joke to be led to move to Beverly Hills, one of the wealthiest cities in the country, only to have no furniture to sit on or clothes to wear. People drove around in fancy limousines, and I had a subcompact that didn't even have a radio or air-conditioning. This situation brought me back to how I felt in my childhood. The elementary school I had attended on Long Island consisted of kids from affluent families who dressed the part. About 5% of the students, however, came from an area of lower-class families. I was one of them and felt like an outsider. I began sobbing at night because I wasn't good enough to have what the other kids had.

It hadn't been long ago that I had worked for Shirley MacLaine, met the city's elite, and eaten at upscale restaurants. I was still the same person, and God was still with me now as much as He was back then. I needed to respect myself regardless of what side of the fence I was on. "I am good enough!" I said to myself out loud. I no longer had to see myself as a misfit. I would practice seeing myself as a person who was as worthy of love and abundance as anyone else. My destitute childhood did not need to hold me back any longer.

I needed to hold my head high, love who I am, and feel good about myself, even if my life was falling apart. Anyone could feel good about themselves when things were going well. I realized that it is not what we have but how we feel about ourselves that makes the difference. Over the next few days, I broke through some internal doors. I grew happier just knowing that my dire situation didn't need to affect me anymore. For the first time in a while, I felt a sense of being okay about myself. I began to laugh as I ate breakfast, sitting in my one folding chair at a folding table in my apartment with a fancy Rodeo Drive address and my famous Beverly Hills, 90210 zip code. During the day, I worked as a weight loss counselor, and at night, I delivered food in the Hollywood Hills.

As I began feeling better, I made a list of the furniture I needed for the apartment. Some items I included on the list were beds, a chest of drawers, a sofa, a file cabinet, and an office chair. I made the list to ensure that God would see what I needed! After I finished it, I put it away and went to work. When I came home that night, I drove my car through the alley behind my apartment building. There, I saw two file cabinets and a TV stand by the dumpster.

They were in great shape. I brought them up to my second-floor apartment.

Then the floodgates opened. Over the next week, I found or was given a combination bookcase desk, a vacuum cleaner, a wicker stool for the bathroom, bookshelves, a living room chair, a lamp, an office chair, a sofa, a coffee table, a full-size bed, and a twin bed. The only repair that most of them needed was a coat of paint. That was easy for me since I used to refinish antique furniture. Some of the pieces even looked like they were from the same set.

Then, one evening, at a friend's suggestion, I went to a codependency meeting. I wanted to know if I was codependent. I sat next to a woman in her early thirties. She didn't say a word during the entire meeting, kept yawning, and seemed unhappy. I made a comment about how strange life can be, and she started talking about not having any money. I told her how I was also dealing with money issues.

She seemed interested in my ideas about breaking patterns. "I must have a real self-worth problem because I don't have anywhere to stay for a week," she said. "I ran out of money and had to sleep in my car."

"You're sleeping in your car?" I asked.

"Yeah, but just for one more week," she responded in a somewhat disinterested tone.

I thought I had money challenges! Impulsively, I offered to let her sleep on my couch. Jean accepted readily. She said she could contribute to my rent when her money came through. Then Jean said something peculiar: she had some China in the trunk of her car. She offered to give it to me if I needed any kitchenware.

I accepted her offer. Was this God reaching out to me again?

I felt a little nervous. After all, my new homeless friend was a stranger. But what harm could come from helping her? I had lived on the edge since I came to Los Angeles. That evening, I heard a car honking its horn in front of my apartment. I looked out the window, expecting to see Jean's old car. Instead, she drove a brand-new, fully loaded Mercedes. I turned away from the window since this couldn't be my homeless friend. Then I heard a loud, crass voice call out, "Catherine, are you there? Where should I park my tank?" It was Jean!

I thought, *Only in Beverly Hills do homeless people drive brand-new Mercedes.*

I went out and showed her where to park the car. Then we brought boxes of dishes upstairs. She had a large Gucci suitcase slung over her shoulder.

I gave her the use of the living room closet. Before she unpacked, she insisted on going through the dishes. She had a beautiful set of Royal Doulton bone-colored China dishes with gold-plated rims—a complete service for eight. Then she opened her suitcase and gave me a bottle of perfume, "Poison" by Dior. I loved the scent, but I should have read the sign. It retailed for about $175 a bottle. She handed it to me and said I should keep it as a gift.

I began to wonder how a homeless person could afford a brand-new Mercedes with thousands of dollars' worth of dinnerware in the trunk. "How did you get all of this and end up broke?" I asked.

Jean told me she had grown up in a wealthy, highly prominent family. She had always had maids, cooks, and chauffeurs, had a huge trust fund, and never had to worry about money. She had done some things her family didn't like. So, in retaliation, they cut her off from her trust fund about a year ago.

"You mentioned you only needed a place to stay for a week. What happens then?" I asked.

Jean told me a long story about her car accident and the drawn-out court case that followed. The settlement was about two million dollars. She added, "When I get my money, I'll happily give you a gift for your hospitality. Maybe it will help pay for a few months' rent so you can write."

She unpacked her suitcase. I watched her pull out things like ostrich-skin loafers and Gucci sneakers. She told me how she would spend $10,000 to rent a jet and fly somewhere in privacy. This wasn't what I had imagined my homeless guest would be like.

It was an odd twist of fate for the two of us to be in this apartment: she had spent a lifetime in material abundance, and I spent a lifetime in lack of it. By the end of the week, I was ready for Jean to leave. Bath towels and dirty clothes were carelessly thrown in the middle of the living room floor, and the sofa bed was left unmade day after day. She even lit up a cigarette after I had told her not to smoke inside. There's nothing like bringing someone home from a codependency meeting to learn how to set boundaries!

The next morning, Jean had a long, loud conversation with her lawyers on the phone. I couldn't concentrate, so I finally asked her to take it outside. That night, Jean told me that she needed to borrow a thousand dollars for expenses before she picked up the two-million-dollar settlement check from her lawyer. After listening to her tale of woe, she added, "When I get my settlement check, I'll give you back $10,000 for all your help."

I had a thousand dollars in the bank, which I needed to pay the rent and buy groceries. My gut feeling was not to lend Jean the money, but her offer was tempting because I wanted a quick and easy fix to my financial dilemma to write uninterrupted by temp jobs.

Against my gut feeling, we went to the bank the next day. I wanted a shortcut to fixing my challenges—a quick, magical solution. I was no longer listening to my intuition. I withdrew the money and gave it to her. We stayed out of each other's way for the next few days. Jean even picked up after herself and smoked her cigarettes on the balcony.

Monday morning, she packed up her things and left for her lawyer's office. She said she'd be back that evening with my money. After dinner, I waited for her to return. A couple of hours passed, and she didn't show up. Finally, the phone rang. It was Jean. She apologized and said she wouldn't have the money until the end of the following week. I got upset and reminded her that my rent was due now. She said she would pay the late charges and come by next Friday.

I found myself worrying all week and was unable to concentrate on anything. What if Jean didn't call? Why didn't she leave a number where I could reach her? On Friday, I waited all day. I didn't get anything done, and she didn't call. The following day, I did the same thing. Still no call. I was beside myself. My landlord called about the rent. I told him I was waiting for some money and would get it that week.

I became petrified that she wouldn't bring me my money. How could I face my landlord? How could I keep the apartment? I was paralyzed with fear. I felt helpless and powerless, waiting for someone to solve my problem. Jean finally called.

"Where have you been?" I exclaimed. "I'm going to get kicked out on the street if you don't pay me back."

"That's what I'm calling about," she said calmly. "There's been a misunderstanding. The case isn't settled yet. The lawyer says it may be two more months."

"What about my money?" I asked in a panic.

"Sorry, I don't have it. I spent it."

"I needed that money for the rent three days ago!"

"Listen, I don't have it. If you're going to cop that attitude, then just consider us even," Jean said, sounding very annoyed.

"What do you mean, even?" I yelled into the receiver.

"Well, I figure you got a few thousand dollars' worth of China at a steal for a thousand!"

"What good will China dishes do me out on the street?" I was appalled.

"That's your problem!" she said and hung up.

I sat in silence, feeling numb from what I had just heard. After about an hour, I got into my car and drove to the beach to sort things out. How could I have been so stupid? How could I have let this happen? The answer came right away. I chose Jean's promise to pay me $10,000, which never felt right, over trusting God and listening to my gut.

Hadn't I always been willing to give to others before my needs were met? I often put myself at risk rather than saying no to someone. How quickly I would give away what I didn't really have. I needed to see my landlord and tell him the truth. I could offer to move out immediately and pay him back as soon as possible. I was not a victim, and it was time I accepted the consequences of my bad judgment call.

I called and arranged to see him the following day. I went to his office, sat down, and told him my whole story. He just nodded. Then he asked me if we could finish discussing this over lunch. Of course, that was fine with me, but I had to wonder why he was "asking me out."

I was waiting for him to get angry with me. He seemed deep in thought, and I couldn't figure out his lack of response.

We drove in his car, and he stopped at the bank. He remained quiet. It felt like I was waiting to hear my punishment. He said he'd be right back. He went inside. When he came back to the car, he handed me two one-hundred-dollar bills.

"What is this for?" I asked, completely confused.

"Well, I figure if you don't have money for the rent, you must not have any money for groceries," he answered as we drove away. "Consider it a gift."

"I don't know what to say." I was not expecting this generosity. He was not the same man I had rented the apartment from months ago. I could feel a tear roll down my face, and my stomach settled some.

"I understand," he said, handing me a tissue. I looked at him and saw tears in his eyes, too. "I've cried a lot lately myself."

"Why? Has something happened?" I asked.

He shook his head and looked down. Our next stop was apparently his favorite Italian restaurant. We went in, sat down, and ordered.

I said, "I'll pay you back for this month's rent. I don't know how or when, but I'll do my best." I told him. He shook his head.

"I can let you stay there for the next six weeks if you agree to show it for me," he offered.

"What about the rent?" I asked.

"Don't worry about it," he said. I couldn't believe what I was hearing.

"Why are you being so nice to me?" I asked. Then I noticed tears welling up in his eyes again.

"You see, my wife died a few weeks ago. We had been married for forty years. I feel lost without her. The money just doesn't seem as important to me now. I've worked hard and saved my whole life but lost the person who made it all meaningful. You know, if you had come to me before I lost her, I wouldn't have understood how the unexpected can happen. My only request is that you help someone else out one day."

I realized that while I didn't have the rent money to give him, I could see he needed a friend. I asked him if he'd like me to cook him dinner some evening. He accepted. We took turns talking the rest of the way through lunch, both of us crying at times.

I thought about all the circumstances, challenges, and lessons that had brought this new friend into my life. Although we had different life paths and backgrounds, we were perfectly matched to help and comfort each other at the moment. I was amazed at the synchronicity God used to bring strangers together under His Grace.

My current problems started when I prioritized the outward signs and ignored my gut feelings. But things turned around when I got honest, put my pride aside, admitted my mistakes, and focused on making things right. Going forward, I decided that synchronistic coincidences or outward signs needed to align with my gut feelings—my inner God's voice—for it to be a direction worthy of following.

When the six weeks passed, the apartment was rented to a nice young couple. I packed my belongings and took great care in packing my new Royal Doulton gold-plated chinaware. I decided to keep it, and one day, when I owned my own home free and clear, I would display them in a beautiful China cabinet in my dining room. They would always remind me of what I learned in my Beverly Hills excursion. Whatever my circumstances were, I needed to be faithful to God's will for me; that way, I'd be in His Grace, and things would work out for the best.

It was time to return to Virginia, where my secret addiction would become more apparent.

8

Relationship Nightmare

Since alcoholism starts with denial, it makes it difficult to recognize the underlying problems in oneself. My mother was an alcoholic. Throughout my childhood, I saw her drink every day, and nothing came between her and that drink. She was a high-functioning alcoholic because she held a job and never drank when she worked. As a child, I knew it would take a heavy toll on her, and I begged her to stop drinking. I even hid her bourbon bottle one night, but that did not go so well, and I didn't try that again.

Drinking was appealing because of the numbing effect alcohol had on my thoughts and emotions, but I believed I was different from my mother because I didn't drink every night. When I drank, I would stop worrying about what was wrong with me, and everything would seem to be all right in the moment. Alcohol gave me relief from emotional pain and a sense of confidence I lacked. Alcohol secretly got me through many difficult situations that I could have never coped with on my own.

When I returned to Virginia, I tried not to feel too discouraged by this venture. I had gone to L.A. with such high hopes, but nothing came to fruition, and I almost ended up homeless in Beverly Hills, of all places. When everything went wrong there, and I had to pull myself together, I feared that heavy drinking would make that impossible. So I tried to drink lightly only when I absolutely needed it.

I landed in Virginia Beach with no money, a home, a job, and little clothing. Fortunately, a friend let me stay in the extra bedroom in her condo for a few weeks while I scrambled to establish myself. Judith sent me a gift of $500, which I used to buy groceries for us and get new work clothes. The following week, another friend called with a job lead. The person in this position had left unexpectedly. The opening had not been made public yet. I immediately went to the company and handed in my resume. It felt like déjà vu—when I applied for the job at the A.R.E, I was interviewed that day and started work the next day. I took the job.

I was the marketing manager for a company that manufactured and sold sound products using binaural beat technology, which plays two distinct beats through headphones. The brain hears the difference between the two beats, influencing one's brain waves. Specific binaural beats can alter brain waves to Beta, Alpha, Theta, or Delta states. Their products were sold internationally and used to lower stress, enhance focus, aid sleep, cultivate relaxation, and stimulate creativity. My position required many of the tasks I performed at the A.R.E. I wrote catalog copy and sought out radio and TV interviews and feature stories in newspapers and magazines for the creator of the products. For what I needed at the time, the job was godsent. I loved my work and was well-trained and suited for its undertakings.

Over the next two years, I worked diligently and finally created some stability in my life. One problem became increasingly aggravating, and I had to contend with it carefully. My supervisor played favorites, and I was treated well since he wanted more than just a nine-to-five business relationship. I never responded to his hints, though. Then, one day, he crossed the line and made a move on me in my office. I rebuffed him and made it clear that I was only interested in a work relationship. From that point on, he made my life there miserable.

I remained careful not to slip up on the job, but forgot to call a client back one day. My boss came into my office in a rage, yelling at me. He said I would be out the door if I made one more mistake. His treatment of me, bordering on emotional and mental assault, was the result of my rejecting his sexual advances. Without thinking, I said, "I'm out of here!" and I packed my belongings, walked out of the building, and entered the terrifying land of unemployment.

I stood in the parking lot, shaking. It wasn't fair that my hard work had ended with my boss bullying me and running me off because of his inappropriate behavior. I had seen that look of uncontrollable anger in my father's eyes more often than I wanted to remember. I knew what it was like to be pounced on mercilessly for slipping up, to be condemned and criticized for every move I made. I was grown now, and leaving my job was the best way to fight back.

My solution to this unhappy turn of events was to get wasted at the local tavern that night. As I revealed, alcohol had been my crutch, my secret best friend for the painful moments in my life. Alcohol got me through the times I couldn't push through on my own. I could not imagine living life without the immediate relief it provided. I did try to play it safe with my drinking, though. Some people who drink have enablers or people who cover for them and take care of them. I didn't have that luxury. So, I followed specific self-imposed parameters to control it and still function. I hoped following my guidelines would hide my drinking from others: I never drank when I worked, didn't drink and drive, and drank more often at home in the evening than when out with people. I used it like medication, so I usually stayed sober through a crisis and drank afterward.

It was hot that summer evening. I called a girlfriend and told her about what had happened at work that day, and she agreed to meet me at a local bar and would be the designated driver for the night. My plan was to get drunk; I desperately wanted not to feel and think about my boss, the day's blowout, and my life. I decided to suspend one of my rules, which was getting drunk in public.

When we arrived at the bar, my friend had one drink and then took to the dance floor. I found myself standing alone and feeling very self-conscious. That's when Jonathan walked over and introduced himself. He was tall, extremely handsome, well-dressed, well-built, and well-mannered. He seemed sweet and sensitive, and I found myself attracted to him instantly. We talked for a while as I continued to drink.

We danced slowly, and I melted into his arms. In my inebriated state, I fantasized that we had been together for years and were madly in love. I imagined us the following morning in our home, the sunlight streaming through the windows and amplifying the already bright and cheerful yellow-and-white decor of our kitchen. I could almost smell the fried eggs, sizzling bacon, freshly brewed hazelnut coffee, and yummy pancakes.

Suddenly, the music stopped, and my reverie ended. The lights flickered—the sign for the last call before closing. As I backed away from Jonathan, I felt unsteady, and he took my arm and steadied me. The air smelled of stale smoke and beer. I couldn't tell whether the room was spinning or I was. I squinted, trying to focus on only one Jonathan, not the two I was seeing. The individual conversations around us started to blend into a single, buzzing sound in my head. I began to feel dizzy and sick to my stomach.

Jonathan asked for my phone number, and I declined to give it to him. He was ten years younger than I, with the face of a model and hair like Fabio. Part of me wanted to collapse into his arms and be taken care of, swept away into my fantasy world where things were beautiful, peaceful, and right. It was one of the toughest *no's* I'd ever given!

Two days later, on Valentine's Day, a dozen roses arrived at my apartment. Jonathan had coerced my friend into giving him my address. She pushed me to call him, which I did, and I accepted a date with him. We had a wonderful time, and over the next few months, we saw each other constantly. He treated me like gold.

During that time, the only job I'd found was as a part-time receptionist, but that didn't pay the bills, so I lost my apartment. I began staying with friends for a few weeks at a time. Some of my welcomes wore thin, but I just couldn't get back on my feet. So when Jonathan urged me to move in with him, I accepted.

Within a few months, Jonathan began to demand more and more of my time. I suspended another rule of only drinking alone and joined him in drinking episodes when he got home from bartending at a local golf resort. He drank a lot more than I did, so I rationalized that my drinking was not so bad. I knew better deep down, but I continued the downward spiral to escape from my depressing situation. I slowly lost touch with my friends, and Jonathan insisted I did not need to work.

One night, I mentioned running into an old friend named Scott, a professional golfer who was single and attractive. It was an innocent encounter. "Scott sends you his regards," I said. Jonathan nodded, knowing him from his bartending at the resort. "Scott also told me about a marketing job that opened up at the resort," I said, "I'm going to check it out."

Jonathan jumped to his feet and punched a hole in the wall with his fist. "Don't play me, bitch. You don't need a job, and Scott needs to stay out of our business," he said. Then, he punched the wall again with a little less tenacity. I froze, holding my breath. He walked out the front door and slammed it behind him. I ran to the bedroom and locked the door. I was shaking. I sat on the bed, stunned.

Fifteen minutes later, Jonathan was at the bedroom door. "I'm so sorry. I love you so much, and I'm afraid I could lose you to some guy. Please let me in. I promise it won't happen again," Jonathan pleaded. He sounded sincere. I could hear him sniffling.

I opened the door. Jonathan stood there looking pitiful. My heart sank and I forgave him. We embraced. I reassured him that I was committed to only him. So, he got a beer, and I poured myself a glass of wine, and we bonded again through drinking after the trauma of his temper tantrum.

His sudden outbursts, followed by quick apologies and then drinking the encounters away, became our relationship pattern. He became insistent on knowing my every move, convinced that any man who talked to me was trying to seduce me. Jonathan's jealousy escalated into insane episodes of accusations and threats.

I kept trying to please him and avoid confrontations. He frightened me. I cared for him, but I couldn't begin to accept that I may have made another mistake or that, this time, it could be worse than all the other past relationships combined.

Then Jonathan's anger turned into fits of rage. Holes were knocked in the wall, things were broken, and threats were made. I had to leave the house on one occasion to protect myself. He had been drinking more than usual and was convinced I had seen Scott, which I hadn't. "You are going to admit it and tell me the truth," he raged at me one night.

"Please, calm down. I didn't talk with Scott or anyone," I pleaded. I stayed and listened to his tirade. He continued drinking and raging. I waited for an opportunity to escape. When he went to the bathroom, I grabbed my keys and purse and ran out of the house. I waited until later that evening to return when I knew he would be passed out. The house was dark. I tiptoed in and could hear him snoring in the bedroom. I locked myself in the extra bedroom and tried to fall asleep. The following morning, he did not even remember his behavior. He had blacked out from his drinking.

I didn't tell my friends the truth because I didn't want to deal with the fact that my situation was not only unhealthy but dangerous. Besides, everyone I knew was impressed by Jonathan's charm and good looks.

But I knew I needed to get away from him, so I told him about my plans to leave.

He grabbed my shoulders and said, "We are soulmates. We are supposed to be together. If you try to leave me, I'll do something so we will be together in the afterlife."

"Are you threatening to kill me?" I asked in disbelief.

"Just don't do anything stupid," he said as he released me.

My heart was racing. All I could think about was getting out of there. I got my keys and my purse and went out the front door. Jonathan followed. I got into my car, and as I nervously worked to put the keys in the ignition, he slammed his fist against the window. It shattered into hundreds of pieces. I was petrified.

He grabbed the keys. Once I was stranded, he dropped to the ground and began sobbing. He begged for my forgiveness. His voice choked with emotion. He said, "I've never felt this deeply for anyone. I've never had real love, and I'll do anything to make things right. Please give me another chance. It's the drinking that's bringing out the worst in me. I promise to stop."

I saw the rage leave him. We both cried. I was scared and confused. I had no money and no job. All my belongings and furniture were in his house. My life had become very small: most of it revolved around Jonathan. I just wanted to blame this situation on bad luck. But I had learned there that it was not bad luck. Instead, I felt like other people's problems were my fault and that I was responsible for fixing them. I thought about the codependency meetings in L.A. and how I lost my rent money to Jean. I remember learning that one person doesn't recognize boundaries in those relationships, while the other doesn't assert their will to enforce them. I was doing more than my share in the relationship with Jonathan, and yet he was hurting me, scaring me, and threatening me. I was staying and putting up with his horrible behavior to avoid abandonment. But I had already abandoned myself. Why didn't I just leave him? Why was I so strongly compelled to stay and hope for change? Jonathan had an intensity level greater than Jean's. But now, I could lose my life instead of just my rent money. Was this codependency again, but worse?

Part of me wanted to believe Jonathan. When he cried and apologized, he seemed pitiful. How could I not give him a chance to get things right? Isn't that what I wanted, too? What if he really would change?

We cleaned up the car, and he agreed to see someone about his anger issues. He promised never to behave like this again. But that's not how it went. His behavior continued to get worse. Little incidents set him off, and he would throw things on the floor or curse. A few times, he even looked like he was going to hit me, but he walked out of the room instead. It felt like I was living with my dad, another rageaholic, when I was a child. I was always on edge, walking on eggshells. I felt like a hostage, trapped. He had threatened to take my life if I left. I could get beaten up if I stayed and made the wrong move. If there had been codependency meetings nearby, I would have gone to one.

Then, I saw a show about how to leave a domestic violence relationship. I put together some gas and food money. I confided in friends about what was happening at home and my plans. I prepared for the day of escape. I had packed some clothes, hidden them, and had them ready to go. I brought an extra set of keys and took those and my important papers to a friend's house. I stopped reacting to things Jonathan said that would have typically started an argument. And I continued to look for an opportunity to leave. Most importantly, I prayed to God for the clarity I needed. I knew this was not what God wanted for me. Again, I had veered away from trusting my Higher Power and was living with the consequences of not trusting and following God's will for me. I had ended up in a situation like my childhood, dealing with rage, alcoholism, and abuse.

Not long after that, my trigger moment came. Jonathan and I were in the car, and I was driving. I began to gently broach the idea of our living apart for a while. There was a short silence. Then, with an intense rage, he threatened to ram his fist down my throat so that I would never again speak of leaving him. He grabbed a bottle of my perfume named "Obsession" from the floor and smashed it against the car door. Holding the broken glass to my face, he said, "And I'll use this to cut your tongue out, bitch."

I had to remain calm. I quickly looked around and spotted four men unloading a truck up ahead on the side of the road. All of them might be able to pull Jonathan off me. I immediately pulled over by their truck and softly asked Jonathan to get out of the car. He yelled a string of vulgarities. His rage and profanities got the full attention of these men. I looked at them for help, pleading with my eyes.

Jonathan knew he was cornered. He got out of the car, still calling me every obscene name imaginable, and walked away. I took off in the opposite direction. Trying to keep my composure but still trembling inside, I drove to a friend's house and told her what happened.

I knew Jonathan would be working the night shift that evening at the resort, bartending, so I could retrieve my things. My friend called five trustworthy male friends to help us; I rented a U-Haul and a storage unit for my belongings. Another friend offered to let me hide out and sleep in her living room for two weeks, starting that night. I would stay carefully hidden and safe. When Jonathan's inevitable phone calls began, I told people not to divulge my whereabouts.

He had no idea what I was planning, convinced I was too frightened to leave him. When I called his workplace and verified that he was there, the five men met me at the house, and within a few hours, we had packed my share of its contents in the U-Haul. By one in the morning, I was safely removed from Jonathan. My whereabouts were unknown to him, and his continued threats were made null and void. Everything had gone smoothly. I left a message that if he ever came near me again, I would have him put in jail.

He called my cell obsessively and left pitiful messages, apologies, and promises. When I had a weak moment, my friends reminded me of how sick Jonathan was and urged me not to feel guilty or to doubt the measures I had taken to protect myself. The key to staying away was to remember daily that the relationship had been abusive and not to speak with Jonathan at all. When you stoke smoldering coals, they can reignite the fire.

In some areas of my life, I was an intelligent woman, an honor roll student, and a college graduate. I had helped many people and read plenty of self-help books, but I had a terrible blind spot. Domestic violence can affect any woman, regardless of her intelligence, because the abuse is rooted in the abuser's need for control, not the victim's abilities or character. The truth was my best attempts at fixing myself had landed me where I was: homeless, jobless, and beaten down again. I even chose to ignore the obvious signs, including the perfume bottles; Jean gave me a bottle of perfume named *Poison* before she stole my rent money, and Jonathan threatened to kill me with a perfume bottle named *Obsession*.

What a price I had paid for getting drunk one more time. No matter how I tried to control the consequences of my drinking, there was always a greater price to pay, and this last drunk had almost cost me my life.

I knew I needed help right then and there. I was willing to change and would take whatever steps necessary to right this sinking ship.

9

Gift of Desperation

Knowing I had no job or place to live and needed to settle down, I called my mother, and she suggested I move to St. Simons Island, Georgia, where they had retired. She offered to help me find a place so I could get back on my feet and maybe help them, too. I had lost everything, even my sense of direction. I cried most of the drive, again having to pull together my few worldly possessions to a new location. This time, I felt a sense of dread. It had been years since I lived near my parents. Maybe we could all heal ourselves.

After settling into a modest home where my mother cosigned the lease, I searched the local job market listings. I applied to the only department store as a cosmetic counter manager for *Clinique Cosmetics*. I had no experience in this area, and it was a far cry from my jobs as a metaphysical marketing manager, but the pay was enough to cover my rent and buy a month's worth of Top Ramen noodles. I applied and got the job.

The next thing I did was to attend a recovery meeting. I was committed to making a change. That first night, the room was filled with about thirty people sitting on folding chairs facing the front, where the chairman stood behind a podium. Toward the end of that meeting, he offered a white chip to anyone who had relapsed and wanted to start again. I was sitting beside a new friend named Jane, the Estee Lauder Cosmetics counter manager, where I worked. Jane nudged me with her elbow to stand up and take one. I nudged her back. She pressed harder. I did not want to call attention to our elbow fight, so I got up and took a white chip. Everyone clapped, and I fought off my embarrassment and shame, having lost the battle to control my drinking.

As I made my way to leave, people said the usual things: "Keep coming back." "It will get easier." "Get a sponsor." A few gave me their phone numbers. I smiled, but all I could think was, *Would it really work?*

As I was walking through the door, I heard, "You know, this can be your only white chip!" I turned and saw Carol, an older, long-timer in recovery, whom I had met on the island.

"True, but what if it doesn't work?" I admitted to her. "What if I relapse?"

"It is 100% guaranteed to work if you work it. It says it in the *Big Book*. If you relapse, it means you aren't doing some part of your recovery. Go back and identify what you were not doing and do it now. Guaranteed!" Carol said confidently, chewing her gum.

Suddenly, I felt hopeful. The next day, I wrote down all the elements of recovery: getting a sponsor, attending meetings, working the 12 steps, reading the *Big Book of Alcoholics Anonymous*, and reaching out to others. I added these tasks and was now doing all the parts of recovery covered in the Big Book and the program. I decided to commit to a full recovery program if it was 100% guaranteed to work. Sometimes, someone can tell you something in one sentence that can completely turn your life around!

It was time to face the beast. One night at a recovery meeting, I met Ruth, a graceful, dignified, and stately woman several years older than I. She sensed that I was unsure how to ask and offered to sponsor me. I accepted the offer without even thinking about it. Ruth was known for her tough love, yet she always extended a gentle hand and had an even tone in her voice. To balance all the bad luck in my life, God had sent me the gift of Ruth. I was proud to be her student.

Ruth said at the very beginning of her sponsorship, "If you are committed to growth, seeking God, and changing, then I'll ride you hard, and you will know victory in your life." But she also warned me, "Recovery is not for the faint of heart! It's for those who are willing to go to any length. Don't waste my time if you aren't willing to roll up your sleeves and do the work."

"You really think I can fix my life?" I asked.

"No," she said. "But I know God can and will if you seek Him out."

"How do I do that?"

"Stop running the show and start following my suggestions. Do the assignments I give you. Call me if you run into a snag. Don't drink and go to recovery meetings. And for God's sake, don't date anybody!"

I felt safe with Ruth. I could trust her. When she asked me questions, I truthfully answered them. I described my experiences in depth. I told her about my fear of the dark and how I'd messed up with relationships. I shared that I felt unloved and unlovable and didn't know how to make good choices. I admitted there were times I thought I was losing it and wanted to break down.

As I heard these words, I cried. I just kept crying and talking. I felt such intense pain and sadness. I was embarrassed, but when I tried apologizing, Ruth comforted me by saying, "There's no better time to cry than when you feel like it."

So, I did it for the rest of that visit and every time we met for the next few weeks. I would meet with Ruth, talk a little, and cry a lot.

Then, my depression deepened. I began to fear I really was losing control. I told Ruth my fears were growing worse, not lessening. At times, I felt terror.

Ruth and I met at the park near the pier. She always bought a cup of coffee for each of us. One night, it was a little overcast with a slight breeze. We sat on a park bench facing the water.

"What are you afraid of?" she asked, immediately adding, "Don't answer. Think about it. Close your eyes and breathe deeply. Be quiet with your thoughts and feel what you're afraid of. Move into it, and when you're ready, try to tell me."

I closed my eyes, and after a few moments, in my mind's eye, I saw a little girl standing alone in a dark, empty room. It was me as a young child. I described her to Ruth. "I'm afraid that what really exists inside me is a dark, empty void, and I'm incapable of love." The pain was unbearable, and more tears came.

"What was life like for that little girl growing up?" Ruth asked.

"My father, who was old enough to be my grandfather when I was born, had just lost a leg to cancer. My unexpected arrival was not good news for him. My earliest memories of my dad are of his blistering rages. He would explode over the slightest of things. One time, I didn't put the milk back in its designated spot in the refrigerator, and my father flew into such a terrible rage I thought he would kill me. Sometimes, in his rages, he would tell me I was stupid, didn't know anything, and would never amount to anything. I was confused because my actions never warranted such a hateful response.

"So, I figured I was the problem since I was the one who provoked my father's anger. I lived in a state of hypervigilance, constantly trying to predict how my father might respond to anything

I did. I came to believe that I was stupid, unlovable, and a pain in the neck."

Ruth put her hand over mine. "I'm sorry," she said. "What was your mother like?"

"She was a 'functioning alcoholic.' Instead of protecting me from my father, she allowed his abuse. She didn't defend herself from his attacks either. Instead, she pretended it wasn't happening. She medicated her hurt feelings with alcohol."

"Did she stay home and raise you?" Ruth asked.

"No, I was left with a series of neglectful babysitters, and when I was nine years old, I was sexually molested by a man."

"What did your mom do?"

"Nothing. I didn't tell anyone," I answered.

Ruth handed me a few extra napkins. I wiped the tears from my face. "Why am I getting worse?" I asked.

"You're not," she said, "You're feeling things you've never let yourself feel."

What Ruth said made sense. Ever since I could remember, I had pushed aside and held in my pain because I thought if I ever let it out, I would lose my mind. Over the years, I drank more and more to numb those feelings.

Ruth suggested I write them down, stop resisting them, and see what is actually there.

I took her advice and stopped fighting this losing battle. I admitted to myself that I was depressed. To my surprise, I got a little relief from not pretending it away anymore. I allowed myself to be miserable without hiding it, and it felt cathartic.

"Emotions don't just disappear when they're ignored. When you bury feelings under drinking, drugging, relationship-hopping, shopping, overeating—you name it—they become like air bubbles underwater, and sooner or later they'll surface," Ruth explained.

When I stopped drinking, I had no way to self-medicate the pain inside me. By the end of my first year of sobriety and working the steps with a sponsor, I still felt suicidal. As the emotions from the past surfaced, they were overwhelming. Without alcohol, I did not know how to handle the insistent pressure. I wanted to live and be happy, but didn't know how.

Every day, I fluctuated between despair and anger, and both responses were out of proportion to the events or situations that triggered them. Ruth claimed, and rightly so, that I still had not dealt with many of my past pains and violations. She said that as I healed my past wounds, my emotions would become more balanced and my reactions appropriate to the present.

One morning, I got to work and thought I was going to collapse. I took a break and called Ruth. "I didn't know if I could stay at work," I said. "I'm exhausted from not sleeping at night, and I wake up so depressed I don't want to face the day. I get angry over nothing, and I'm ready to blow up. My mind is so muddled that if someone asks me a question at work, I struggle to think clearly and answer it. My fear of being alive is almost transcending my fear of death. I'm really frightened. I can barely function. I'd never kill myself, but I think about my life ending a lot. It's the only way I find relief."

"You need professional help outside of recovery. Would you let me help you get it?" Ruth asked.

I agreed, and Ruth wasted no time making arrangements.

In the meantime, I was afraid I would lose my job. What would they think of me if they found out? So I called my new recovery friend and coworker, Jane, at the department store. She suggested

I call the human resources manager. I remembered when I told the truth to the landlord in Beverly Hills, everything worked out for the best, so I called the manager. She understood and reassured me that I would have my job when I felt well enough to return.

At 4 p.m., I was signed into a mental hospital.

Ruth turned me over to the inpatient assessment nurse. After the intake interview, the nurse and the doctor tagged me with *suicidal ideations* and put me in a room where I would be monitored. They went through my suitcase and took away my razors, belts, and mirrors. I was relieved to be there and committed to doing whatever they asked of me. I was ready to face myself. I was scared, but this was my only hope. I told the nurses I did not want any medication.

That evening, I took out Ruth's assignment to write a list of the fears and resentments I had been suppressing. The point was to take an inventory of what I was feeling, just as a store takes inventory of what is on its shelves. She suggested that, when I had completed my list, I should speak it out loud, first to myself in a mirror, then to God, and finally to another human being.

10

Breakdown and PTSD

Unable to fall asleep in the suicide watch room, I continued working on my list of fears and resentments. When I finished it, I went to a fake plastic mirror and recited my list aloud. At that point, the nurse opened the door and saw me talking to myself in the mirror.

Startled but knowing what this must look like, I turned to explain. But the nurse didn't listen and quickly excused herself, shutting the door behind her. That felt uncomfortable. I wasn't crazy, just depressed. But it wasn't the first time my process had been misunderstood, so I finished in front of the mirror and continued the exercise.

I set a chair next to my bed for God, sat on my bed, and began reading my list aloud, imagining God sitting in front of me. The door opened, and again, the nurse eyed me as I sat talking to an empty chair. Again, I began to explain, "This is not what it looks like," I started, but she said it was okay and left again, shutting the door behind her.

"God. Sorry for the interruption," I continued, a little faster this time, listing my part in the wrongs created in my life around fears and resentments. "I've listed the shortcomings I have been ashamed of but want to heal and change: I stuff my feelings. I run from speaking up for myself. I'm insecure and often think people are mad at me for no reason or that they don't like me. Trusting people is hard for me. I don't feel safe. I do self-destructive things. I have been harsh and critical of myself. I feel overly responsible for other people's problems. I feel like everything is my fault, and I apologize incessantly to others. I feel guilty standing up for myself. I isolate myself from others and try to deal with my loneliness. I feel inadequate, worthless, and unimportant. I have trouble expressing my honest feelings. I'm intimidated by angry people and panic when I make a mistake or have a problem. I am a people pleaser and approval seeker. I have been afraid of abandonment, yet I have jumped into relationships with abusive men. I'm worried I won't know You or Your Love.

"I don't like admitting all of this to You. I wish it would all go away. I know I sound like a mess. Please help me. Look where I am at! Thanks for listening."

So, regardless of its appearance, I told my true feelings and experiences to myself and God. I would complete the exercise during my stay there by telling a counselor. Ruth had me doing step 5 in recovery: identify our character defects by looking at the fears and resentments we listed and reviewed in step 4. We can see our part, or how we have contributed to the fears and resentments we have held. Then, by admitting them to God, yourself, and another person (whom we can trust), we acknowledge what we want to change and heal. In recovery, we learn that secrets can make us sick. So can shame. By admitting our shortcomings, we are releasing the secrets and shame into the light. By accepting our character defects, we acknowledge what we want to change and release the shame from our secrets into the light.

I did feel some peace afterward. I got into bed and turned the lights off. The nurse opened the door again, and I pretended to be asleep. In the suicide watch room, you get checked on every hour.

BREAKDOWN AND PTSD

The following day, they let me out to the patio. I met the other five men and two women from my unit there. "What kind of work do you do?" one of the men asked.

"I wrote a self-help book," I said proudly.

"Must not have been too good if it landed you here," he answered. Everyone laughed. He was right. For a moment, I had forgotten I was in a mental hospital.

"Actually, it was about how people in your life are road signs to self-discovery. It turns out I didn't have the whole story back then. I'm here working on my follow-up," I said, claiming my truth. The others nodded, which made me feel better. They understood.

Each day, I participated in intensive group therapy sessions aimed at helping me return to the most frightening and damaging experiences throughout my life, mainly in childhood. As I relived each episode, I reexperienced the deeply suppressed emotions I had been too afraid to feel back then. Sometimes, I was so frightened that I wanted to run out of the hospital, but fortunately, I was in lockdown.

The staff helped me express and release a lot of pent-up rage. One day, they handed me a plastic bat to hit a picture of the molester I had drawn earlier. I was told to hit the face and yell out what that person had stolen from me. I felt embarrassed and self-conscious at first. I told the psychologist and nurses that I couldn't see how this silly act could help me. I was stuck in my logical head.

They encouraged me to try it. Eventually, I picked up the bat, swung it, and made some comments about the drawing I made of an abuser. Then I did it again, this time with a little more feeling. Then again, with some anger. And after a few more tries, a rage pulsed through me, and I let out a guttural cry so loud it rang through all the halls of that hospital ward. All the violations from the men in my life, all the criticism and rage directed at me by my father that I had swallowed as a child, all of that came pouring out of me after decades of silence and isolation.

I collapsed on the floor with the doctors and nurses holding me. One nurse stroked my head. "You did great," she softly whispered.

I lay on the floor, tingling from head to toe. It was like the relief that comes from throwing up after hours of intense nausea—miraculously, you feel better.

It was freeing to experience my emotions in front of and with other people. Those same people honored me with their trust as they opened and bared their souls to me. We honestly shared what we felt and believed about ourselves, our deep, dark secrets, pains, and fears. Together, we helped each other heal.

I learned that four of the five men on my ward had been prisoners of war or had served overseas and were being treated for Post-Traumatic Stress Disorder (PTSD). The two women were dealing with the effects of childhood sexual abuse, and they, too, were being treated for PTSD. One of the women was going through her fifth divorce. She had been promiscuous from a young age and allowed alcohol and drugs to cloud her judgment. Her marriages were all short-lived. She was worn down by her life and baffled by her choices. During her stay at the hospital, she got in touch with the sexual abuse she endured from age 8 to 12 by an uncle. This therapy was the first time since childhood that she felt safe enough to process what had happened to her. She got in touch with her rage, fears, and pain. As she relived her childhood experiences, I saw her revert to an eight-year-old frozen in fear. As she came out of the relived past trauma, she said this was why she felt so empty inside as an adult. I could relate to her story.

I soon learned that PTSD is a disorder that affects people who were victims of traumatic events. After years of trauma and distress, painful memories can become stored in our minds and bodies. Events that cause PTSD produce such a high state of threat that our body chemistry changes. Long after the danger has passed, the person with PTSD stays on "alert" to prevent or foresee future events that could retrigger the fear of the original traumatic event.

Some of its symptoms include living in a state of hypervigilance (constant monitoring) of our surroundings, being startled easily, and experiencing flashes of panic. The therapist at the hospital explained that many adults who had childhood experiences like mine constantly surveilled their homes or relationships, always on the lookout for anything that resembled the threat of the initial event or events.

Toward the end of the third week, I was ready to return to my life. I was feeling better, relieved, lighter. Something had begun to fill that hollow space inside me. I felt more connected, freed up, and more real inside me.

Two days before I left, I met with my counselor.

"I'm sorry," the counselor said, "for the things that happened to you in your childhood."

"Thank you," I cried. It was the first time anyone apologized to me. It felt good to admit the truth to someone and feel heard at last.

"Can you forgive yourself for doing the best you could with what you knew at the time?" the counselor asked.

I thought about her question. I wanted to forgive myself. "Do you think God could forgive me?"

"I think God is love and forgiveness," she answered.

"Then I forgive myself," I said.

11

Breakthrough and Recovery

When I returned home from the hospital, my parents called. I wanted to scream at them for all the things they had or hadn't done to me growing up. I was furious when realizing I had settled for so little from the men in my life, which started with my father's abuse. I was enraged about the abuse I had endured and how I had begged for crumbs of attention from everyone in my life. Instead, I pushed through the brief conversation, knowing this was not the time to express those feelings.

I knew I had more pent-up anger to express. One night, I bought a plastic bat and went into the garage to hit an old mattress I had leaned against the wall. As I hit it, I yelled out what angered me about my past. Not long into my at-home exercise, there was a knock at the door. My next-door neighbor heard me yelling and asked if she should call the police. I reassured her that everything was okay and stopped this exercise.

The following day, I was walking on a trail in the woods. I had not seen anyone in a while. So, I found a big stick, used it like a bat, and hit a tree trunk, again yelling how I felt. It was very cathartic from not having expressed my anger through the years of my father's emotional abuse. I turned around and saw a father and son walking toward me on the trail. For a moment, we locked eyes, and before I could explain myself, he turned, and they quickly walked away. I must have looked like a madwoman and frightened them. I threw the stick away and went home.

The following night, I came up with an anger-release method I still use on occasion. I took a pillow with both hands, hit it on the bed, and whispered what I was mad about each time. This way, no one calls the police, and I don't look crazy or frighten others.

While at the hospital, I missed Ruth. She felt more like family to me than my parents, but the hospital had strict rules: only immediate family members could come one afternoon a week, but they had to attend a two-hour group family session. My parents came to the hospital, but my father refused to come in. It was a lockdown facility, so my mother had to be escorted inside. She greeted me with a hug. It was good to see her, but it felt awkward. She looked around anxiously at the stark white walls and shiny, waxed grey tile. "I still don't understand why you are here," she said as some of the patients from my wing passed us going into the group therapy room.

"I think you will get a better idea once the session starts," I said, pointing to the door.

"I can't stay for this; your father is in the car and won't come in. Besides, I don't think you have a problem." She left abruptly afterward, saying we could visit when I got home.

I couldn't wait to meet with Ruth again and thank her for all her help. I told her I was amazed at all the time and wisdom she had poured into me without receiving any money or recompense.

"Just paying it forward," she said in a gentle voice. "Years ago, a woman took me under her wing, guiding me and teaching me to make healthy choices and be free. One day, you'll do the same for others. That's how God's light stays bright."

Each week, Ruth and I met. She saw my commitment to recovery and brought me closer to her personal sphere, which meant meetings at her house. Ruth mentored many women but was protective of her personal space, privacy, and business. We had coffee and walked on the beach. I called Ruth often for all kinds of advice and suggestions, and that was new to me. I could be vulnerable with Ruth. She pointed out, "Your biggest problem *is* your thinking. When you let God renew your mind, everything changes for the better."

Ruth would tell me, "Behaving in new and healthy ways often feels uncomfortable at first, but with practice, healthy behaviors will become natural." She reminded me not to put too much stock in my feelings. "Feelings," she said, "are not facts."

Then, she got right to the root of the matter. Because of my abusive relationships, she said that I should commit to one year of no dating while we explore recovery principles. "If you start a romantic relationship now, it will take the focus off your growth and recovery. Now is a sacred time, a space to develop yourself."

I didn't like what she told me, but I understood and agreed to give it a try. She wanted me to realize that love starts with God and comes from within yourself. "If you let others determine your value, you give them the power to lift you up or knock you down. Self-esteem is an inside job," she added. "As your relationship with yourself becomes complete, your relationships with others will also become whole."

Ruth tried to give me a vision of a healthy relationship. "They don't drain you. They give you a safe place to express love and to share who you are. When you care for yourself first, you can give to others from the overflow in your life."

"Why have I always been attracted to the bad guy?" I asked Ruth.

"My friend, often the people and places that caused terror in our childhoods still attract the same in adulthood. There is a link between what we learn about ourselves as children and how we live as adults. We go after people and situations that replicate the unmet needs from our childhood. If you are in a relationship with someone who doesn't respect you and you stay there or keep going back to them, you are emotionally addicted. What you were taught about love early on—namely, the fear and adrenaline rush from the danger involved—set you up to seek those same experiences with men later on. Your needs are never actually met, but, just like an alcoholic, you stay in search of the high, even without gaining satisfaction or results."

Ruth had nailed it. She was making sense of the dynamics and reasoning behind behaviors I'd experienced in my relationships with men that had baffled me all my life.

"You can't expect abusive men to heal you and fill your emptiness. That emptiness can only be filled by God. The way to stop and heal from obsessive, abusive relationships is to have a deeper, spiritually grounded love for yourself. When you realize you are created by God *for* God as His daughter, you change how you act and what you choose to allow in your life."

"Ruth, how did you learn all of this? You are in a long-term marriage, and you seem happy," I said, noting what I had observed.

"I think Mark Twain sums it up for me: 'Good decisions come from experience, and experience comes from bad decisions.' Let's just say I had 'bad' experiences before I did this work on myself and then met my husband," Ruth graciously explained.

What I was learning had worked in her life and the lives of all the other women she mentored. For a year, I committed to avoiding relationships and instead looking to God and myself for love and healing. I eagerly anticipated the healing that would come with the new phase of this spiritual journey. Learning to live sober and healing added another dimension to my growth and self-awareness. I'd read hundreds of how-to books and tried endless self-help ploys, but now, through recovery, I was finding God more profoundly.

One day, I arrived at the coffee shop and found Ruth sitting at a table off to the side by a window where we would have some privacy. Ruth wanted to talk about my love life. I had shared with her about Jonathan and other failed relationships. It was a pattern I wanted to break, a relationship turnstile that I wanted to be free from. Ruth told me that if I put the work in on myself, I wouldn't get into another bad relationship. I assured her that that was what I wanted, and I was committed to that.

"How can you recognize a counterfeit bill?" Ruth then asked.

"By comparing it to a real one?" I guessed.

"Precisely," Ruth affirmed. "It's the same for love. You can tell real love by knowing what love is. You're a writer. Is love a noun or a verb?"

"It's a noun. It describes a feeling," I said without hesitation.

"You are half right. Love can describe an affection we feel for another, a noun. It is also a verb, something you do. Real love is a choice. It is an action word. When you love someone, you respect them, listen to them, empathize with them, appreciate them, and affirm them. When we love someone, we choose to make sacrifices and compromises because we care about them and consider their best interests. Love involves truth, trust, and faith. It is not selfish, and it brings hope." Ruth painted a picture of what I lacked in past relationships.

What I had experienced with men and called "love" was the opposite of what Ruth described as love. I could see that my relationship problems had come from not knowing what love was, what it looked like, and how it should act. Ruth gave me a new healthy standard to gauge real love against and to measure how lovingly I was behaving.

What I had called love wasn't love at all. Life had taught me incorrectly. I had considered lust and feelings based on physical attractions, and primitive in their instinctual drive and intensity to be love. The magnetism, the pull, the lure of those erotic experiences had a life of its own, and like momentous tidal waves, they had overpowered any attempts at logic and reason. I had so desperately looked for love in the wrong places. I had a lot of work ahead of me, comparing what I had thought love was with what it really was. Ruth said that the only thing that matters is to discover a personal relationship with God so that you *experience* the love of God. I was all in.

The following week, Ruth invited me to her home and told me to bring an apron to help her make a wedding cake for a client. Ruth had a small at-home baking business. I felt honored. Her asking me to help bake for a client was highly unusual, and I came with an apron in hand.

She greeted me at the door, and I hugged her warmly. I was comforted simply by entering her house, decorated in light, airy colors. Its rooms were painted soft yellow with bright white trim, with big windows in every room. There was a flow to her house, and the details of all her furnishings complemented each other. Plants, candles, paintings, sofas, accent pillows, and side chairs all came together as part of a mosaic, exuding peace and comfort, just as her presence did for me.

BREAKTHROUGH AND RECOVERY

She led me into the kitchen, where the usual aroma of freshly baked goods was missing. I had gotten spoiled from eating a tantalizing homemade dessert each time I came over.

"Tonight, instead of giving you a piece of cake, I want you to see what goes into making a wedding cake." Ruth poured us two cups of coffee and offered me a seat at the kitchen table.

"Ruth," I asked, hurrying on, "I know I've committed to not dating, but why can't I stay open to meeting someone while I grow and heal? I'm not a kid anymore."

"Most of us want to be in a good, loving relationship. We want to be in love. But first, we need to figure out how to get there and with whom to join our lives. We have the right intentions with healthy desires, but in our ignorance, we make disasters out of our love lives. We create families and divide those families repeatedly. It doesn't have to be that way. You can find true love."

"But how?" I asked, intrigued.

"Let's start making that cake," she said, changing the subject. Ruth began reaching into her cupboards and handing me various ingredients to put on the counter: flour, sugar, baking powder, and vanilla. Then she walked over to the refrigerator, talking as she went.

"First, there is nothing wrong with marriage. It's quite beautiful when you're with someone perfect for you. The problem lies in picking the right person, and you have a *broken picker*. So, I am going to pick for you." Ruth began handing me more ingredients: butter, milk, and eggs.

My muscles tensed at the very idea of Ruth picking my mate.

She grabbed two big mixing bowls from the cabinet. She asked, "Would you like to be married to someone who will never leave you, someone who will listen to your most intimate thoughts, someone who will understand and meet your ever-changing needs, someone who will be strong for you yet comfort and love you in the way you have deeply desired?"

"Who wouldn't? But does that kind of man even exist?"

"That's true love, and it exists. But much like baking a cake, there are some preparations you can make that will position you for success in your love life." Ruth got out the blender, mixing spoons, and two baking pans.

"You've lost me," I said. "How is getting a love life like baking a cake?"

"I'll show you," Ruth said.

She asked me to measure out and sift together all the dry ingredients. I carefully mixed the flour, sugar, salt, and baking powder. Then she had me mix the eggs, the milk, vanilla, and the butter into another bowl. I greased the baking pans and checked the oven temperature. All that was left to do was to combine the bowl of dry ingredients with the bowl of wet ingredients. But as I reached for the bowl with the eggs, milk, vanilla, and butter, Ruth took it and left the room. She returned empty-handed. The only thing left on the counter was the bowl with the other ingredients.

"How do you think the cake will come out with just these four ingredients?" Ruth asked, pointing to the bowl.

"Not good."

"Why would you want to make a cake without the key ingredients that hold it together and give it substance and moisture? Why would you want to do something, knowing ahead of time it won't come out?" Ruth asked.

"I wouldn't. You took the bowl away," I said, puzzled.

"Well, if you look at the history of your love life, it's as if you're still wanting to bake a cake without the main ingredients that create the foundation and form of it," Ruth said. She disappeared from the room again and returned with the missing ingredients. She continued to make her point.

"My brother is a home builder. There's a fundamental principle in home building: the size and strength of any house will be determined by the size and strength of its foundation. You must lay a strong, spiritual foundation within yourself before you can build on it through a relationship with another person. Just like eggs added to flour are the keys to building cake layers, a personal relationship with God is the key to creating a love relationship with someone else.

"Patience and a renewed mind are two more key ingredients of a strong base to live by, just as milk and butter are keys to our cake. By laying the proper foundation first, whatever you try to build will stand the test of time. We live in a society that wants everything to happen quickly. But God has His divine timeline for us and is not in a hurry."

Ruth and I finished mixing all the ingredients and poured the batter into a cake pan, which went into the oven to bake. I took off my apron, and we sat at the table.

"God is your Heavenly Father to whom you can surrender, follow, and commit to a committed relationship. God wants to be your foundation, your everything."

I felt resistant and uncomfortable hearing God referred to as Father. "Ruth, I have all these negative feelings associated with the term father. I don't know if I can think of God in that light."

"That's fair, and I know this is challenging. But your perceptions about the roles men play in your life need to be healed so you can receive the truth of *God's* role in your life," Ruth explained. "God is the rock upon which our spiritual life must be built. It takes effort and work daily to seek and do God's will. Until now, you've focused on the *men* you could match up with. If God is the ultimate matchmaker, why don't you consider aligning yourself with Him?"

I was beginning to feel overwhelmed again. In relationship after relationship, I had continually surrendered my life to and put my confidence in a man instead of in God.

Ruth said, "Marry God in your heart and seek to love Him fully. He can be your true first love." Ruth continued, "You can have a forever love relationship with God. He's what you've looked for in the wrong men your whole life. He's the right one."

Ruth's excitement and enthusiasm were contagious.

"But what do I have to offer Him that He would want me so much?" I asked, my low self-esteem clicking in again.

"It's not *what* you offer Him, but *who* you offer Him. He has everything except one thing: you! Give Him yourself." Ruth explained.

I sat quietly with all this wisdom for several moments. "Do you think this will stop the pattern of bad relationships I've had, with the last one being the worst?"

"You can't get where you need to go if you're on the wrong road and driving in the wrong direction. Backtrack to where you missed your turn and get on the right road. Making God your first love is getting on the right road," Ruth added.

Ruth brought our meeting to a close. She said my assignment for this week would be to consider how I could practice making God my first love. Before I left, she said, "Whatever we put ahead of God, we lose. There is a promise found in Matthew 6:33: '*But seek first the kingdom of God and His righteousness, and all these things shall be added to you.*'"

I went home, excited about the prospect of being married to God. I seemed to have nothing to lose and everything to gain. I felt more committed than ever to following Ruth's suggestion to make an unseen, spiritual husband more tangible.

The following morning, getting ready for work, I reached into my jewelry box for earrings and noticed an engagement ring I had worn years ago. It was a simple, one-carat stone (cubic zirconia) in a white gold band. When the relationship it represented ended, I put the ring away. I had never considered wearing it again for fear that it would scare off potential prospects by suggesting to the world that I was engaged.

That morning, though, I realized that it didn't matter if a ring made me look unavailable because I *was* unavailable. I was choosing not to date, flirt, or even interact alone with men. I was free to wear this ring and decided it could symbolize my commitment to God. Excitedly, I put it on. It sparkled. It held rainbow prisms of hope. I wore it proudly as a statement about my marriage to an ethereal husband. I decided to believe by faith that God's presence would be as real as a husband as the physical chair beside my bed.

The following night after work, I made dinner. I put an extra place setting at the table for my unseen husband. I felt a little self-conscious, but I did it anyway. By the end of the meal, though, I had the strange sensation that I wasn't alone. I felt peace and comfort. I decided to consciously take God, my invisible love and provider, with me wherever I went.

The following day, when I woke up, I greeted Him. I had breakfast with Him. On the drive to work, I confided in Him about my cares and concerns for the day, for my life. At times, I got carried away in our conversation: I'd pull up to a red light and be embarrassed when the passenger in the car next to me saw me talking to myself. Then I would hear what Ruth told me many times: *What other people think of you is none of your business!*

When Wednesday rolled around again, I couldn't wait to tell Ruth what I had done to make my marriage to God more real. I showed her my engagement ring and told her I now went everywhere with Him.

"So, commit to finishing the course, Catherine. God has called you to be His." Ruth pointed to a passage of scripture familiar to me by now, Isaiah 54:5-6: *'For your Maker is your husband . . . He is called the God of the whole earth. For the LORD has called you like a woman forsaken and grieved in spirit, like a youthful wife when you were refused, says your God.'*"

"So, God will never forsake me?" I asked. The implications were astounding.

"A hole in your heart can't be filled with a relationship, Catherine. The emptiness in your heart is a God void; only God can fill it. Your marriage to Him needs never to end!"

God became my source of joy, hope, comfort, peace, direction, resources, finances, and wisdom. All I had to do was spend time with him and let God determine how my prayers and needs are answered and how I can help others.

Ruth rose from the table and walked me to the front door. As I was putting on my coat, she asked, "Why do you think you have repeated abusive relationships?"

Her straightforward question threw me off guard. I didn't have a short answer. It was part of my past that I felt ashamed of, and I tried to hide my failures and mistakes.

"Don't answer that now," she said. "But I want you to review your patterns with men and write down your understanding of why you had these kinds of relationships."

It was a good assignment that held promise for making sense of and understanding my relationship with my father and the other men who followed after him. Maybe I could finally put the pieces of my life together so I could heal and create a different experience.

Then, one day, I went to Walmart. Christmas songs played as I walked through aisles stocked with seasonal items and caught sight of a Santa suit for sale. My spirit leaped inside me as I felt the strong urge to buy it. *What would I do with a Santa suit?* I couldn't imagine why I felt led to buy it, but I had learned to follow my intuition, no matter how illogical it seemed. So, I bought the suit!

The following night, the week before Christmas, I went to a recovery meeting, where I shared about having bought a Santa suit, saying that if anyone needed it, please let me know. After the meeting, an older woman with a slight handicap approached me. She told me her daughter had gone out on drugs again, had been arrested, and was now sitting in jail. This woman now had full-time custody of her four-year-old grandson.

She teared up as she told me how badly her grandson missed his home and mother. The woman asked me if I would consider dressing up as Santa and surprising the child with a present she had already bought for him.

In my depressed state, it was the last thing I felt like doing. Yet, looking into her tear-streaked face, the words, "Sure, I will," came out of my mouth. I told her I'd be at her apartment the following day at 4 p.m.

An hour before I arrived at her apartment, I started dressing up in the Santa suit. I stuffed pillows around my stomach, rear, and anywhere needed to take on the persona of the big jolly ole fellow. Glancing in the mirror on my way out the door, I decided that, from a distance, I looked convincing. However, I felt self-conscious and was not in a festive mood.

It was early afternoon when I walked to the woman's apartment door and knocked. She greeted me and led me inside. In her living room, the cutest little boy sat on the couch. His eyes opened wide, and a big smile of amazement and awe spread across his face. I said, "Ho ho ho!" and called him by name. That was all the proof he needed that I really was Santa Claus. I gave him his present and said I needed to get going to visit thousands of other little children in town. The truth was, I didn't want to chance his figuring out I was actually a short, forty-something woman struggling with insecurities and a bout of depression. The little boy hugged me, and I was on my way.

Walking to my car, I heard a child yell, "There's Santa!" I turned around and saw five children running toward me. My heart raced as I fumbled with my car key and unlocked the door. But the children caught up to me just as I got into the car. They were eager to tell me what they wanted for Christmas, and I listened and assured them I would put their wishes on my list. Just before I drove off, one of the children said, "Santa, why do you have long nails painted red?" I just said a few more "Ho ho hos!" and a "Merry Christmas!" and drove away.

I did not want to tell them the truth about Santa. As I drove home, I realized that people in passing cars were either waving or honking at me. With my newly acquired ho-ho-ho attitude, I smiled, honked, and waved back at them.

When I arrived home, I ran into the house. Relishing the reflection in the mirror of myself as Santa, I laughed at what I had just done. Then I noticed a surprising thing: I wasn't depressed anymore. I felt lighthearted, like the Santa who had just brought good cheer to a needy child. I had stumbled into the solution to my depression that day. All my praying, talking, thinking, and inventorying alone had not been enough. These practices had prepared me for the ultimate solution to my preoccupation with myself: helping someone else.

    The Santa suit allowed me the freedom to choose the persona of a cheerful giver. To become that, I don't need a costume; I just need to give what I can, using what I have, to keep what my recovery has brought: love, acceptance, and peace of mind.

12

Love and Self Worth

The following week, I returned to Ruth's for our meeting. As I walked through her living room, I noticed a soft glow of lights. She had put up a Christmas tree wrapped in white lights and red bows. I could smell the pine scent. We sat at her kitchen table, and she poured each of us a cup of coffee. There were a few raspberry macadamia nut cookies on a plate left over from a catering event the previous day.

I told Ruth about my Santa escapade and how it changed my day and mindset. Ruth was glad to hear about my new insights. "Let's talk about how we see ourselves and gaining confidence," she started, "What we hear about us when we are young, we believe, even if they are lies. If *you* believe them, that's the person you see when you look in the mirror."

I thought of all the negative messages I had received about myself throughout childhood. I had been constantly criticized and came to believe that I was bad and the cause of my family's problems. I tried harder and harder to please my parents and avoid doing anything that would upset them. I felt responsible for their feelings and at fault for everything that went wrong, and invariability, something went wrong every day.

Ruth asked me to follow her into her bedroom, where she had a full-length mirror in the corner of the room. She positioned me in front of it and stood behind me. Ruth steadied me, holding my arms, and poked her head over my left shoulder. Together, we looked into the mirror as she said, "I want you to say, as you look at your reflection, 'You are beautiful, and I love you.'"

"I can't do that!" I exclaimed and turned my head aside to hide my blush. "I'm too embarrassed, and I don't feel that. Obviously, I never have."

"Let's change that," she said with a smile.

It was evident that Ruth would patiently wait until I did just that. Her firm grasp on my arms wouldn't allow me to wiggle my way out of this acknowledgment. I wanted to run and hide, but I finally managed to blurt out, "I'm beautiful, and I love myself."

My loud voice and forced words, spoken desperately, showed how much work I had to do. I knew I didn't believe what I had just said. On the other hand, I could see how far I had come over the past couple of months: I had never looked myself in the eyes.

"Good, that's a start!" Ruth said as we went back into the kitchen and sat down again. "Correcting how you think about yourself is essential since your level of worthiness affects how you allow others to treat you. Real and lasting self-worth is not based on anything outside yourself. Another person's approval, bank accounts, and employment status can change in the twinkling of an eye, so you cannot let them determine your self-worth."

When Ruth said employment status, I remembered what I learned with the Do-Nothing-Club. I was now getting a clearer picture of how my father's rage had contributed to my low self-esteem. I needed to banish the lies that lived in me. I was forever hearing critical voices in my head that told me, *You're unworthy* and *unlovable*.

I felt genuine despair. "Ruth, is it possible for me to ever feel real confidence?"

Ruth got up to refill our coffee. When she returned to the table, she leaned closer to me and began whispering about her past. "When I was younger, I also struggled with low self-esteem. Then I met a man named David, and we started a long-distance relationship since he lived across the country. For the first several months, we wrote letters to each other. I fell madly in love. Being in love gave me a good feeling about myself. I loved my newfound confidence. I thought David was the source of it.

"When we finally got together, I realized David was not who I thought he was. We split up. When that happened, my new confidence disappeared, too. Why? Because *I stopped giving myself permission to feel good about myself.* For the most part, that relationship had existed in my head. It wasn't David who had generated my confidence; I had done it!

"Gaining *self*-confidence is an inside job. You must do the work. Confidence comes from how you think about yourself, and no person or circumstance can alter it unless you choose to let it," she shared.

I appreciated Ruth's experience in helping us change the way we see ourselves. "My negative self-image seems so deeply ingrained. Is it possible to change it?" I asked. It was hard to imagine that, in her younger days, Ruth had struggled with low self-esteem. I wanted to be comfortable in my own skin and have the dignity and confidence that she had.

"Deeply ingrained patterns of behavior usually don't go away overnight. Confidence comes from doing the next right thing. Doing esteemable acts raises and builds our self-esteem, beginning with how we see ourselves. If you could see yourself through God's loving eyes, you might feel differently," she explained.

Ruth's first assignment for me was to acknowledge who God says I am and to regard myself with love so that I could view myself differently. She suggested I speak aloud and often make affirmations based on scriptures, confessing to my true identity. I took note of the numerous examples she gave me, such as:

- I am loved
- I am forgiven
- I am a new creation
- I am God's own child
- I am God's creative, handy work
- God is for me, and He is on my side
- God has prepared good things for me to do

Listening to Ruth, I felt a new sense of pride. I wanted to develop a different view of myself. Ruth suggested I start looking at myself through God's eyes and accept and love myself where I am now.

"Not only can you change how you see yourself, you can change how you treat yourself. It helps to practice acts of love toward yourself rather than waiting for someone else to do it for you," Ruth explained.

For my second assignment, Ruth gave me numerous suggestions to incorporate into my daily life to practice love and self-care, such as:

- Eat right

- Drink plenty of water

- Get enough rest

- Exercise

- Be creative

- Focus on my attributes

- Spend time with uplifting people

- Read inspirational books

- Pray and meditate

"The third part of raising your self-esteem is practicing doing esteemable acts, and specifically, giving to others. As you do, your love and confidence will naturally grow, as when you played Santa for that little boy. You'll see more miracles unfold as you act on your intuition to do random acts of kindness. The more anonymous you can be, the more God shines through. Kindness is doing little things that seem scarcely worth doing and yet mean a lot to those for whom they were done," Ruth explained with contagious enthusiasm. I could feel her excitement and passion as she spoke.

"So, here's the third part of your assignment," Ruth continued. "Implement *random acts of kindness* into your daily life."

"How do I start?" I asked.

Ruth rattled off several ideas to help me:

- Cleaning out my closets, giving away whatever I don't use

- Calling someone who's having a hard time and just listening

- Buying groceries for a struggling family and anonymously leaving them on their doorstep

- Calling the local shelter for abused women and finding out what they need

- Offering to babysit for a single working parent

- Paying for someone's shortage at the checkout line in the grocery store

- Spontaneously giving away something of mine that someone admires

- Letting someone cut in front of me during rush-hour traffic

- Giving away smiles during the day to people who need them

"Can you see that you won't have time to pine away for a missing boyfriend because you'll be so busy helping others?" Ruth asked, driving home the contrast between a selfish life and one lived for love. "From here on, the longest time you get for a pity party about being alone is one hour! Cry all you want for sixty minutes, then put the tissues away and get busy. God and this world need you to grow the light of real love in your spirit."

Ruth stood up from the table. I was grateful to have a concrete plan for how to develop into the kind of person I would want to be with.

13

Provision and Safety

In the weeks ahead, I became busier than ever, just practicing these three assignments. Every day, I faced myself in the mirror and spoke aloud the affirmations detailing who God says I am. Initially, I felt self-conscious and awkward, but I continued the practice. I began to feel better. The power and meaning behind those words started to have a noticeable effect on how I felt about myself.

The second assignment, practicing more self-care, helped me focus on developing a better attitude by consciously being more grateful and hopeful each day. I made it a point to get plenty of sleep, walk more, and eat healthier meals. I drank more water and generally tried to be kinder to myself.

For my third assignment, doing random acts of kindness, I met with a pastor from an inner-city church, himself a recovering drug addict. He told me the church was planning a clothing giveaway for the people in the area, but the donations were light, and he had only a week to go.

I volunteered to find clothing donations. I made up a flyer asking people for clothing donations, stressing the looming deadline, and passed the flyers out to everyone I knew or came across. Within days, I had accumulated so much clothing that I had to rent a truck and hire help moving it all. The pastor was thrilled. At the giveaway the following day, I watched people with smiles as they found items they needed and liked. I loved knowing that, in some small way, I had participated in the process. It drove home that one person, one gesture, can make a big difference in someone else's life.

God was moving behind the scenes in my life. It was as if a veil had been lifted from my limited vision of everyday life. Recovery and Ruth taught me to practice laying down my personal will and seeking His will more often.

I had difficulty surrendering parts of my life to God as much as I wanted to. I feared turning things over to God because I feared what could happen if I lost control of my life—or, at least, the illusion of control. Then, the thought had occurred to me that if I had more faith, perhaps I would feel less fear. And if I had less fear, maybe I would have more peace.

One night, several women I worked with invited me to dinner with them and their husbands. Usually, I would have declined, feeling uncomfortable as the only single person, the tag-along. But then I reminded myself that I was married and could bring my invisible Heavenly Husband to the restaurant, too. Even though the other couples couldn't see Him, I would know He was there.

We went to a very lovely Japanese steakhouse. Seated around the chef's grill, I noticed that the chair to my left was empty. I set my Husband in it, in my mind's eye. The menu was a little pricey for my budget, and I worried my bill might use up my cash flow for the next few days. So, I trusted God to see me through the rest of the week.

I had a really lovely time, and the food was excellent. The checks were handed out to each couple at the end of the meal, but I didn't receive mine. I asked the waiter what happened to my check, and he said that my meal had been taken care of. I asked who had paid for it, explaining that I wanted to pay that person back. He left and returned, saying, "It was a gentleman seated on the other side of the restaurant. He didn't explain why; he just insisted on paying for your dinner anonymously, and then he left."

I couldn't help but wonder: Did God love me so much that He would send an unidentified stranger to pay my meal ticket? Immediately, the thought came to me that my Husband may be invisible, but He takes care of me just like the other husbands sitting at my table cared for their loved ones. I felt a warm, loving presence. I could feel my self-esteem rise a notch as I experienced firsthand how God is our source. I recommitted to seeking what I sought in God instead of the wrong men.

How freeing that would be to know God was my trustworthy source and, at times, moving through people as His surrogates. As I left the restaurant, I looked around at the people eating and conversing. I smiled. A miracle had just happened, a breakthrough from the unseen to the seen, and no one else seemed to be aware of it. God was letting me know He loved me from afar and could show up for me through other people and circumstances in my life; He was orchestrating things from behind the scenes.

I wondered how many more undetected miracles happen around us all the time.

Money remained very tight for me. I was working paycheck to paycheck with no leeway for unexpected expenses. Then, without warning, my air conditioner died. An expensive part had to be replaced. It was at the height of the summer in South Georgia, so it couldn't be put off. I panicked. I didn't have the extra money. I called Ruth, and she reminded me to take things one day at a time.

She asked, "Have you talked with your Husband yet?"

Her question caught me off guard. I almost retorted with, "What husband?" before I remembered to whom I was married. I was not used to thinking of God first in a panic. My knee-jerk reaction in a crisis was still fear, not faith.

I got off the phone, and I prayed. I just told God, *I'm doing everything I know how to do, but I need help. I need the air conditioning fixed and money to pay for it. I appreciate your paying my restaurant bill, but this is serious. Thank you! Amen.*

Then Ruth called me back and referred me to an air conditioning repairman she knew. I called, and he agreed to come over after the day's scheduled appointments. By that evening, the air conditioner was fixed and running. He gave me a bill for $995 and told me I was lucky the whole unit didn't die because that could have cost a few thousand dollars.

When I asked if he could bill me, he said he usually got paid at the time of service but would give me thirty days to pay due to the circumstances. I thanked him and breathed half a sigh of relief.

Now, I just needed to come up with an extra thousand dollars in thirty days. So, I started talking to my invisible Husband: *Okay, God, you're my provider. Here's the bill. I need an opportunity to pay for it.*

Two days went by as I tried to put my financial concerns aside. Then I got a call from a friend who worked as a sales rep for a furniture rental company. She told me she unexpectedly needed major surgery and had to take a medical leave from her job for one month. Knowing I had had that same job in another state years before, she asked if I would consider filling in for her twice a week for a month. All I had to do was check on her existing accounts and follow up on new leads. She offered to give me any commissions and salary she usually made. She said they would pay me to come in for a day of review training, after which they would send me out on the street two days a week while my friend was gone. I took the job. Then an unusual thing happened.

I went to a few appointments, had some lunch, and then found that I still had an hour until my next appointment. I headed in the general direction of that lead and was stopped at a red light when I noticed a sign across the street: *Whispering Winds Nursing Home*. I felt the strongest intuitive urge to go in there. I resisted it for a moment, but couldn't ignore it, so I pulled into the parking lot. It would be good to go in and leave a business card.

I knew nothing about this nursing home, nor did I have an appointment with them. I got my briefcase, went inside, and spoke to the receptionist, introducing myself and telling her I was with the furniture rental company.

"Oh great!" she said, to my surprise. "They're expecting you. They're waiting for your presentation in the meeting room." She motioned for me to follow her. I didn't know what she was talking about, but I followed her with my briefcase in hand.

In the meeting room, I introduced myself to the two men there. Both seemed to be expecting me. I gave them a presentation I had prepared for another nursing home the week before, and it went very smoothly. I learned that this company had just taken over the nursing home and wanted to refurnish all the units with rental furniture. So, I made a bid.

Toward the end of the meeting, I learned that each of the two men had thought the other had called my company and a competitor to get bids. As it turned out, neither man had called anybody, and neither one knew it. When we all realized the truth, there was a moment of silence. We were puzzled about how this meeting had occurred at all, considering everyone's mistakes.

They decided to accept my offer on the spot, and I landed a large deal just like that! By the end of the month, I was able to pay off this unexpected debt.

Only God could have guided me to the perfect place at that perfect moment in time!

I could see that with God's direction, I could accomplish in moments what I could spend hours or days trying to do on my own. Not only did I thank Him, but I asked for His help in remembering these moments of His faithfulness, provision, and protection so that I would continue to trust Him more. Thank you, God.

The first five months of my year-long commitment to avoid men went by quickly, with dramatic changes in how I felt about myself. Then, when a new guy showed up at a recovery meeting I attended regularly, I felt an immediate attraction to him. He was tall, dark, handsome, and well-dressed, obviously a professional in the community. My heart raced as I fought the lure to approach him. But then our eyes met, and he walked over to me. We introduced ourselves, and he said he was new to the area. He was an ophthalmologist who was looking to start a new practice here. I started to flirt with him, and he responded with interest. I began questioning my agreement to abstain from dating for the rest of the year.

Suddenly, I realized I was acting as I always had around men. Part of me felt the excitement and high of meeting someone new, while another part of me heard Ruth in my mind saying, "What are you doing? Don't act impulsively on feelings of attraction. Remember your commitment: It's you and God right now. Time to find yourself first. Keep God in charge."

The eye doctor kept talking, but his words faded into the background noise of the conversation in my head with Ruth. Truth and Ruth knew how to spoil a relationship prospect and take the fun out of flirting.

I excused myself and left the room. I needed some air, and I needed to regroup. I felt like I did when I first gave up drinking or smoking. I used to rationalize my addictive urges by telling myself *If I felt this strongly about doing something, I must need to do it.* Now, I was learning that just because something felt right didn't mean it *was* right.

I called Ruth and told on myself. I admitted how drawn I felt to the eye doctor and wanted to quit my year-long commitment to no dating. "If you want to see our work through, don't act on your attraction to him. Step back, wait, and watch him over time to see what happens. He will show you the truth about his character from a distance. This perspective will give you knowledge about yourself that can change your life forever," Ruth said with these kind and clear suggestions.

"But Ruth, what if I miss the opportunity to meet the one?"

"If he is the one, he will still be there when you are ready, and nothing can stop that. If he isn't, you can't make that happen," Ruth explained, comforting my fears.

It was a powerful message, so I agreed to follow her suggestions over the next few months. I regularly attended the same meetings as the eye doctor but didn't converse with him or flirt; I just watched him from a distance. I continued to feel strongly attracted to him, and of course, I continued to feel conflicted. But even though I was lonely and longing for the fun and excitement of getting to know someone new, I stayed true to my commitment. I just waited and watched.

Two months later, the eye doctor relapsed into alcohol and drugs. The night before his relapse, he slept with a woman from the meetings whom he had pursued with determination. He had a one-night stand with her, relapsed, and then bailed out on her by leaving town. She became pregnant from that one night of poor judgment and was left to raise her baby alone.

That could have been me. I felt compassion for the woman, as though she had taken the consequences of what could have been my disastrous affair, left to my old devices.

The truth stared me down: I was still attracted to the same kind of man who offered the same potential hazards as I experienced in my past. I was attracted to men based on lust, not love. The people that frightened me most in my childhood were exactly the kinds of people I was constantly attracted to as an adult.

Being mentored under Ruth's *Love Gone Wrong Recovery Program* had just saved me from another go-around of disappointment, disillusionment, heartache, and single parenting.

I resolved to let any future such attractions just wash over me like a nice summer breeze and let them go. This was another monumental, defining moment for the future of my love life, and I couldn't wait to talk to Ruth.

We met at the beach for her late afternoon walk. I always felt special when I was with her. She was fully present to me in our conversations. Her cell phone was turned off, and when we were in public, she would acknowledge people who knew her in a way that let them know she wasn't available to socialize with them right then.

I met her in the beach parking lot, where we took our shoes off. The warm sand under my feet and the cool ocean breeze were refreshing. The wind rinsed off the last two months of inner struggles about resisting my attraction to the wrong man. I filled Ruth in on the eye doctor and how he had used and abandoned that woman in recovery. I told her that if it weren't for her counseling and God, that woman could have been me.

"You forgot to thank someone else."

"Who?" I asked.

"Yourself!" she added enthusiastically. "You have a part in shaping your destiny. What you do today does make a difference tomorrow. Your willingness to be healed determines how long you drag your emotional baggage around. That's what this preparation time is for.

"In the Bible, great men of God are instructed not to fall prey to the traps of the enemy. The traps are found in human weaknesses that have yet to be disciplined and put under the authority of our Higher Self. Addictive desires for things such as alcohol, drugs, sex, food, you name it, need to be worked out, or they will be in the driver's seat of your life."

I glanced out over the ocean and spotted two dolphins frolicking in the surf together. The moment was magical. Then Ruth and I turned around to begin our walk back. We talked so much that I didn't realize the distance we had covered.

"There's a time in our walk with God when He puts us in a place of waiting," Ruth explained. "A place where the past no longer relates to the present, where we are being prepared for a future we've never experienced and for which we have no point of reference. It is a time of stillness, and it can feel unsettling if we forget that this is only for a season. It is a time to grow deeper with Him, a time to pray, and a time to practice your faith.

"When we are used to making things happen ourselves, it's hard to let go of the steering wheel, but it's only by doing so that we can see who the real driver is. I'm proud of you for letting God steer you through your attraction to the eye doctor. Nobody breaks a lifelong behavior pattern without much discomfort and effort. You are like a caterpillar growing in a small, dark cocoon. To get out, it has to struggle hard, and just when it thinks its life is over, it blossoms into a butterfly."

I liked her analogy. As we walked, I let those thoughts sink in for a few minutes.

"Ruth, this guy, like the others in my life, had me fooled. I don't ever want to go back to that place. How do you stop that kind of relationship?" I asked.

"By saying *no* to them and *yes* to yourself. These men can't have any power over you unless you give it to them. You really threw this eye doctor off by pulling away and exercising self-control. It was clear to him that you were not vulnerable, even if only subconsciously, and he needed to look for someone less healthy."

"I'd been fooled by other men. Do you think I could recognize an abuser in the future?" I asked.

"Don't be in a rush. Wait and watch what a person does over time. Talk is cheap, and actions speak louder than words. Pay attention to your gut feelings and any red flags."

I felt a surge of confidence, for that is precisely what I had done: waited and watched the eye doctor.

"Another hint," Ruth said. "Protect yourself. Consider it a warning sign if you hold a guy you're dating accountable, and he dodges and defends himself. Consider it a double red flag if he gets mad and blames you. A healthy relationship allows two people to confront, discuss, and take responsibility for their actions."

When we returned to the parking lot, I hugged Ruth and went to my car. I thought about how rarely I had ever felt safe and protected in my life. Much of my waking energy had always been spent anticipating hidden dangers lurking around the corner. But what if God ultimately had my back? Couldn't I learn to relax and live in peace in a way I never had?

14

Tragedy and Troubles

My life was finally coming together, when a few days later I got a call from the hospital that my mother had just had a near-fatal stroke and was clinging to life in the intensive care. I immediately drove to the hospital. On the drive over, I thought about our mending relationship. Over the last year, my mother and I have been experiencing a lot of healing. While her drinking had not stopped, nor had her life much changed, I had learned how to reach out and love her as she was. Recovery taught me to practice unconditional love and forgiveness toward her by accepting her and loving her the best I could. She could no longer garden outside, which she loved, so I would spend an afternoon with her every week. She would sit in a folding chair and direct me to plant seeds, weed, and prune her plants. It was my way of keeping my side of the street clean, and it always warmed her heart, and while she never said that, I just knew. We didn't discuss the past; we just agreed on cultivating a new normal. I had learned that it wasn't up to me to try to change my Mom, and I just loved her.

A few nights ago, my phone rang. It was my mother. "I just wanted to tell you I love you," she said.

"I love you, too, Mom." We were off to a great start on a new phase of our relationship. I had been so excited about our visit that day. I had thought it was the beginning of the fulfillment of my lifelong fantasy of a normal mother-daughter relationship.

How could my mother have fallen so critically ill now? Everything seemed surreal. I hoped it was a mistake.

When I arrived at the hospital, Mom was hooked up to all kinds of tubes. Her eyes were open but unfocused, and she was moving involuntarily from side to side. Seeing her this helpless seemed more than I could handle.

I stayed with her for the rest of the night. In the morning, the doctor said she had had a severe stroke that paralyzed her right side, also damaging certain parts of her brain and affecting speech, memory, and emotions. They would work to stabilize her over the next week in hopes she could be moved to a rehab hospital in Florida. Her need for full-time care in a nursing home would depend on how extensive the damage was and how much she could recover in rehab.

I was overwhelmed.

My thoughts turned to my father. He was eighty-nine years old and depended on my Mom for everything. She was his life. My father adored my mother, even though he always yelled at her. If I argued with her, he immediately came to her defense. No one else had a hold of his heart like my mother.

He was all alone now. There were no friends or family members who could help with his care. I had to wonder, *What is he feeling?*

We had been estranged since I was a child. He argued about everything I said. Even if I agreed with him, he would fight with me about it. It didn't take much for him to go into a rage around me. As a child, I tried to stay out of his way. As an adult, I walked on eggshells with him. I continually returned to my father to see if, *this time,* I could earn the approval he continued to withhold from me.

I knew he needed me now. Things may be different.

Leaving my mother attached to all her tubes, I drove to their house. As I got out of my car, even after all these years, I still fantasized that he might warmly embrace me and realize his profound love for me, his only daughter, who was there for him in this most vulnerable time of need.

When I entered the home, I found him sitting at the dining table, drinking coffee and reading a newspaper. He peered over his reading glasses and shrugged, acknowledging my presence. I sat down at the table.

"She's not here," he said as he focused on the newspaper.

"I know," I answered. My father was acting as though nothing had happened. "Aren't you upset?"

"I don't need to show how I feel in front of you." His words stung me. He lifted the newspaper back up, blocking my view of his face.

"I'm going back to the hospital. Do you want to come?"

"Give me a minute," he said. He left the table and retreated to his bedroom. By now, I had forgotten the fantasy of a warm embrace from him.

As I waited for my father, I noticed a picture on the bookshelf of myself at the age of ten. I looked so depressed. Guilt was a hallmark of my childhood. At that age, I remember feeling guilty about even going to a friend's house. My father would constantly remind me that, being sixty years old, he might die at any moment. He implied I shouldn't leave the house or ask for anything because he might drop dead soon. That was thirty years ago, and he was still going strong.

On the drive to the hospital, he crossed his arms and looked out the car window. He could barely look at me. *How can he be so cold to me amid this tragedy?* I wanted to run away from him, but I couldn't.

The thought of having to take care of my father by myself was fast becoming my worst nightmare. My dad was thirteen years older than my Mom, so I had always assumed he would die before her. It had never occurred to me that my mother could end up helplessly bedridden and my father solely dependent on me. Now, it was just Dad and me, with me also looking after Mom during this crisis.

Indeed, this must be his nightmare, too.

I felt overwhelmed by and unprepared for the long-term challenges now facing me. My brother lived several states away, and I knew he wouldn't be able to help much.

When we got to the hospital, my mother could not focus her eyes and was unable to communicate with us. The doctor informed us that she would soon be transferred to a rehab facility in Jacksonville, Florida. They could determine the extent of the damage the stroke caused and her capacity to regain any of her lost functions. We stayed by her bedside the rest of the day, even though she was incoherent.

A few days later, my mother was moved to that hospital. It was just outside Jacksonville, a 90-minute drive away. My father came with me as I drove there. He badgered, demeaned, and criticized my every move as we drove along the interstate. "I'll never forgive you for what you did," he said, bringing up one of his many resentments toward me.

"What did I do?" I asked, too surprised to say anything else.

"You quit a job after only three days of working there," he said, and got angry all over again.

I barely remembered the incident, which had taken place over twenty-five years earlier. "I was a teenager! I'd been working as a dog groomer since I was eight," I defended myself. He was referring to a retail job I tried for fun, and because it interfered with my other job, I quit. I was flabbergasted.

"There's no excuse! You're irresponsible," he said with shaming disapproval.

Who holds a resentment that long over something so petty?

Then, we drove in silence for about fifteen minutes while I tried to collect myself. "Can I ask you a question without your getting upset?" my father asked. It was a clear signal that I would probably get upset, so I braced myself.

"Who will take care of me when you die?" he asked.

Was that a relevant question from a *loving* father approaching ninety to a daughter of forty-one? Why was my dad more concerned about his well-being than his daughter's? I pointed out that there was a greater chance that he would die first. Still, he pressed on about who would take care of him.

"You could easily die before me. You make many bad decisions!" my father said, challenging me coldly.

"Haven't I been there for you through all of this?"

"Well, we've always been there for you!" my father said proudly.

I just shook my head and didn't respond.

We arrived at the hospital and went to Mom's room, and Dad stepped over to her bed to check on her. He gently reached for her hand through the guardrails. "My poor Frances," Dad said. "I wish it could have been me instead of you. I promise I'll stick around as long as you do." He spoke softly, leaned over her, and kissed her forehead. I was moved. But when I went to the bed to comfort Mom, she grabbed my arm and jerked it, shrieking the only word she was able to say: "No, no, no!" She looked at me with what appeared to be all the anger and rage she could muster. I pulled loose from her and ran into the hallway, crying. I wanted to collapse from all the emotional pain that caused me.

A nurse came over and wrapped her arms around me. It was a much-needed embrace, quenching my deep thirst for a mother's love. I soaked it in. She explained that Mom's emotional instability, frustration, and anger were the effects of the brain stroke's physical catastrophe.

As the nurse comforted me, I began to understand that it was my Mom's condition that caused her violent response to me. She had a lot of damage to her brain and body. Mom could not speak, read, write, or get the "good side" of her body to follow mental commands. Being wholly trapped in her body, she was at the total mercy of the hospital staff. If anything happened to her or anyone mistreated her, she would have no way to report it. I became consumed with helping my Mom with her vulnerability. I stepped back into her room, determined not to take anything personally. I wanted to be strong for her.

This visit was only one part of the nightmare.

Dad slept through most of the drive home that day. It was quiet and peaceful. Even though the visit wore him out, he would not miss the opportunity to see my mother. He pressed through his physical limitations and pain to make it to her.

Just before we returned to his house, I ran through a fast-food restaurant and got a cheeseburger. My father was awakened by the cashier's voice through the loudspeaker. Our eyes met, and he immediately looked away. There were a few minutes of silence as I returned to the road.

"Why the hell are you eating and driving? Do you want to get us killed?" he shouted. I was so startled I almost dropped my burger.

"Okay, I won't eat and drive while you're in the car." I put the cheeseburger down. We returned to an uncomfortable silence.

Finally, I pulled into his driveway.

"I've never seen anything so stupid in all my life. Were you trying to kill us?"

"It won't happen again," I said patiently. This incident should have been a closed case, but Dad continued to berate me with all the anger he had always directed toward me. After what I had been doing for him since Mom's stroke, his laundry, food shopping, and attending to his medical needs, his raging at me for eating a hamburger was intolerable.

I had been abused by him my whole life. I couldn't do that anymore. I knew I would have to set boundaries with him, or I would end up having a nervous breakdown again!

"I'm all you have left. If you keep treating me like this, then I'm not going to help you, and you can go into your house and die by yourself," I informed him. I grasped the steering wheel. I had been terrified to speak up to this man my whole life.

Nothing more was said between us. My father got out of the car. It was the scariest thing I had ever done. I had finally stood up for myself and set my first boundary with him. The rest of the afternoon, I fought off feelings of incredible guilt for talking back to him.

My dad is a survivor. After assessing the situation, he called me that night. "I'm too old to be different, but I'll agree if you don't eat a cheeseburger in the car, I won't yell at you," he said and hung up. It was a start, barely.

For three years, I had worked diligently on my recovery. I had reached a place of sanity and peace. I had gained some self-confidence, and I thought I had healed from a lot of my childhood

THE FATHER NOBODY KNOWS

pains. One therapist I had seen in the psych hospital suggested that my relationship with my dad was so highly toxic that it would be best to stay away from him.

But that is not what happened. A few years after leaving the psych hospital, I found myself again enmeshed with my father and doing the opposite of what I had been advised regarding him. What wouldn't leave my mind were the questions: *Why was I now with him, helping him seven days a week? What choice did I have?* There was no one else to take him off my hands, and he did not have the money to hire help. I wanted to be free of him and from the hurt he caused me. I was tired of feeling helpless and victimized by my father.

Since I believe that nothing happens by accident, then technically speaking, what had caused me to spend so much time with my dad was a "God Thing." It just didn't feel like a blessing because of what it brought up in me.

The critical question was, "Was I willing to do what was right before God?" As bad as it felt being with Dad and absorbing his abuse, I knew this was God's will for me. But none of my therapy had truly prepared me for confronting all this original pain with my father.

After rehab, the first nursing home my Mom was transferred to was a nightmare. While it was in an affluent part of town, during the first week of her stay, I found evidence of possible physical abuse. Upon further investigation, one of the employees confirmed my suspicions. With a few friends, we went there, put her in my car, and took her to another nursing home, one with a long-standing good reputation.

After that, my life became consumed with insurance companies, social agencies, medical bills, doctors, hospitals, rehab facilities, and nursing homes. Still, during this stressful time, my father continuously poked at my weak spots to get a rise out of me. He seemed to find satisfaction in successfully baiting me into reacting to his jabs.

When my father could no longer get a reaction from me, he attempted new blows. He knew my reverence for God's love and truth was sacred to me. One day, he said, "I'll tell you my favorite quote from R.G. Ingersoll: 'It can be truthfully said that hope is the only universal liar who never loses his reputation for ferocity.'" He watched me, waiting for me to react.

I held back. "Well, I believe God saves us through hope and truth," I said.

"What a bunch of crap! There's no God that saves you, and I don't need you preaching to me," he shouted. Before I could utter a word, he yelled at me again. "This is my Bible. You should be reading this every day." He lifted a large-print Webster's dictionary. He reminded me again that the Greeks invented everything, including the alphabet, so his first love was the dictionary. He opened it to where he had last placed his bookmark. Once again, I felt angry, but I didn't react.

"Today's new word is phlegmatic," he said, preaching arrogantly to me. "That means having or showing a slow and solid temperament. Maybe you need to become more phlegmatic!"

"You're rude, and I'm done!" I stood up to leave. I forgot to pause for a moment when upset. He was a master at bringing out the worst in me. Was there no end to this abuse? Conversations between my father and me were more like mental bungee jumping than fruitful exchanges. One minute, my father would seem docile, and then he would hurl verbal assault bombs at me.

As I left, he picked up the can of Lysol (not Windex, like in the movie *My Big Fat Greek Wedding*) and sprayed the glass tabletop where

I had been sitting. He used Lysol incessantly on tabletop counters. One time, I caught him using it as a deodorant. For some people, the aroma of freshly baked cookies reminds them of their childhood. For me, it is Lysol.

I called Ruth and cried on her shoulder when she arrived at my home that evening. I updated her about the never-ending, never-changing saga between my father and me. I also told her about my mother's increasingly debilitating condition.

"I feel so overwhelmed. How is all of this going to turn out?"

"Everyone has uncertainty in their life in some area, be it finances, children, marriage, or health. The key is to trust an unknown future to a known God."

Ruth picked up her Bible and opened it to the *Book of Job*. "Job was a good man whom God blessed with abundant wealth. Then, one day, Satan came before God in Heaven and accused Job of serving God for purely selfish reasons: for protection and prosperity. Satan challenged God to take away all of Job's physical blessings, hoping that would prove the hypocrisy in Job's heart. God accepted the challenge and permitted Satan to afflict Job. He was only allowed to take away Job's possessions but was prohibited from harming Job himself.

"So, fire fell from Heaven and killed Job's sheep. Raiders captured his camels and killed all but one servant. Then, the worst occurred. While Job's children were dining together, a great wind came and struck the house, and it fell on the young people, and they died. This cruel tragedy was intended to break Job's faith."

"Did it?" I sipped my tea and let it calm my nerves.

"No, instead, Job tore his robe, shaved his head, and fell to the ground in worship. Through all this, Job did not blame God. Instead, he prayed, worshiped, and accepted God's sovereign design and purpose, even though he did not know why he was suffering. Job clung to God," Ruth explained.

"Did God bless him for this attitude?"

"Not yet. Satan wasn't through with him. He accused Job of remaining faithful to God just to protect the only thing that was left: his health. Once again, God permitted Satan to afflict Job, but he was restricted from taking his life. Satan plagued Job with painful oozing sores from the soles of his feet to the top of his head. His condition was so bad that his wife urged Job to curse God, but he refused to do so."

"Ruth, this is not cheering me up!" I exclaimed.

"I'm telling you this because we all have Job moments. Job still didn't know why he was suffering. He cried out to God. But Heaven remained silent," Ruth said as she reached for her tea.

"I feel like a female Job," I said. "I've been praying for relief, and God is not answering me."

"Life is easy when God answers prayers how you want Him to. The challenge is when His answer is not what you want. Sometimes it is 'no' or 'not yet,'" Ruth added.

"Honestly, I've had thoughts of wanting to drink lately," I said, and felt good about admitting it.

"You can stay sober through any situation when you trust in God. We usually see suffering as a tragedy," Ruth went on, "but suffering can lead to spiritual maturity. And spiritual maturity comes from accepting God's will. You don't have to understand His ways; that's where faith comes in. When we are powerless over circumstances, we must give our lives to God's care. He will lead us out of any painful situation we are facing."

After a few moments, Ruth added, "You must trust that there is a bigger picture. One you can't see or understand right now. If Job knew the higher purpose of his trials ahead of time, it would have been easier to bear them. But then the test would not have been a test."

Ruth had a way of helping me see things from a different perspective. I began to see that taking care of my father and suffering through it could contribute to my spiritual growth.

"Now, do you really believe God has forgotten about you?" Ruth asked.

"No." My thoughts turned back to Job. "So, what was the bigger picture with Job?"

"Job had been chosen specifically by God to demonstrate the meaning of full surrender and to prove to God that his commitment was based on something higher than self-interest. Sometimes, through our struggles, we come to know God more deeply. Job, for example, came away with an increased awareness of God's greatness and the necessity of submitting to His will no matter the cost. What Job learned by standing humbly before God was that God is still with us even when suffering leads us to doubt."

I clung to Ruth's words. I wanted to complete God's assignment with my father and stay sober while doing it.

"What finally happened to Job?" I asked.

"After Job's terrible trials, God gave him twice what he had lost and blessed him more in his latter days than in his early years. When God restores what was lost or stolen, it is always increased, multiplied, or improved so that its latter state is significantly better than its original allotment," Ruth explained. "I know you don't understand why you must endure all this abuse. Can you follow Job's example and trust God's goodness and sovereignty?" she asked.

I nodded and committed to doing just that.

We stood up, and I walked Ruth to the front door. "One day, you will be the wiser and stronger for it. You'll see how even tragedy can be a part of God's grace, allowing you to help others who will be going through what you are experiencing now," Ruth said, and hugged me. I watched her walk to her car.

That night, I got into bed and wept while complaining, "God," I said in the darkness of my room, "why are you allowing this heartache in my life?"

Then I caught myself and thought of Job. I wiped my tears and remembered my commitment to Ruth earlier in the day. Then, I prayed:

> *"God, I don't understand what You are doing. I will place my hope in You and put my life in your powerful hands. I hope that one day restoration can take place as it did in Job's life. Amen."*

15

Gratitude

One morning, I arrived at my father's house and noticed a loud, persistent chirping sound. "Dad, what's that?" I asked.

"It's a cricket. I'm trying to find it to kill it," my father answered. He always spoke with such authority, like a drill sergeant.

I walked around the house and spotted a smoke alarm. It was a repeating chirping alarm. "Dad, it's the battery in the smoke alarm. I can disconnect it and change it out later," I offered. I was pleased to find the source of that irritating sound. I started to get the ladder.

"Don't touch the smoke alarm," he said adamantly. "I know the sound of a damn cricket when I hear it, and that's a cricket!" My father's pride seemed to permeate every exchange we had. He argued with me over everything.

I took a deep breath. My body tensed. I tried one more time to reason with him. He became so mad that he left the room. At least he was honoring our agreement not to rage at me.

"Don't touch that alarm. I'll find the cricket!" Dad shouted again just before he slammed the bedroom door shut.

When I left the house, I was shaken. I sat in my car and calmed myself down. I had always wanted a win-win with him, but every exchange became a lose-lose. My father would never let me be right, no matter the circumstances. There wasn't anyone who could shake the core of my being so profoundly over nothing. Attempting to resolve the issue with him only led to more disharmony. Now I had to solve the dilemma of fixing the smoke alarm without him knowing I helped him.

Later that evening, after he had removed his wooden leg and gotten into bed, I sneaked into his house and quietly changed the battery in the smoke alarm. For the first time in two days, the house was finally quiet. I left without saying anything to him about it.

The following morning, I checked in on him. "The chirping stopped," I commented.

"That's right! I found the cricket early this morning and killed it," he proudly announced.

My Dad's pride made him stubborn and unteachable. There was no room for change in his world. Every encounter was based on his self-absorbed domination. I was beginning to understand why self-confidence had been such an elusive quality for me to acquire in childhood.

Yet, change came faster than I expected. When I arrived at my father's that morning, he wasn't sitting at the dining room table, having coffee and reading the dictionary, as he did every day.

I found him still in bed. "What's the matter?" I asked, alarmed.

"I'm too dizzy to sit up. I feel sick to my stomach," Dad answered with a surprisingly sweet and humble voice. I quickly called the ambulance. I gathered some of his belongings and went with him to the hospital. We got him checked in, and they did some tests.

The following day, he remained frail. The doctors felt he had an intestinal blockage and put him on a liquid diet. They didn't know how long it would take him to recover or if he would recover.

When I saw my Dad, he was sweeter than ever. Seeing this tenderness in him, I let down my defenses.

GRATITUDE

When I spoke to the doctors, they ruled out any surgery and told me he would be unable to live alone again. They said he would need to be discharged in a few days and that I should make arrangements. I had promised myself I would never let my father move in with me because of our difficult relationship. I felt I could survive my father's constant harassment as long as I had my home to retreat to at night.

My father's continuing sweetness that morning caused me to renounce my promise never to let him live with me.

I reasoned that his toughness enabled him in his younger years to keep his job. After he had lost his leg, he still commuted each day to and from Manhattan to his job as a waiter. He would walk one mile to the train station, switch to a subway, climb two flights of stairs, and walk another set of city blocks to a job that kept him on his feet all day. He did this year-round, even with snow and ice on the ground.

Sometimes, I would cry at his heroic struggles in life. I longed for an exchange of warmth and affection with him. But the same hardness that drove him to endure such hardship kept him at arm's length from those who tried to love him. It was all he knew. It was how he survived.

So, over the next few days, I cleared out his home. I only kept his bedroom furnishings, clothes, books, photos, and small personal memorabilia.

I brought him home to my haven and began the journey of nursing him back to health. Without the resources to hire a nurse, I had to change his catheter, help him into the bathtub, and give him his medications. These were tasks I never thought I could do with him.

Since I couldn't work full-time, I found part-time work with temporary agencies or house cleanings for a friend's business that managed short-term rentals. The physical work helped relieve the stress, and the pay and flexible hours were good. I could work on the days when neither of my parents had health emergencies. It was not work I aspired to do, but it paid the household bills.

By now, we had accepted the grim news the doctors told us. My mother showed no signs of improvement, and they did not see her getting any better. The insurance coverage for her rehab was going to be discontinued. My father was in no condition, either physically or financially, to maintain the house they had lived in, so he agreed to sell it.

I began cleaning and painting the house so I could sell it. I knew that whatever money I could raise to help with the mounting medical and living expenses would be needed.

As I completed its renovation, I decided to get rid of the last of Dad's household furnishings, so I called Goodwill to pick up two worn couches, end tables, a kitchen table, and a couple of wooden chairs. None of the items matched anything in my home, and in two months, my father never asked for them.

The following day, I brought my father his coffee. I felt relieved and satisfied with all my hard work in dismantling their house. "Did you save my favorite chairs?" he asked, referring to the two old wooden chairs I had just donated to Goodwill. "If you got rid of my chairs, I'll never forgive you. They're the only chairs I can sit in comfortably. I'll never find others like them," he added. I had no idea how much they meant to him, and was glad he didn't know they had gone to Goodwill.

"Sure, I saved those chairs! I'll go get them right away," I lied, if a white lie.

GRATITUDE

"Good," he said, suspiciously staring at me.

My next mission was to track down the chairs at Goodwill. Since they weren't that nice-looking, they should still be at the donation center. I hopped to it right away.

To my dismay, after looking over everything at the Goodwill Center, the chairs weren't there. Panic set in. I did find the employee who loaded the truck that day. He remembered the chairs being purchased the moment they hit the sales floor. I felt butterflies in my stomach! This was getting worse.

"How much were they sold for and to whom?" I asked him.

"They were sold to a local antique dealer for five dollars each," he answered.

I breathed a sigh of relief. "Sold to which dealer?" I asked.

Neither he nor the manager knew her personally, and she paid cash.

I began to look up all the antique dealers in our county. There were at least thirty. Overwhelmed, I closed my eyes and uttered a foxhole prayer to God. It was simple:

Please help me find and recover my father's old wooden favorite chairs before he kills me! Amen.

Instantly, an image of a locally owned antique shop came to my mind. It was one of the largest in the area. I had nothing to lose and everything to gain. I drove right over. I walked through each aisle, looking for any sign of those chairs. I reached the last aisle without seeing them and wanted to fall in a heap on the floor and cry. Then I turned my head and saw two chairs that looked like my father's, except they had a coat of white paint on them, giving them a shabby chic look. I looked underneath one and found the same finish as my Dad's chairs.

I found the price tag. The set of chairs was $150. I brought one to the store's owner and told her my predicament.

"How much do I need to pay you to get them back for my dad?"

"The ticket price," she said without hesitation.

"But you only paid $10 for them," I objected.

"I had to slap a coat of white paint on them. Besides, it's not my fault you let them go." She would not budge. So, I bought my father's two chairs for $150. Then I went to a man who stripped the paint off the furniture. He charged me another $150 to bring them back to their original wood grain finish.

Finally, $300 later, I brought home my father's favorite chairs.

"I was beginning to think you might have been stupid enough to throw away these chairs," he commented when I brought them into the house. I just breathed a sigh of relief.

I called Ruth and told her about my chairs' adventure. She started laughing. "Expensive chairs!" I heard her say.

"It's not funny! How am I supposed to keep doing this caregiving by myself?" I said, half-complaining, half-whining.

"You're not doing this alone. Who do you think led you to the chairs? Remember your prayer? Try thanking God in all your circumstances. Gratitude will draw you near to God and help you truly know Him, and you need to know Him now more than ever.

"If you stay in God's presence, He'll give you ideas you couldn't think of and the wisdom to see things others don't, just like finding the missing chairs. Catherine, you'll need God's guidance and presence to walk through this trial. Stability in tough times is born of living in complete trust in God instead of yourself," Ruth explained.

"How am I supposed to be thankful when I don't feel the least grateful?" I asked.

"You don't have to feel it; you just have to do it. In time, the feelings will follow your actions because events will unfold and reveal a new perspective on your present situation, or it will cause a change in you."

"When you praise God and thank Him, what do you say?" I asked.

"Try saying,

'God, I thank You for being who You are!'

'God, I thank You for what You have done!'

'God, I thank You for what You will do now!'

'God, I thank You for what You continue to do!'

'God, I thank You for what You have brought me through.'

"It is one of the most powerful invocations you can say in times of trouble," Ruth said.

Before I got off the phone, Ruth suggested I keep a gratitude journal. Finding anything to be grateful about in caring for my father would be a real stretch. But there was nothing easy about my current assignment. I decided to continue applying the spiritual keys Ruth taught me to my earthbound predicament.

16

The Art of Surrender

I could find no refuge anywhere. Only a few weeks after the house was sold, my father's health returned, and so did his negative attitude toward me. He was now taking over my household.

The only place in my house my father would not go was the garage, so I got the bright idea to fix it up as my getaway place. I bought and laid down outdoor carpeting, painted the walls white, and had a cable TV connector installed. I moved my desk, TV, and workout equipment there. My father's presence had squeezed me out of my three-bedroom, two-bath house, so I decided to live in the garage as much as possible.

Everything I tried to do for my Dad became a battle, even the simplest things, such as replacing worn-out pajamas. He wore an old, stained pair of pajamas every night. Whenever I mentioned getting a new pair, he said he didn't need them and didn't want to waste money on something he didn't need. But these pajamas were getting beyond acceptable. With trepidation, I broached the subject of the new pajamas one more time.

This time, when I suggested new pajamas, to my surprise, he said I could get them for him. He gave me the details: the style, material, color, and size.

I went to the department store to find the exact specifications for his pajamas. I found them. I was thrilled with the prospect of doing something right that would please him. Even at this late stage, gaining even a morsel of his approval would be healing.

Filled with excitement, I brought him the new pajamas and took the tags off after unfolding them. He looked at them and looked blankly back at me.

"Aren't they nice?" I asked, trying to change an awkward moment.

"I told you I didn't want new pajamas, and you shouldn't be wasting my money!" he scolded me. He was receiving Social Security and a small pension from his union job as a waiter in a Manhattan luncheonette.

"But you told me to get them! Besides, you need them," I said, defending myself.

"I never said such a thing. Stop talking foolishness and return them. You didn't even get what I would've wanted. These are ugly, and I would never wear them."

"Nothing I do is ever good enough for you!" I said, grabbing the pajamas. I was so angry that I had fallen for his ill-tempered deception. Why did I always think he would be different?

"When will you act like a grown woman?" he asked.

"You're the one who needs to grow up! Don't you appreciate anything?" I was so angry that I had taken the bait. I knew it was too late to take back my words and reaction.

I gathered the tags from the pajamas and left the room, trembling. I tried to shake off the argument, but there was no winning with him. I called Ruth and asked if I could stop over on my way back to the department store.

She greeted me and led me back to her kitchen. She had made hazelnut coffee, and a plateful of homemade chocolate chip cookies sat on the table. I filled her in on the pajama fight.

"I can never please him. He's always losing his temper with me. He yells at me, is impatient and angry, and constantly criticizes me. Ruth, I don't know if I can handle this!"

"You can do this and come out the better for it," she said reassuringly.

"Why do I feel like God's punishing me?"

Ruth retrieved her Bible from the reading table across the room. "There is someone in this book that you will relate to. His name is David. He went through great trials with a man named Saul. Let me tell you about him."

I took one of the chocolate chip cookies and sipped on my coffee. I was eager to gain more understanding.

"David, as a young man, was visited by a prophet of God and anointed to be the next King. Before his time to rule came to pass, he was employed by King Saul as a worship leader. One song written about David became extremely popular everywhere on the streets. The lyrics referred to the thousands more slain by David than by King Saul. Every time King Saul went out, he heard people singing it, which ticked him off because he did not want to be number two in the public's esteem.

"David had done nothing to deserve the King's anger. From the moment he entered Saul's service, he had been courageous and honorable. But no matter how much David tried to please the King, he turned on David.

"So, David had to flee the palace to save his life. Then, while David was on the run, he and King Saul's daughter, Michal, fell in love and married. Saul seemed to soften a little for a short time and tried to get along with his son-in-law, David. He even invited him back to the palace. David resumed his duties as the King's assistant and resident musician. Is this sounding familiar?"

"Yes! Please continue."

"Once again, the tortured King fell victim to the darkness in his mind and tried to kill David, but he ran away. He knew his career in King Saul's Royal service was over, and there was no going back.

"David went on the run again and was forced to hide in the wilderness. He kept rehearsing the events in his head over and over. He questioned what he had done. What was his crime? Why was King Saul trying to take his life? But while he had lots of questions, he had few answers. These were tough days for him, being misunderstood, questioning his motives, and being selected arbitrarily as the target of another person's evil nature and jealous arrows.

"There was nothing to break the loneliness of David's silent isolation. Days stretched into weeks, and months, and then years. Saul became obsessed with killing David, who continued running, dodging, hiding, and not wanting to take the offensive—but not wanting to die either.

"Now I feel like a female 21st-century David," I exclaimed, reaching for another cookie.

"Do you think David understood what his travails were about? Did he understand what God was doing? Did he grasp how God would use his unfair persecution to teach others for thousands of years to come?" Ruth asked.

"I doubt it!" I answered. I saw Saul as being like my Dad, and, of course, I related to David. I knew what it was like to be confounded trying to figure out something that made no sense.

Ruth opened her Bible. "We don't have to guess what David was thinking back then because he wrote it down in Psalm 142. God wanted it written for future spiritual warriors like you and me, for when we aren't feeling great about our lot in life under God's control. David probably wrote it while hiding in a cave, scared and confused. In it, he poured out his desperate cry to God to help him."

After I read Psalm 142, I was amazed at how much I related to the feelings and predicament of a shepherd who lived thousands of years ago. David cries out to God as he sinks to his knees in despair. He feels left alone and forgotten as his enemy hunts him down. His only hope is to appeal to God for help. Psalm 142 (NKJV):

> *I cry aloud to the Lord; I lift up my voice to the Lord for mercy. I pour out my complaint before him; before him I tell my trouble.*
>
> *When my spirit grows faint within me, it is you who know my way. In the path where I walk men have hidden a snare for me. Look to my right and see; no one is concerned for me. I have no refuge; no one cares for my life.*
>
> *I cry to you, O Lord; I say, "You are my refuge, my portion in the land of the living." Listen to my cry, for I am in desperate need; rescue me from those who pursue me, for they are too strong for me. Set me free from my prison, that I may praise your name.*
>
> *Then the righteous will gather about me because of your goodness to me.*

"So, what did David do?" I asked.

"He became a great King of Israel. And through his lineage, Jesus was born! In Psalm 142, David offers us a guiding principle for overcoming great trials and dealing with dysfunctional relationships. Do you see it?" Ruth asked.

"Not really," I admitted.

"David cries aloud to God. Then, he begs for God's attention and help. David tells Him he can't take it anymore, and he tells God about his troubles—that he has an enemy who is tormenting him, one who hates his guts.

"David was overwhelmed and at the brink of exhaustion. He thinks he can't take another step. Just at that point, a truth dawns on him. David reminds himself that God knows his way and the path he's been traveling. He tells God that it doesn't make sense to him. David then affirms that he needs to focus on God and God's character to make it through this horrible mess! He commits to changing his perspective and attitude. From that moment on, he will walk straight ahead, trust God with his heart, feelings, and soul, and entrust his future to God.

"David is on the path God placed him on. He hasn't wandered off it. We can see that God allowed David's enemies to set a snare for him. David then asks God, 'Why?' and admits that it feels as if God and everyone else are against him. This is the worst, loneliest, most miserable time in the desert of the unknown for anyone. When you reach this level, you're usually not thinking straight," Ruth explained.

"I feel like David: alone and sorry for myself. How do I apply the principles David used?" I asked Ruth.

"David surrenders completely into God's arms. When the going gets tough, the tough run straight to God! Don't give in to discouragement and self-pity. You can't afford to do that, or you'll die in the battle. Refuse to go down with the blows." Ruth put her hand over mine.

"Just because something is not presently prospering doesn't mean it's not from God. He uses many things to test the hearts of men and His chosen leaders. David did not return evil for evil but good for evil. Saul continually tried to kill David, but David would not raise his hand against Saul. Instead, he waited patiently, even during intense persecution and injustice, for God to establish him in His time. Retaliation is not God's way. Don't let the 'Saul' in your Dad bait you into retaliation, or you'll be retaking the test again." Ruth stood up and opened her arms to me.

I hugged her. I knew I had gotten what I needed. "One more bit of advice," Ruth gently directed me. "Stop trying to get the last word in. God knows the truth."

We walked to the front door, and she closed it behind me.

Finally, when the day ended, I heard my Dad yawning in his room. I was grateful to be in bed, and the house felt peaceful.

I thought about Ruth's suggestion that I give up having to have the last word, since God knows the truth. So, I swallowed my pride and took the high road. "I'm sorry for getting mad at you earlier," I blurted out to my father in the dark. I felt proud of myself for apologizing even though I didn't feel like doing it. I lay my head back down on the pillow.

"Thanks for saying you're sorry," my father called out from his bedroom.

"Sure, Dad!" I said as I felt a moment of warmth between us.

"I'm glad you knew you were wrong!" he said. The mocking voice was familiar.

I continued to feel like David, and he continued to act like Saul.

17

Overcoming Trials

Money continued to be tight. I lived in a small home with minimal expenses. There had been no significant crises for a few months, so I looked for a full-time job. I was offered work in a drug court program, something I was excited to take on. It was 8:30-5 with a lunch break. I started on the following Monday. It was great to get back to meaningful work with others. Everything had gone smoothly. When I returned to work the next day, my father called me. "I'm dizzy and can't get up. I need you to come home," he said and hung up. I knew it was serious if he called. I left work and went home. I managed to get him into the car and to emergency care. After waiting three hours, the doctor told us one of his medications was causing an imbalance in his equilibrium. So, we got a new prescription, and I brought him back home.

I returned to work on Wednesday, and on Thursday afternoon, I received a call from the nursing home. "We just sent your mother by ambulance to the hospital because her blood pressure rose to a dangerous level. We need you to meet her there," the nurse said. I spent the rest of the afternoon speaking on behalf of my mother to the doctors and nurses as they worked on stabilizing her. Once they did, we returned to the nursing home, and I got her tucked into bed.

Friday, I returned to work, and the director called me into his office. No surprise! He explained that he thought my elderly care situation would not lend itself to full-time employment at the facility, citing my need to miss two days of my first five days at work. He apologized, and I handed him my office keys. I understood. Time was ticking away, and I worried about my inability to pursue a career and establish meaningful work caring for both my parents.

When I let my father know I had lost my job, he insisted I use whatever I needed from his Social Security and pension. I didn't like taking money from him, but I was limited by what I could earn while caring for them. Neither of us wanted to depend on the other for anything, and yet here we were depending on each other for basic survival. So, I set up a monthly allotment from his endowment to cover my household living expenses.

Next, I turned my attention to another passion, which was becoming a therapist. I wanted to help others who experienced what I had, and I wanted to do something meaningful for myself. I discovered that the closest college offering a Master's in clinical mental health counseling had a fast-approaching deadline for the next semester. I gathered referral letters, test scores, and undergraduate transcripts and completed the lengthy application form. As an honors graduate with a four-year degree from Adelphi University, I thought I had a good shot at being accepted. I was willing to take out student loans and seek scholarship awards. I was pleased with my plan and sent it off priority mail.

As we approached the deadline, I still hadn't heard back from the college. I called and was told that they never received my application and no longer had any openings. The department program director suggested I resend it for the following year. What happened to the easy flow of things I used to know in my life?

I called Ruth. "Other friends of mine who have helped their parents have had their situations resolved, but nothing has changed for me. Why is there no end in sight?" I asked.

"God says that you are blessed if you persevere under trial; you are growing and maturing spiritually," Ruth responded. "An athlete's endurance does not increase until they exceed their previous limits. Our faith doesn't grow until we are placed in conditions requiring more faith than before. Our love doesn't grow until we are placed in a situation where we must give more than before. The same is true of our patience, peace, etc. You can expect to undergo some trials if you want to grow spiritually. Trials should not be avoided; they should be embraced as opportunities. God uses crises in your life to teach you about Him, who He is, what He can do, and how much He loves you," Ruth said.

I closed my eyes for a moment to let that truth sink in. "Does it have to take years to happen?"

"It takes what it takes. You build endurance and discipline by repeatedly practicing the work until it's complete. This training corrects and molds your character. Life gives us what we need to develop to attain victory through our challenges," Ruth shared.

"Isn't there another way?" I was still hoping this obligation would all magically disappear.

"There are infinite ways, but only God knows your unique needs."

"I wish I could feel God's presence in this situation," I conceded.

"When a child is learning to walk, his parent will back away, so the child has to take more steps to reach them. God backs away so we can learn to walk, fall, and get up again. There is no quick fix to spiritual maturity," Ruth added, then got off the phone.

I felt like a race car in the Indy 500, poised at the pit stop, refueled with Ruth, and having tires changed for the next ten laps around the track with my Dad.

As much as I didn't want to hear that truth, I knew I needed it. Ruth wanted me to see the benefits of going through my hardships.

It had taken me years to understand that the spiritual growth I prayed for lay outside my comfort zone. All buckled in, I felt like I was on a roller coaster ride. Once it had begun, I had to see it through to the end, the only safe place to get off.

I was already having a bad day and had gotten some sad personal news, so I kept it to myself. I could feel my father's negativity as I walked into the kitchen that morning. It was a real, tangible force.

"You're getting fat!" Dad blurted out, glaring at me.

I needed to catch my breath. My father's words stung because I had gained some weight, so I excused myself. As I walked through the dining room to head outside, I noticed his calendar on the table where my father sat most of the day. On the front cover was a big picture of a wolf, my father's favorite animal. Like the predatory wolf, he could sense when I was a weakened prey and always went in for the kill. How could so many years have passed since I started taking care of him? How did my Dad always know when I was at my weakest to come at me the hardest? How could I resist letting him affect me at such times?

In a moment of clarity, I decided that I would no longer feed on the lies my father had fed me my whole life. I had to start proactively feeding myself God's love and truth instead. I needed to give myself pep talks the way Ruth always did. "Stop taking things personally," Ruth had told me with certainty in our last conversation. "The journey of receiving God's promised benefits includes suffering and waiting for them. If you expect this reward, you don't have to feel discouraged or deviate from your course. You can keep doing the next right thing, even though wrong things happen, because God is on your side. God is your strength and will give you victory."

I thought for a long moment about Ruth's affirming words and felt some of the toxicity come off me. I was ready to face my father again and determined to have a good outcome.

I returned and found Dad eating his lunch at the dining room table. "Dad, you're right. I've been overeating from the stress, and I have gained some weight," I confessed, trying to open a heart-to-heart conversation.

"You don't know what tough times are. As a child, I worked for my parents at their store, and I carried coal daily to heat their house through the cold winters in Maine. I was only able to get a third-grade education. So, stop your complaining. You've got it good," he said.

"That's true! Look at how well-read and self-educated you are," I tried to compliment him. We may be making progress. Dad remained silent and continued to eat. Even his silence was better than his badgering me.

"A friend of mine in recovery relapsed and died yesterday," I told him. "She overdosed." At this point, I had been in recovery from alcoholism for years. Sometimes, I felt like a soldier on the front lines battling the enemy of addiction and alcoholism. I had seen many lives lost to it. Even though my father and I had fought on two different battlefields, I hoped he could see we both had lost our comrades.

"That's nothing compared to what I saw in World War II," he said.

"What did you see, Dad?" I asked.

"No need to talk about it. Tough it out. You're a grown woman. Your friend brought it on herself. Besides, you're not an alcoholic;

you're a weak-willed person. Don't get any fatter. It won't make you feel better," he said, and he picked up the newspaper and started reading it, blocking his face from my view.

I abruptly jumped up and ran out of the house, crying. In only fifteen minutes, I was reduced to tears again. I needed to see Ruth. My best efforts weren't enough to keep my peace while handling him.

So I called Ruth and drove to her house. She greeted me and led me to her kitchen. She had placed a freshly baked blueberry muffin on each of our plates. The aroma of the muffins and brewed coffee permeated the air. After she filled our cups and sat down, I filled her in on today's "battle."

"How can he be that cold? Where is his compassion?" I asked, my voice choked with emotion.

"Don't expect him to give you what he doesn't have," Ruth said.

"But why do I have to be the one to help my miserable father?"

"Maybe you're the only one God has to pick from right now," Ruth smiled. "Maybe you are in the Refiner's Fire."

"That doesn't sound good," I said with a gulp.

"It's a process like refining silver. Silver must be heated to a liquid state so the impurities can be separated and taken out. Then, once cooled, it is put in the fire again to be hammered and shaped into its intended form. This is what God does for us. He has to remove the lesser things that keep us from our greatness. God will put us in the fire to separate the impurities we must deal with. Those trials will burn up everything holding you back if you use them to purge what no longer serves you."

Ruth went on, "We are tested by our greatest weakness. If we are impatient and pray for this trait to be lifted, we'll have many opportunities to wait in grocery lines, in traffic, and with people. It is not an attack of bad luck; it's an answer to our prayers to refine our impurity of impatience. Tests will not destroy *us*; they will destroy our limitations, fears, and insecurities if we embrace them and walk through them.

"You only have two options: trust God or fear trouble. If you fear trouble, running away will only lead you from defeat to defeat and growing in self-pity. The biggest battle is to maintain your peace at all times.

"Once you learn the sweet victory of overcoming a trial, you will not choose to leave a situation in defeat. The greater the trial, the greater the victory. You can never become who you are supposed to be without a victory, and there's no victory without a trial."

I knew I was guilty of trying to pray away the challenges I faced daily. I wanted to come through the fire and become more like Ruth, whose patience enabled her to remain in charge of her reactions to people, places, and things. The ability to rule our emotions so we don't lose our tempers is one of the surest signs of true wisdom, maturity, and great spiritual strength.

I was learning to count to ten and pause when I was angry. Then, when I felt neutral enough to talk, I could say what I needed to say. My goal was to *say what you mean, mean what you say, but don't say it mean!*

I would no longer be controlled by my father's disposition and actions. I had to learn to keep my serenity even if my situation with him didn't change. The more I could accept my flaws, the less my father could use them against me.

I knew I must learn not to let my father's anger dictate my quality of life if I were going to survive the Refiner's fire. Yet I wondered: Could I maintain a calm attitude in my father's presence?

I knew I was not where I wanted to be and was determined to do better. After hearing Ruth, I made a commitment to start praying the following:

God, help me to want what I have and
give me the strength to do Your will. Amen

Ruth cleared the dishes from the table, signaling the close of our time together. She walked me to the front door and gave me a hug. I thanked Ruth for her wisdom. She had a way of broadening my perspective and grounding me in the truth. I left feeling ready for another lap around the track with my Dad.

I always felt steadier after spending time with Ruth. She knew things would always work out because God was in control. Stability is one of those outward signs that we trust God.

It was a new day. Would I have a breakthrough? The smell of bacon sizzling in the frying pan and coffee brewing reached my bedroom. Dad was cooking a breakfast of toast, bacon, eggs, and coffee. He called for me to eat with him.

After breakfast, Dad insisted I leave him alone in the kitchen so he could clean up. I went into the living room to work at my desk. A few minutes later, I heard him yelling for me to return to the kitchen. Something about the tone of his voice was off—really wrong! It was the same tone he'd used in my childhood when he was getting ready to rage at me.

I slinked into the kitchen, feeling childishly insecure. Dad held my plate with a small piece of bacon on it. He began yelling at me for not finishing it. Then, he started to cut me down with a barrage of accusations. "You never think . . . You're childish, selfish, and immature . . . You have no respect . . . You're never going to amount to anything! You don't even have the decency to finish this bacon . . . You act like the world owes you . . . You're lazy, and you waste everything!"

This time, I didn't react. Instead, I calmly asked my father if something else was bothering him. It was the first time I responded to his attacks with love and compassion. After many years and a lot of help, I no longer believed what he said about me when he was in a rage. I saw myself through God's eyes, not my father's diatribe. I was determined not to let it bother me, at least not outwardly. My lack of response got him madder than ever. He stormed out of the room. I followed him as he went into his bedroom. He slammed the door in my face.

"Go away," he yelled.

So, I did.

I walked right out the front door and kept walking. I must've walked for two hours, thinking about this verbal assault the whole time. I felt for my father. He was so stuck in his own mind, in his own feelings. For the first time, I saw his rage wasn't about me. How could all of this anger be about a slice of bacon?

The next time I met Ruth, I shared the bacon story.

"I didn't react in the same old way! I passed the test."

"Congratulations!" Ruth said and gave a nod of approval.

"But why do I feel so shaky?" I asked.

"It's because a moment of fear or anger consumes as much energy in the body as hours of hard labor. That's why staying bitter keeps one from moving forward. Holding resentment is like drinking poison and hoping the other person gets sick. You are called to something much higher: forgiveness and walking with God," Ruth said as she got up from the couch and returned with her Bible. She quickly found the passage she wanted to share with me.

She opened her Bible to the book of Genesis, chapters 37-45. "Let's look at Joseph's life. He was one of twelve sons, the favorite of his father. When he was young, he talked about how, one day, his older brothers would bow down to him. Because of his youthful boasting and his father's favoritism, Joseph's brothers became jealous and angry enough to trick him, staging his death to fool their father and then selling him into slavery in Egypt.

"As a slave, Joseph devoted himself to his master and was quickly promoted. He was gradually entrusted with the responsibility of the entire household. The master's wife was attracted to Joseph and propositioned him, hoping to get him into her bed. When Joseph refused, she falsely accused him of rape, and her husband had Joseph thrown into prison with no hope of release.

"Again, Joseph did his best to serve with a good attitude. He was trustworthy and dutiful and soon ran the prison administration. When the Pharaoh (the king) sought the meaning of several of his dreams, word got back to the king about Joseph's dream interpretations. He was summoned and led by the Spirit of God, and Joseph accurately interpreted the dreams and their meaning.

"Finally, after many years in prison, Joseph was freed. The Pharaoh appointed him Prime Minister of Egypt. Only the Pharaoh was above him. Thirteen years had passed since Joseph had been sold into slavery by his brothers. Even through Joseph's years in prison, he had lived according to God's Word, and after several setbacks, he was rewarded.

"Then a great famine hit Egypt. Joseph's brothers needed food and traveled to the Pharaoh's Prime Minister for help, not knowing he was their brother Joseph."

"Joseph must have been angry at them for what they did!" I said and felt for Joseph.

OVERCOMING TRIALS

"No, from his new position of power, Joseph tearfully revealed himself to his brothers, who had sold him into slavery many years before, and forgave them. He explained that he had sought a higher purpose for all that had happened to him. In Genesis 45:7-8a, he said, *'But God sent me ahead of you to preserve you for a remnant on the Earth and to save your lives by a great deliverance. So, then it was not you who sent me here, but God.'* He told them not to feel guilty about what they had done. Joseph could see how God had used their misdeed to save thousands of lives, including their own."

Ruth put her Bible aside and edged a little closer to me. "When we look at the bigger, long-term picture and see that God is always working in our lives, it becomes easier to forgive the people who have wronged us. God wants our relationships reconciled. Sometimes, our suffering is preparing us for our future success. Joseph's pain from his abandonment, slavery, and false imprisonment prepared him for power later. He repaid his brothers' betrayal with love and became the agent of change that brought his family together. Maybe God has chosen you to be the agent of change in your father's life," Ruth said.

"But I haven't seen any changes," I admitted.

"Neither did Joseph while he was in prison," Ruth explained. "When you're in a testing season, it usually means a miracle is coming. So, your challenges can signal good news up ahead! Maintaining a healthy attitude when life isn't fair takes serenity, courage, and wisdom. We can't change people, but we can choose our attitudes. We need God's help to change our responses to the injustices of life and be optimistic when we are treated unfairly. We need God's wisdom to know whether to fight an injustice or to make the best of a bad situation."

"If I forgive my Dad, he will get off free, while I've had to pay dearly for his abuse of me. Growing up with my father's rage has had its effects on me. So, how do I excuse what he did for all those years?"

"When you forgive someone, you are not freeing them from their endless wrongdoing. They still must deal with the consequences of their choices. Forgiveness does not excuse anything. The last thing your father is is free. Forgiveness frees you, thus freeing your energies to be better used by God.

"How do I forgive when I don't feel forgiveness?"

"True forgiveness is a choice. You may need to claim it one hundred times on the first day and again on the second day. On the third day, you will need to claim it less often, and then, one day, you realize that you have forgiven him completely. You can pray for God to give him wholeness and for God's love to burn all negativities from his life. One day, you may well know your father in a very different way.

"Forgiveness is not a feeling. You'll never wake up one day and think, 'Wow, I feel like forgiving my wrongdoer today!' Our natural human tendency is not to forgive the ones who hurt us the most. Sometimes, we take a perverse pleasure in feeling that we deserve to be angry with that person. We like the feeling of holding on to the right to strike back. Obviously, those feelings are not from God.

"When we do decide to forgive the person who has hurt us, we sometimes expect to feel differently right away, and, when we don't, we think that perhaps we haven't forgiven the person, after all. As you continue choosing to forgive, you'll feel less pain. It all starts with the decision to forgive.

"Forgiveness is for *your* benefit. We shall be forgiven as we forgive. Every time you react to your father by holding resentments, you are hurting yourself. God has the power to heal your memories."

Listening to Ruth, I realized how little I had understood about true forgiveness.

"When you forgive, you're releasing yourself from a job that isn't yours. God is the only one who can deal with that person because He is the vindicator and judge who will fight our battles."

Ruth always told me the truth, even if it was hard to hear. She was right, and I certainly wanted God's forgiveness for all my wrongs. I needed to let go of the questions that kept going around in my mind: Why should I forgive my father when he never apologizes? How could I forgive him for having raged violently at me as a child, for having constantly beaten me down with abusive insults my whole life?

But I could see that resenting my father and continuing to suffer from him only perpetuated my problems. It was time to give up wishing he would become patient, loving, and kind. Those qualities would have to come from me. I could no longer justify *my* reactions based on *his* wrongful behavior.

"When you give up wishing your past with him was different," Ruth continued, "you can better forgive him."

It was a tall order, but I knew it was the only means to navigate my way to peace through all the strife my Dad continuously stirred up in me.

Ruth stood up to hug me. "On his own, your father is unable to grow in love. If you can stop being hurt by him, you can walk with the kind of love that will lead him to God one day. Your challenge is twofold: practice self-control in response to the offenses and pray for your father."

When I got home that evening, my father was in bed with his door closed. I quietly peeked in on him. He was sound asleep. I was more committed and motivated to practice forgiveness instead of reacting to him. He was my assignment and my opportunity to grow and heal.

The following morning, I went for a beach walk and then returned home. Feeling calm and detached, I walked into the house. We had not talked since the bacon fiasco when I walked out on him. I heard my father open his bedroom door and looked up to find tears in his eyes. It was the first time I'd ever seen him cry.

Taking my face in his hands, Dad looked straight at me and said, "Forgive me. I don't want to die thinking you don't know I love you. I can't help myself. I'm an old man with little time left and too old to change, but I promise I will try to be better."

You could've knocked me over with a feather.

18

Passing the Test

At age 99, my father's cognitive functions were declining, and his symptoms of dementia were escalating. Even though he refused to live in the nursing home where my mother resided, I knew it was time. After lunch the following day, Bill, the social worker from the nursing home, came to assess the situation without discussing Dad's potential new residence. He was a younger man, very pleasant, with a gentle demeanor. He took a seat across from us.

My father looked at the mild-mannered social worker and said, "Now, what the hell do *you* want?"

"Just to get to know you," Bill answered.

"I'm mad, and it's all her fault. I gave her all my money, and now she's trying to do away with me!" my father told Bill, even louder and angrier. The social worker just quietly listened.

Dad lowered and softened his voice. Pointing at me, he said, "She needs help. Can you help her?"

"I'll try," Bill said.

Bill's gentle answer to my father's question brought Dad's emotional pitch down another notch. He perceived everything in terms of himself versus me. He didn't understand that I was on his side, so I stayed out of the conversation.

He talked to Bill about the Spartans and their militaristic culture.

Then, my father looked directly at Bill and crossed his arms. "What do you want from me?"

"I just want to be your friend," Bill said.

I was now sitting on the couch in the living room. My father looked at me, then back at the social worker. "She's contaminated," Dad whispered to Bill. "She's not a real Greek, but don't tell her." My father thought I was out of earshot. Why did he mock me for the one thing he was most proud of—his Greek heritage? I was Greek, and I was his daughter. Why did he try to deny me my own heritage? I had to ask myself again, what was my father's lifelong contempt toward me based on? Sometimes, I thought it would have been easier if he were a drunk. Then, I could have attributed his ill feelings toward me to his drinking, but he had always been sober.

Would this saga ever end, and when it did, would my time spent being tested and pruned end in a breakdown or a breakthrough?

Later that day, I got comfortable at Ruth's house, where she made us tea. "Every day is a test for me to stay emotionally sober and choose whether I'll act out on my angry feelings or deal with them," I said, sipping on the hot, soothing tea. "I need to vent!"

"I'm all ears," she said.

"When my mother became ill, I was not expecting such hardships. I thought my efforts in recovery would be rewarded by the absence of troubles. It has taken me years to understand that God was more concerned with my character than my comfort level.

"But now it has been ten grueling years of battling an angry man who refuses my help and care every step of the way. Dealing with his personality and dementia has been exhausting and beyond anything I could have imagined.

"I've done everything I could to care for him and keep him safe. He treats me atrociously one minute, and in the next moment, he's pouring on the charm for a pretty store cashier. For the first few years, I didn't even realize he had dementia because he'd been acting the same since my childhood. He'd always had rages, outbursts, and willfulness. His trying to dominate and intimidate me was nothing new." I paused and took a deep breath.

"To stay strong, I've read countless stories of men and women who struggled and matured through their wilderness seasons. I found hope in their eventual breakthrough when God released favor, as their problems turned around and their dreams suddenly came to pass. It spurred me to read how others had overcome their hardships. That's what I want!" I took another sip of tea. I looked down for a moment.

I continued, "So, when trouble came and stayed, you taught me to say, 'I'm not going to panic; this is only a test. This will pass, and I'll pass the test.' And when I didn't pass the test, I got to retake it. And you helped me learn to trust and rely on God, even if what transpired didn't make sense. I've stopped trying to figure things out and asking, 'When God' or 'Why God.'

"I'm constantly choosing to believe that God is the way when there seems to be 'no way,' and when the front door of my life appears closed, God may be opening a back door. I'm trying to live right and do right so I can have the breakthrough.

"So, Ruth, where's my breakthrough?" I burst out crying. Ruth handed me another tissue to dab the tears running down my face. Ruth scooted closer and held me like a mother would a despairing daughter.

"You've come too far, for too long, to collapse under the weight of your emotions now. Keep your perspective and refocus. I think you are in the last phase of this storm," Ruth said encouragingly. She paused for a moment. "God promises you ultimate victory in the end. Don't lose heart; your breakthrough is coming." Then Ruth's husband came into the room and gave her a sweet smile, signaling it was time to call it a night.

I stood up and thanked them both. I knew the only way out was through perseverance.

Sometimes, situations aren't what they seem. I thought it was a miracle to find my father sitting at the dining room table listening to a preacher on the radio. I was surprised because my father didn't believe in God.

"Do you like this sermon?" I asked, hoping he might be changing in his old age. He paused for a few minutes, looking like he was deep in thought, as he listened to what was being said on the radio.

The preacher spoke about having hope because nothing was impossible with God. My father remained quiet. Was he turning toward God after all these years? Was he beginning to open to the spiritual life?

"What a bunch of crap!" he said, startling me out of my momentary fantasy. I walked over to the radio and turned it off.

"How can you call a message from a preacher about hope in God a bunch of crap?" I asked, aghast.

"Because hope is a lie," my father retorted.

I felt my blood pressure rising. *How does my father manage to always get me upset?*

"It's you that's hopeless . . . not God!" I stormed out of the front door, demonstrating my lack of self-control, tolerance, patience, and love, and being non-responsive. I did what I didn't want to: I responded to his verbal attacks by attacking back. This only fueled the fire. It was a vicious cycle.

I called Ruth, who invited me over for another mentoring session. She greeted me at the front door and led me back into the kitchen. I could see from the white flour on her apron that she had been baking. I stood at the kitchen counter as she formed the dough into cookies and placed them on the baking sheet.

"How am I supposed to lead Dad to God? He could die any day, and I'm still yelling back at him. What's worse, I'm yelling at him about God!"

"Are you still living in the fantasy of how you wish your dad could be?" Ruth asked.

"I suppose so," I answered.

"Your father doesn't want to hear about God. He believes only in his opinions and likes to upset you for the fun of it. Only God's Spirit of truth can penetrate the veil of blindness in him."

Ruth put the pan of sugar cookies in the oven to bake. We sat down at the kitchen table. "Your job is to remain peaceful and monitor your behavior instead of trying to control your Dad's."

"How do I respond to my father without provoking him?" I asked.

"When he says something offensive, you could say, 'If I were you, I'd feel that way, too.' It is a neutral statement. You're not agreeing or disagreeing, but the other person feels you are on their side. Remember, it's only a test!" Ruth reminded me.

"If God is testing me, I don't want to know my G.P.A.," I admitted, laughing nervously.

"I have prayed for years for God to stop my father from verbally attacking me, all to no avail. Why is that, Ruth?"

"Since God can move mountains, he must not want to move this one yet," she laughed gently. "If God intends to teach you not to get provoked, you are right where you need to be. If it weren't your father, there would be someone else to take his place! I've found that if I figure out the lesson in a situation and learn it, I can be freed from it and move on."

I could hear the doorbell and Ruth's dog barking in the front entryway. We stood up, and she walked me to the front door. The UPS man was waiting for her with a package. She turned to me after she signed for it, and he left. "Face your circumstances with a good attitude and stay where God has you until He releases you. The promotion comes after you pass the test." Ruth hugged me and said goodbye.

As much as I didn't like it, I knew this situation was where God wanted me to be. I no longer said, "Oh God, I don't want to do this anymore—this is too hard." I was now committed to the hope that things would change for me and my father even in the eleventh hour because of God's oversight.

Riding in the car one day, I brought up the forbidden subject. I decided to try one more time with my father. "Dad, what would it hurt to talk about God at this stage of your life?" I asked. An expression of rage and indignation came over him.

"I told you if you mention God again, I'll report you to the authorities for elder abuse!" he threatened.

I wasn't going to give up, but I wouldn't bring it up again on my own. I wanted my father to be touched by the sweetness of God's love, an experience that I knew would melt the hardness of his heart. Rather than resentment, I felt compassion for him.

I thought of a favorite saying: *Don't quit five minutes before the miracle happens!* I knew my father needed a miracle. I just didn't know which five minutes would lead up to it, and I didn't want to give up moments before it happened, especially after investing so much time and heartache over it. So, I held onto God's promise day after day.

After a decade of waiting on God's timing, I learned to stay out of the way. None of my spiritual entreaties had worked, so I had no more expectations. I was resigned to do my caregiving with love and leave the outcome to God. I was a slow learner, but I was finally starting to get it.

It had become impossible to deny that, between his falls and the threat of him accidentally starting a fire, Dad was now a danger to himself and others. It was time for my father to join my mother in the nursing home. I knew it was the next step to keep him safe and me well. I had no more guilt or fear about it.

The day finally came. My friends and I packed, unpacked, and arranged Dad's new room in record time. It was like a home makeover TV show where some lucky person goes out to dinner and returns to find a newly remodeled kitchen.

When I took my father into the nursing home, the nurses clapped. And when we rolled him into his new room, he was sweeter and more appreciative than I'd ever seen him. It was a bittersweet ending to ten years of difficult caregiving.

Afterward, I walked out to my car, and while driving home, I gradually realized that my father's life and safety were no longer directly dependent on me twenty-four hours a day. I had been so consumed by his life and needs that letting go of all that would be a major adjustment. I felt like I had been in a dark and isolated place for a long time. Suddenly, the bright light of freedom shone through. Was I really free to walk out of that prison cell?

Everything about caring for my father had been an intense, hands-on crash course in manifesting unconditional love. Learning and practicing real love taught me that sometimes you must make sacrifices. When children don't get what they want, they have a temper tantrum. Real love doesn't give in to the irrational impulses of our emotions. Real love is a choice for goodness beyond the focus of self-gratification. How ironic to realize that through all the years of emotional turmoil with my father, he had been the one teaching me about real love! I was left with a bittersweet feeling.

When I came home from the nursing home and walked into his empty bedroom, I was moved by the peace, calm, and emptiness I now felt there. How could one person pack so much emotional energy into a house? My dad had always been the thorn in my side. After ten years, the chains that bound us were broken in a moment.

I began cleaning up his bedroom at home. I had really wanted to keep my father's war medals, feeling they would somehow acknowledge, maybe even honor, the war between us for years. I had felt particularly disappointed a few years earlier when I learned he'd given them to an acquaintance. But as I was cleaning out Dad's old newspaper clippings from the bottom of a small box, I found a metal of his that must have gone unnoticed. The Medal of Good Conduct and Efficiency was engraved on the front, with *Honor and Fidelity* on the other side. What a treasure to find that metal now! I started crying. I missed the person he could have been and the meaningful father-daughter relationship we might have had.

My peaceful reverie over my father's absence did not last long. When I moved my father into my mother's room at the nursing home, I just hoped he could get along with her. After sixty-three years of marriage, I knew old habits do not die easily. I figured their fights couldn't last long because of my mother's limited speech. In ten years since the stroke, all she had been able to say was "No" and "Shut up"—the three words she hadn't said enough in their years of marriage. On the other hand, those words could keep my father arguing for a long time. I especially didn't want my father to get kicked out of the nursing home because there was now no place else for him to go.

I got the dreaded phone call from the social worker at the nursing home. "Miss Lake, we don't know if we can keep your father. There is an issue that we can't resolve." My heart was racing. The issue was that they constantly fought over the remote because you could only have one TV in each room. I asked the nursing home not to do anything until I got there. Then I prayed. I gathered my purse and keys. The idea came to me to buy two universal remotes and give one to each of them. My mother was unable to operate a remote due to the sustained brain damage from her stroke. She could push the buttons with the hand that was not paralyzed, but she did not know what show or channel she wanted because she couldn't follow them. I took the batteries out of hers so that it would not change the channel when she pushed the buttons. She did hold onto the remote most of the time because it made her feel like she was in control of something. It worked like a charm. My mother had her remote, and my father could use his to watch what he wanted. Each thought they had won the battle. I had to wonder what kept them arguing for more than half a century, and why I had been in the middle of their battleground for years.

After three months had passed, Dad had adjusted to the nursing home, relieving me of a lot of the stress. He remained ornery, and I visited them every other day, bringing whatever they needed. I would cut my father's hair and manicure my mother's nails. I was kept busy keeping track of all their medical expenses and reporting to the various government agencies.

My father continued berating me whenever he saw me, but I had learned to ignore it. I had passed that test! I continued to pray for God to touch my father and heal his heart.

19

Wailing Wall Prayer

It had been years since I traveled and took time away from caretaking duties. I needed this break. I have always wanted to travel to Israel, so I decided to plan a trip. I was amazed at how everything came together to facilitate this trip and was excited about what I would discover.

Early in the trip, we went to the Jordan River, where John the Baptist baptized early believers and Jesus. Baptism is a Christian tradition in which you are publicly immersed in water to symbolize burying your old way of life and being reborn with a new life in Christ as you rise. We were offered the opportunity to be baptized, and it was a timely ceremony for me, so I accepted.

It was a beautiful morning. We were given a light white robe to wear and walked single-file down to a calm river, pale green in color. It was only a short distance to the opposite shore. The pastor was waiting for us, and one by one, we were prayed over and then fully immersed in the water. When I rose, I imagined the start of a new beginning and the next season of my life. This would mark the moment when I released my past and continued to move forward on my spiritual journey with God. The sun shone through some overhead trees, its rays glistening on the water's surface.

We went on a walking tour and followed the steps Jesus took, leading us to some of the holiest places on the planet. We went to the Mount of Olives, viewed the Dome of the Rock, walked through the Garden of Gethsemane, entered the Lion's Gate into the Old City, and passed the Pools of Bethesda. We walked the Stations of the Cross, the path Jesus had taken while carrying the cross to Calvary. Being within the ancient city walls and in the location where King David reigned in Jerusalem, I felt that the Biblical stories were coming to life for me.

We took a boat ride and had a worship service on the Sea of Galilee. We visited a kibbutz, a communal farm living situation common in Israel, and we walked around Megiddo, identified in *Revelation 16:16* as the final site where the battle between good and evil is fought at the end of time.

The place that drew me in the most was the Wailing Wall. It is near the Temple Mount's southwestern corner, facing a large plaza in the Jewish Quarter. It is a portion of the ancient limestone wall built by Herod, made up of large stone blocks, and the visible area is 131 feet high. It is the closest location to the Holy of Holies, which is believed to have held the *Ark of the Covenant* that housed the stone tablets on which the Ten Commandments are written. The Wailing Wall got its name because, during the Roman rule over Jerusalem (324-638 AD), Jews would weep over the destruction of their two temples.

It has been an ancient prayer spot for Jews up to the present day, and it is believed to be holy and blessed by God. The prayer notes to God are removed twice a year, just before Rosh Hashanah and Passover, and buried in the Jewish cemetery on the Mount of Olives.

People of all faiths journey to the Wailing Wall and either recite prayers or write them down on a piece of paper and put them in the gaps of the large stones. The Wall has two sections, one for males and the other for females. There were a lot of people praying that day.

When I approached the Wall, I was struck by the power of the place and its emotional impact on me. I felt for all the people who had come to this Wall before and the many standing there today. Soft-spoken prayers were being lifted to God, and many written missives were placed in the wall cracks. I closed my eyes as I faced the Wall and held my prayer in the palm of my hand. I had written:

Dear God,

Please save my father and heal his heart, so that he will know You and Your love. Please heal our relationship before he passes. Thank you.

Love,

Catherine

I placed it on the wall. Feeling overwhelmed, I cried. I had sought my father's love my whole life. He was now ninety-nine years old, and there had never been any emotional change in him toward me. With so little time left, this prayer seemed like an impossible request to God. But I believed in God and His miracles. In faith, I gave my prayer to God. I placed my hand over it on the Wall and then backed away, and as is customary, I did not turn my back to the Wall within a few feet of it. This approach felt like the most powerful of all the ways I tried to resolve things with my father.

One night, two weeks after returning from Israel, I was awakened from a sound sleep at 3 a.m. I sensed I was being asked to write a letter to my father, inviting him to turn to God and ask

Christ into his heart. The guidance was to write the letter, take it to my father, and ask him to pray with me.

Not again! I said out loud.

I wrestled with my Higher Power's request, but eventually reminded myself that God knew what was happening. Intuitively, I sensed *this time it would be different!* I had to trust God and have faith. I had nothing to lose except being yelled at one more time.

So, I wrote the letter.

At 10 a.m. the next morning, I went into my father's room at the nursing home and closed the door. They had taken my mother to be bathed, so Dad and I had the room to ourselves. His hearing had worsened, so I was glad I had typed the letter. I gave it to him, and he started to read it. He saw the reference to *God* and stopped. "You may not know this," he said, "but I went to church from when I was eight to fifteen years old."

"This has nothing to do with church and religion," I assured him. I didn't know if he was trying to bait me. "This is between you and God today."

Then, I quietly asked him to read the last paragraph, telling him how much it would mean to say this prayer with him. Here's the letter I gave him:

Dear Dad,

I want you to know what is in my heart. I love you, truly.

I believe God loves us all the same. It doesn't matter if we have been good or bad; we can't earn His love. God's love for each of us is a free gift.

WAILING WALL PRAYER

I also believe God provides a place for us called Heaven when we transition from this life at death. It is a place where we will be made whole spiritually. A place where we can see loved ones, family, and friends, and where we will be conscious of our connection with God. Maybe the richness of Heaven can be glimpsed in this world by turning to God here and now. I want to see you in Heaven one day, and I want us to have that kind of time together here, too. We got robbed of it in this life.

With all the gifts God offers us, He only asks that we invite Him into our lives. A simple prayer to invite God in could be as follows:

Right now, I confess that you, Jesus, are the Son of the Living God. I believe that You died for me and rose again. Please come into my life and heart. Wash me, forgive me of all my sins. You are my God. Thank You for saving me. Amen.

Dad, maybe this is selfish, but I could have no greater, sweeter moment or memory than of praying this prayer together. My one desire is to have this special moment with my dad. Could we pray this together?

With Love Always,

Catherine

"Would you pray with me?" I asked when I saw he had completed reading the letter. He looked at me. There was humility in his eyes that I had never seen before. "Yes," he said as he stretched his hands toward me. We held hands and prayed. I could feel God's loving presence permeate the room.

I thanked God for the miracle that had occurred and for our being together.

As I left the nursing home, I thought, *When Dad dies, he's going to be so blown away by Heaven! Maybe he and Mom will finally get a chance to have some joy!*

Over the next few months, my father had a complete change of heart. He became a warm and tender person, especially toward me. He never spoke another negative word to me, constantly showering me with compliments and loving-kindness. He would take my hand and kiss it when I saw him. "You know how much I appreciate what you've done," he would tell me.

One day, the staff told me my father had wheeled himself down to the nurse's station the night before and started singing for an hour straight, 'Glory, Glory, Hallelujah' from *The Battle Hymn of the Republic*. They said he has a great voice and enjoyed him bellowing out that melody. I told them I had never heard him sing. His vocal cords were damaged as a child, and he could never carry a tune. The nurses looked perplexed, but not me.

Watching the changes in his spirit as he let God into his heart at the age of 99 was remarkable. Even the relationship between him and my mother was better than ever. Anyone who knew my father before and after this changeover knew God's Spirit was moving in him.

Suddenly, I remembered a prophecy that had been delivered to me over thirty years earlier when I went to the A.R.E. (Association for Research and Enlightenment) research conference:

> *One day, you will give a gift to your parents that will be far greater than the seeming life they gave to you.*

I had always remembered those words, though I had only just now understood their meaning. The gift was knowing the love of God, and our eternal life is even greater than the gift of life we are born into here. The ramifications of my father's rebirth, which I had just witnessed, are the true spiritual birth we all seek.

I was so glad I hadn't quit (at least 1,000 times) five minutes before the miracle happened.

Even though my mother continued to have occasional bouts of frustration, for the most part, she remained calm now and resigned to her limitations and conditions. She seemed pleased with the peace that settled in her relationship with my father and seeing the peace between my father and me.

Then the call came. It was 8:15 a.m. "Your mom's blood sugar is up to 316, and her blood pressure is very low. Her pulse is barely detectable, and she is cold and clammy," the nurse said.

"I'll be there immediately." I hung up. I was shaking. Seconds counted. I grabbed my keys, ran to my car, and drove to the nursing home as fast as I could.

When I got there, I saw Mom still breathing but taking very shallow breaths. A nurse hooked her up to an oxygen tank and placed a mask on her face. Her eyes stared off into space; her hands were cold to the touch. I put one hand on her forehead, which was still warm. Her slow, rhythmic breathing was labored. Her eyes shifted in my direction.

"Mom, you're free to go on. I love you . . ." I was whispering to her. Everything seemed surreal.

Her eyes moved and looked again in my direction. Her hand squeezed mine. Then her breathing softened, becoming ever so slight with long pauses.

She had always told me how reading poetry calmed her mind. I picked up my mother's favorite book of poetry, lying on her nightstand. I randomly opened it to a poem she had placed stars in years ago.

VICTORY IN DEFEAT

Defeat may serve as well as victory
To shake the soul and let the glory out.
When the great oak is straining in the wind,
The boughs drink in new beauty, and the trunk
Sends down a deeper root on the windward side.
Only the soul that knows the mighty grief
Can know the mighty rapture. Sorrows come
to stretch out spaces in the heart for joy.

—Edwin Markham (1852-1940), *Poems that Live Forever,* Selected by Hazel Felleman. Printed by Doubleday 1965)

I fought back tears as I read that poem to her. I hoped her joy was coming.

I hung onto each small breath she took. It became hard to tell if they were hers or if they were the oxygen machine continuing to pump air into her lungs. The nurse came in. There was now no heartbeat, no pulse, and no breath. The nurse pronounced her dead. She was gone.

I drew open the curtains separating my parents, which I had kept pulled to shield Dad while Mom was dying. Because of his dementia, he sometimes experienced confusion, and I didn't want him to interrupt Mom's transition. I wanted her to be able to go peacefully.

I looked over at my dad. He looked back at me, concerned.

"She's gone, Dad," I said as I went to his bed. After sixty-six years of marriage, I was grateful to be there for him in this tender, painful moment. He had just lost the love of his life.

"She's really dead?" he asked, with a look of disbelief on his face.

"Yes, Dad," I said. He broke down and cried like a baby. I'd never seen him cry like that. I held him. After a few minutes, his dementia kicked in, or maybe it was reality taking its toll. He started talking about unrelated, made-up stories. I just listened. It didn't seem fair that at his age and in his condition, he would also have to endure such grief. Life is hard. Maybe we go through the rough stuff in old age so that it's easier to surrender this life as we prepare to move into the next and better one.

Thirty minutes later, the funeral home came and put Mom on a stretcher with a plush black blanket over her. I wheeled her to Dad's bedside since he had been unable to get out of bed to go to her. I motioned for everyone to leave the room. Dad reached out to touch her head as he tried to say goodbye to her before breaking into tears again.

How do you say goodbye to someone you've shared your life with for that long?

Then they wheeled Mom out of the room, and I accompanied her to the funeral home. I asked if I could be alone with my mom to say goodbye. They showed me to a large room, wheeled her in, and shut the door behind me. Mom lay motionless on the table, her face peeking out, her body covered by the plush black blanket.

"Mom, there's so much that went unsaid between us. I love you. I'll see you again one day." I kissed her forehead and then pulled the blanket over it.

I had years to prepare for her death, but when it happened, I did not feel prepared. I was intimately tied to her my entire life. For all the challenges we faced from her drinking, our complicated relationship, and her tumultuous marriage, she was still my mother, and I loved her. I thought I would feel relieved after years of caretaking and seeing her suffer. Instead, I felt overwhelmed by the loss.

I went over to Ruth's. When she opened her front door, I fell into her arms. I wanted a mother's hug. She held me for a few minutes while I cried out another wave of sadness and grief. Then, as quickly as it came, it subsided. I collected myself, and we went into the den and sat on her couch.

"It's so sad. Now my parents have finally reached a peaceful place with themselves and each other, and it's over," I said.

"The longer you live, the more you'll see how we can't judge whether something that happens is good or bad because we don't know the bigger picture that God sees.

"One day, you'll see all the good that has come from this situation with your mom and dad that *seems* to have sidetracked your life!" Ruth said. "When you've done everything you can, believe that love controls the plan and put it in God's hands," Ruth said.

"I understand. It's like the story of the man stranded on a deserted island and his hut caught on fire. It seemed like the worst thing in the world had happened, but that afternoon, a Coast Guard boat saw the plume of smoke, found the man, and rescued him," I said, having heard that story in a recovery meeting.

Before I left, I decided to resist judging events as good or bad. I recommitted to letting God run the show, knowing He would continue recycling things meant for harm into experiences used for good.

20

Heaven's Gate

Dad was now 101. It had been two years since the Wailing Wall prayer, and my father continued to show me unending kindness. It had been three months since my mother passed peacefully in their room at the nursing home after many years of suffering. I was by her side as she slipped away, and I comforted my father as I broke the news to him. With the recent passing of my mother, he had been having more episodes of confusion along with dementia.

When I checked in on my father that morning, he looked sad and helpless. His right hand was riddled with arthritis. His eyelids were very red and swollen. I cleaned him up and cut his hair. He looked at me and began to cry like a baby. In fifty-four years, I had seen him cry this hard only twice—once when my mother passed away, and at that moment. "I'm so glad you're here," he said. "I should've been better to you. Forgive me, your mom had an affair," he said with his head hanging low.

"It's okay. I know all about it." I tried to reassure my father that all was well. Since my mother passed away, my father made up stories. I learned the easiest way to handle them was just to go along and pretend they had really happened.

Then he asked me for a mirror. I gave him one. He strained and struggled to get a glimpse of his face. He looked at himself in the reflection for a few minutes.

"How old am I?" he asked. I told him he was 101 years old. He looked back at the mirror. I wondered if he would exclaim in shock at how badly he looked from the passing of time and aging. He used to be very vain about his looks.

"Well, I look pretty damn good, don't I!" he said to my surprise, and he blew me a kiss.

The following day, I went to visit him. His face looked sunken, his skin was grayish, and his breathing was raspy. I sat on the bed and put my hand on his arm. He felt cold to the touch. It felt like his body was shutting down and beginning its descent into death. He opened his somewhat swollen eyes slightly, and he recognized me. "Oh, Catherine, I've always loved you," he said. Then he faded out of consciousness again. Sitting on the edge of his bed, I noticed a sense of peace filling the room.

He came around again. "Who's the nice gentleman standing by your side?" he asked. I was startled because I could see no one else in the room, so I asked him if he knew the gentleman.

"No, but he's smiling and waving at you!" Dad said. I told him he must be a friend of ours. My father may have made up stories, but he never imagined seeing people.

Dad slipped back into a sleep state again, breathing lightly with a rhythmic raspy sound. The room remained peaceful. I sat looking directly at his little bookshelf and the mementos of what was left of his life. There were a few photos I had seen since I was a little girl: the picture of my parents in uniforms when they first met, the one of my mother in her early thirties posing next to their 1950 Hornet Hudson car, the WWII photos of my father in the Philippines, and one of my brother at age ten. A lifetime had come and gone now, and what was left for him were these few items, representing over one hundred years of living, as he lay in a bed attended to by one visitor—me.

My father came to again, and I became acutely aware of the peace in the room and between us. "Thank you for coming. Where's your mother?"

"She's gone, Dad."

"Where do you think she is?" he asked.

"Heaven," I said with a smile. A big grin came on his face, and he softly sang an old Greek song in his native language. With his good hand, he took mine and kissed it. "Opa, opa . . ." he said, closing his eyes and fading away again.

I watched my father, the Spartan, the old Greek warrior, the man who had survived a severe handicap, the Great Depression, and a brutal world war, as he courageously faced death. I felt the peace again. What a contrast to the years of fighting, struggle, anger, and pain I had experienced with him. It was all coming to a close. All that was left was this peaceful surrender. I knew he had decided to let go. He wanted to be with my mother, the woman who was the love of his life. He welcomed death and, with it, the hope of seeing her again.

Why couldn't we have had this relationship throughout my life? I had always wished to feel this closeness with him from childhood on. At least I had been given these last, precious moments with him, even if he was on his deathbed.

That night, I looked up the meaning of the Greek word *opa*. *It is a declaration of the celebration of life itself. It is another way of expressing joy and gratitude to God and others for bringing us into a state of wisdom where we acknowledge what matters: health, family, and friends. It is a declaration that you are well and where you're supposed to be. It signals that you need to stop and celebrate life.*

Opa! It would be my father's last word to me . . .

It was the beginning of his journey to Heaven's Gate. It started when my cell phone rang at 4:30 a.m. "Your father's vitals have changed," the nurse on the other end of the phone informed me. It was like hearing a pregnant woman's water had broken and labor was imminent. "I'll be right down," I told her as I quickly dressed and slipped into my shoes.

I had often prayed that God would allow me to be with my dad as I had been with my mom when she died. Dad had been emotionally alone so much of his life, and I didn't want him to feel alone in death.

As I drove toward the nursing home, thoughts and memories flooded my mind about my father. It was dark and quiet on the streets during the early morning hours. I felt very alone. About ten minutes into the drive, a car pulled out in front of me. Its license plate startled me as it caught my attention. It spelled out "COSTA" in big letters, my father's Greek nickname. What were the odds of that happening? It reminded me that God was at work in this mix, orchestrating the unfolding events. I felt less alone as I pulled into the nursing home parking lot.

I walked into Dad's room to find him lying on his back. I immediately recognized his labored breathing as the death rattle: rhythmic, shallow breaths that sounded like rattling, caused by the buildup of fluid in his lungs. He was unable to talk but was aware and conscious. He looked over at me and nodded his head to let me know he knew I was there. I took his hand in mine. He squeezed it. I sat next to his bed so I could be close to him. I continued to hold his hand and keep eye contact with him.

I noticed his lips were parched and chapped. Dampening a small sponge, I moistened them, then returned to holding his hand and stroking his arm. His skin was cold to the touch.

He continued to look at me. "I love you, Dad. I'm right here," I told him. He squeezed my hand. I said I wouldn't leave him. He squeezed my hand again—an hour passed. The nurse rolled in an oxygen machine and put the mask over Dad's nose and mouth. She secured the mask around his ears.

I followed her back into the hallway. "Does my father need the oxygen feed since it's clear he's in the last stages of dying?" I asked.

"It's standard procedure," she said. I remembered that they had done the same with my mother, too, as she lay dying. With the oxygen continuing to pump into her, it had been hard to know if Mom or the machine was still breathing. I wanted to know when my dad's real last breath occurred. Birth and breath are connected. A baby's birth is wrapped around its first breath. At death, our birth into the life beyond is wrapped around that last breath. I wanted the glory of my father being birthed into Heaven to be a natural transition untampered by man.

I went back into the room and sat by his bedside. He nodded his head again, acknowledging my return. I held his hand, and he squeezed it hard. Then, he let go and pulled the mask from his nose and around his ears. His hand came back to mine, and he squeezed it again. We had eye contact.

"I agree, Dad."

We both knew he was about to die, and he wanted to embrace it. He was a fighter, and he was courageous—many people at this stage of dying slip into unconsciousness, but not him.

Three hours had passed when he released my hand and put it on my neck. With what little strength he had left, he pulled my head to his chest and held onto me. It was the most genuine, deep, all-embracing hug I had ever received from him. It carried all the years of love he had felt for me but had been unable to express for so long, the love I had craved so desperately from him and had sought elsewhere throughout my life.

I fought to hold back my tears. This was my time to be strong for my father. The love he was communicating through his embrace washed away all the fights and turmoil we had experienced over the years. It was a beautiful culmination of the changes God had worked in my father's spirit since he had received Him two years earlier, at age ninety-nine.

I held back my tears as he suffered through his last breaths, a look of humbled helplessness in his eyes. I wanted to absorb every detail of my last experience of him.

Two more hours passed. Dad was still conscious. We continued to hold hands, and I stroked his arm from time to time. Mostly, he would look at me, and I would nod back to him, signaling that everything would be okay. I wondered how long his suffering would go on. I prayed to God under my breath continuously. Time seemed to stand still. Eternity hung on the edge of each breath.

Dad had been hanging on for five hours now.

Another hour passed. I continued to hold my father's hand and pray. Suddenly, his eyes opened wide as if startled by a loud sound. I looked into his eyes and firmly said, "You're going to be okay. Everything is going to be okay."

As soon as I said that, his eyes lit up and he smiled. He began looking around the room in all directions, a childlike expression of wonder and awe on his face, like a kid glimpsing Disneyland for the first time. The hair stood on my arms, and I felt a powerful presence envelop the room.

Then, my father let go of my hand and reached out to touch someone I couldn't see. Whoever he saw was more real to him than I was at that moment. A look of joyful wonder remained on his face. Then he looked at me, dropped his hand, exhaled softly, and was gone.

The room turned quiet and still. What had felt like a vortex of God's presence, a Heavenly escort to greet my father, had come and was now gone, my father in tow. I had become so caught up in the rapture he was experiencing that I had momentarily forgotten that he was in the process of dying, and in a flash, he was gone.

Suddenly, I felt the emptiness of the room. I wanted to talk with my father now more than ever. I wanted to know: Who had my father seen? Angels? Jesus? Did he see my mother? All the above?

It felt as if he had been slowly moving out of his house all morning and suddenly had taken his last bag and left. But before he left, he had been allowed to see the mystery of God in time and space; the Great Mystery was confirmed for him while he was still in his earthly body, even if for just a moment. By staying conscious until the end, he had allowed me to witness him witnessing God; he let me watch his birth into eternity. Before he left, Dad had brought me as close to Heaven's Gate as possible. What an enormous gift from him and God to me.

I closed his eyes. "Opa, opa . . ." I whispered.

Seconds after my father's last breath, I ran into the hall to get the nurse. She put the stethoscope on Dad's chest. She pronounced him dead at 10:10 a.m. Then, the childhood memory returned of me waking up every morning to my father's alarm clock, set to a local New York radio station's news report called 10:10 W.I.N.S. I knew it was a message: WINS! We won! We overcame the struggle.

Ms. Clara, the 101-year-old lady from across the hall, came in with her walker. I told her what happened. She burst out crying. "He was my friend. I'll miss him," she said. "I'll be right back," she told me, abruptly leaving the room.

She returned with a silver pin. She insisted on giving it to me and wanted me to wear it. "It's important for you to have this," she said. So, I reluctantly agreed and pinned it on my jacket.

The funeral home director came and picked up my father's body. I drove to the funeral home and sat with him as he wrote up the death certificate. He filled in the time of death. "Seems like my mother died around this time, a few months ago," I told him. He went to his files and pulled out her death certificate. Incredibly enough, the time of her death was 10:10 a.m.

"I've been in this business for thirty years, and I've never had a married couple pronounced dead at the exact same moment three months apart," he said.

"10:10 WINS!" I exclaimed, standing up from my chair. My parents were leaving a message. We all won. Love prevailed in the end!

At home that evening, I thought back over the day. It occurred to me that there must be some significance to Ms. Clara, the 101-year-old from across the hall, giving me that pin immediately after my father's death. I took it off and stared at it. It was a lovely hummingbird. I searched the internet for the spiritual significance of the hummingbird.

In some cultures, the hummingbird symbolizes *resurrection*: When the temperature drops, hummingbirds become lifeless, appearing to die. But when the weather warms up, they come back to life again. The swift movement of the hummingbird can often be compared to the 'here one moment, gone the next' appearance of passing on through death. It is the only bird that can fly backward, so it is closely linked with accomplishing the impossible.

The hummingbird symbolized the miracle of my healed relationship with my father, and then his death. Ms. Clara could not have picked a more fitting gift for me on my father's death. It was a treasure from my lifelong trial and our resurrection.

PART TWO

Genetic Identity

21

Date with Destiny

Between my time spent with Ruth's counseling and dealing with my father, a lot of healing transpired regarding men, relationships, and father issues. Staying clear of romantic entanglements enabled me to focus on my growth and recovery rather than getting distracted by someone else's needs, wants, hang-ups, past baggage, addictions, sexual infidelities, anger issues, and selfish desires.

When I met with Ruth during this period, I told her I felt great joy watching other women heal, grow, and change in recovery. I could see that Ruth was pleased.

"Do you know what today is?" Ruth asked.

"Your birthday?" I guessed, seeing a small birthday cake on the dining room table.

"No, it's yours!" she said, pointing to the cake with a single candle.

"My birthday is not until July."

"I'm not referring to your *belly button* birthday. We're celebrating your commitment to staying away from men and finding God and yourself."

Ruth lit the lone candle on top of my cake. "This honors no breakups, chaos, or abuse! I wish you many more!" So, I made a wish and blew out the candle.

"Thank you, Ruth," I said, holding back tears of gratitude.

"I didn't do it; you and God did," she said, humbly declining to acknowledge her shepherding my recovery.

"With your guidance, I've learned the difference between love and lust and what love was and was not. You helped me get off the turnstile of unhealthy relationships and see that just like substance addictions, it has cycles of withdrawals and relapses."

Ruth had helped me stop seeking short-term gratifications with their downturns and, instead, to wait on God's timing for a long-term stable relationship. I learned that when I hung onto an abusive man in hopes of changing him, it was an unconscious attempt to fulfill a childhood need for the acceptance and love I had never received from my father. The abusive men in my life were not rejecting me personally; they were sick people, too, who had nothing to give back.

Through Ruth and my recovery, I became part of a spiritual support group that I adopted as a spiritual family. I learned to have fun, play, be spontaneous, and embrace and heal my inner child while staying sober.

I'd started meditating and practicing more self-control. I learned to get out of my way and spread the message of hope by volunteering at local healthcare organizations, mentoring other women, and doing simple random acts of kindness. As I reached out to others and did the next right thing, my confidence grew, and my low self-esteem diminished. At the time, it was part of the process of learning to detach from my father's battering and stay focused on my new truths about myself.

Ruth had taught me about spiritual maintenance or how to be accountable for my actions daily, as I prayed, read scripture, confessed, forgave, made amends, and meditated. Whether it was my drinking and attraction to unhealthy relationships, whatever God miraculously changed in my life happened only when I completely let go of my self-will. Even when I was saying, "I let go," but was secretly still holding on, God knew the truth, and nothing changed. I had to walk a path through loss and loneliness and grieve the death of my old self and its personal desires. I had to surrender and let God take charge of my life.

"Well, I'm finally okay with being alone for the rest of my life. How can you top that for the miracle of transformation?" I had no more expectations or delusional dreams of being whisked away in a fairytale romance.

"Maybe God doesn't want you to spend the rest of your life alone. Did you ever think He may have picked out someone for you and been preparing you for them?" Ruth asked. "Maybe, for you, having a healthy relationship would even top the miracle of being happy alone!"

"It's hard to imagine since I've never been in a good, healthy relationship," I laughed.

"I know you've turned your day-to-day *life* over to God. But have you also completely turned your *love life* over to Him? Have you allowed God to choose your partner if that's His will for you?"

"No, I haven't," I acknowledged. Ruth's question made me nervous; I had finally made peace with being alone and was actually enjoying it.

"Well, if you are to have a partner, why not let God choose that person? Write a letter to God, telling Him the kind of husband you would have liked to have."

I agreed to do this appeal.

"Visualize what a good mate would mean to you. Set a high standard; imagine having one with the best qualities, not the least.

This can be your faith walk because it won't be based on your past experiences with relationships."

Ruth and I sat in silence for a moment. I didn't know what to say; I felt a little stuck.

"I see you with a God-loving man who is successful, stable, kind, and wise. Now build on that," Ruth said.

Soon after, I wrote a letter to God detailing an imaginary mate spiritually, mentally, physically, and emotionally. I described how I wanted to be treated, how we would spend our time together, and aspects of his career profession that included community involvement. At the end of the letter, I added a sign to know that God sent this person, if and when he showed up.

The following week, I went to see Ruth. When she greeted me at her door, I was hit with the aroma of fresh vanilla. "Let me guess! You're making a vanilla wedding cake?"

"Yes, I am."

Ruth asked me about my letter to God about an imaginary mate. So, I read it to her. She instructed me to put it in a lock box when I got home and forget about it.

"Being faithful and having integrity during tough times reaps great rewards when we're ready. One of my favorite biblical stories is in the *Book of Ruth* about Ruth and Boaz.

"Naomi was an older married woman who had two married sons. Her daughters-in-law were Orpah and Ruth. Shortly after Naomi's husband died, her two sons died as well, so within a short period, Naomi and her daughters-in-law all became widows. Naomi turned bitter and lost touch with the virtue of her namesake, which means *beautiful*," Ruth said, retelling the story in her own words.

"Naomi, feeling she had nothing to offer these two young women, encouraged them to return to their original families. One of them, Orpah, agreed and left. The other daughter-in-law, Ruth, remained faithful to Naomi in her time of grief. She made a commitment to stay and look after Naomi, even in a foreign land and in a seemingly hopeless situation. She wouldn't let present troubles determine her future."

Some aspects of this story struck a familiar chord. I, too, had chosen to care for a family member and put aside personal plans for my own life because it seemed the right thing to do. "So, what happened to Ruth?" I asked, eager to see how her story ended.

"Ruth's vow to Naomi was a beautiful commitment of selfless love. Moving to Bethlehem to care for her mother-in-law meant renunciation of her own heritage. But Naomi and Ruth's relationship was centered on God's will for them. They were committed to each other and trusted God to guide and care for them. Eventually, they were led back to Israel. Naomi arranged for Ruth to work in the wheat fields of her relative, Boaz, a wealthy, kind, and gentle man.

"Boaz would leave the edges of the crop for the poor. Many poor women flirted with the reapers and then tried to steal grain, but Ruth did neither. She soon gained a reputation for such honesty and integrity that Boaz became quite taken with her.

"Ruth liked him as well, and the first night Ruth became involved with Boaz, he asked God to bless Ruth. In time, he became her husband and richly blessed Ruth."

"So, everything worked out well for Ruth in the end."

"God used Ruth's sacrifice and commitment to Naomi and her diligence in doing what was right to lead her to a new life filled with promise that only He could have orchestrated. Ruth's son with Boaz became the grandfather of King David. Ruth's simple acts of faith led to the blessing of millions upon millions of people."

When Ruth finished the story, I was filled with hope and excitement. When my parents became ill, I committed to looking after them in obedience to what I believed God wanted of me, despite an estranged relationship with my father. At first I couldn't see how my decision would benefit me, but I eventually put my trust in God. "I loved how things had ended for Ruth," I said.

"God honors faithfulness. He allows difficulties as opportunities to develop character. Ruth's faithfulness yielded an abundance of God's blessings through which Naomi's initial bitterness was redeemed. God's unseen hand met the desperate needs of both women."

"More than that, I feel some special blessing of God is near for me," I confided.

"If one day God sends you a Boaz, you will recognize him from the description you've already written in your letter to Him. It's quite a list!" she added, laughing.

I thought a moment about some of the highlights of my description, reminding myself that I wanted a man who would treat me as an equal partner, support my endeavors, and not feel threatened by my achievements; someone who would hear my needs and respond to them with care because he, too, knew of God's love. He'd enjoy giving, loving, and blessing me and would recognize me as a special gift, knowing that God had brought us together. My Boaz would honor his commitment to me through all kinds of challenges and be my best friend. He'd protect me, romance me, and ultimately be willing to lay down his life for me.

"I agree! It's a tall order." I had to laugh out loud.

"I'm glad you've developed high standards," Ruth said. She walked me to her door and gave me a hug. She held onto me a moment longer and whispered in my ear, "I, too, think something special is around the corner for you!"

So, when I got home, I folded the letter and put it in the little compartment of my jewelry box. *What could come from a locked-up letter?*

A few days after the lockbox letter exercise, a new friend in recovery invited me to spend time on a boat. She was a few years younger than I and was working as the first mate of the captain on the Zapala, an old 1920s riverboat owned by a local resort. Since the boat was mostly made of beautiful old teakwood, it constantly needed waxing, and much of her free time was spent cleaning it.

The first time my friend invited me down to the boat, she just wanted me to keep her company as she worked, which I did. It was a welcome change from the daily stress of caring for my parents. Just sitting on the boat, feeling the wind blow over us, and hearing the lapping of the waves against its sides was very relaxing and calming.

She began calling me daily, inviting me back to the boat. The next time I went, she insisted on showing me how to work on such a vessel and take care of it. She taught me to tie knots, use lines in docking the ship, throw out fenders to protect its sides from banging against the dock, and how to clean the deck. I thought it was odd since I knew nothing about boating and wasn't asking to learn such things. But I believed God sent people into my life for a reason, even if I didn't understand what that was, so I learned to do these tasks.

"Now you're ready to be a first mate soon!" I nodded, even though her comment made no sense to me.

The next day, I got an unexpected call from the job I'd had after I left Clinique and worked until my mother's stroke. It was a job offer for a temporary 8-5 desk job in the County Commission office. It paid a little more than I was making at the department store with excellent benefits, but it involved doing monotonous tasks, like endlessly copying files and handling dry reading materials related to code enforcement and county ordinance books. It was work that endlessly frustrated me; I felt ill-suited and mismatched for it. I was creative, free-spirited, with a marketing and sales background. I had never understood why God had placed me there, besides learning much about local and county governments. As a result, I became proficient at crossing t's and dotting i's, as well as record keeping and copying.

I wondered, *Would I ever be done with this job?* However, I accepted without a second thought based on that strong, now-familiar God-prompting feeling. So, the following Monday, I reported to the County Commission office to fill in temporarily. The County Clerk was the same woman I had worked with in the past. She had a strong spiritual life and a deep connection with God.

One day, I was assigned to choose the menu for the Drug and Alcohol luncheon hosted by the new commissioner everyone called "Cap." I was impressed that this commissioner was addressing humanitarian issues in addition to everyday responsibilities like water and sewer, repaving and repairing old roads, easements, abandonments, and liquor licenses.

As I began working on a menu, Cap walked in the door. I felt a strange familiarity with him, though I'd never seen or met him.

Cap introduced himself and asked, "Have we met?"

I thought, *Must have been in some other lifetime!* I smiled, feeling self-conscious as our eyes remained locked.

"I don't think so, but it's nice to meet you," I said, and then there was an awkward silence. I went over to the copy machine and pretended to make a copy of something. Cap eventually left.

"What was that between you and Cap?" asked a friend who was working there.

"What do you mean?" I asked while aware of the unusual sense of recognition I had with him.

"There was energy between the two of you! I felt it."

I was surprised she had picked up on our familiarity.

"I've never seen him act like that," she said. "Cap's normally self-confident, but he was fumbling for words!"

Something was up. I returned to my desk and reviewed the menu and the agenda for the Drug and Alcohol luncheon he was orchestrating. I knew people in our recovery community who I thought could contribute significantly to the discussion and should be invited to the luncheon. I decided to call Cap about my idea.

Moments later, my friend came by and said, "The Commissioner is on line two, and he wants to talk about the luncheon." Realizing I was almost too nervous to answer the call, she stepped over to the phone, pressed the right extension, and handed me the receiver.

"I'm glad you called," I said, taking a deep breath. "I have a few questions about the luncheon meeting." I was amazed I had said that much.

"Why don't we discuss it over lunch today?" he asked.

Two hours later, I walked into his office at the marina. I felt weak at the knees. We went to a little restaurant overlooking the water and talked for a while about the luncheon meeting. He liked my idea of inviting people from the recovery community and insisted that I attend as well.

As we ate and moved off that topic, Cap shared that he had been divorced. Since then, he'd been casually dating other women, but only socially. Cap added that he really didn't have a lot of time for dating because of his business, children, and responsibilities as county commissioner. He ended by saying that he followed his own calling, believed in destiny, and that his favorite book was the Bible.

He stopped and apologized for talking so much, but I was grateful to hear him out since I still felt at a loss for words, which was unusual for me. Over the course of our lunch, I learned that he owned a boat, bus, and trolley-tourist transportation business, and was a certified Coast Guard captain. Cap loved his work and enjoyed entertaining the tourists on land and at sea.

"I almost feel like we're old friends and need to catch up on our lives," Cap said. "Could we keep in touch?"

Everything Cap said, and even how he looked, reminded me of the imaginary person I had created on paper just two weeks earlier. I felt like I was in the *Twilight Zone*, and Cap Fendig was a figment of my imagination. I was almost speechless.

I accepted his invitation to stay in touch, and we exchanged phone numbers. We both agreed that, at the very least, we were kindred spirits. That night, when I got home, I had a message on my answering machine from him.

"Hi. This is Cap. I really enjoyed lunch today. Thank you!"

The next day was Friday, my last day of temp work in that office. My final task was to drop off an agenda book at Cap's office on my way home. Just before I left my office, Cap called to see if I was coming. When I arrived at his office with the book, he invited me to join him for dinner and meet his parents. This connection was moving rather fast. It seemed like God was responding quickly to answer my husband's letter.

We went to the same restaurant where we'd had lunch earlier in the week, and I found his parents to be charming and easy to be with. They had only been married to each other for almost fifty years. They'd raised four boys. All of Cap's brothers were married, had graduated from college, and each had three children. Throughout our meal, I noticed that Cap's dad, Neal, was very attentive to his wife, regularly showing her little signs of affection. Occasionally, I glanced at Cap and could feel warmth in my heart and an admiration for the kind of man he seemed to be. It was different from the uncontrollable, lustful physical attractions of the old days.

When we finished eating, Cap walked me to my car. I told him I was going to meet a friend at a coffee shop, which, it turned out, was only two blocks from where he lived. He invited me to stop by his house afterward. I was intrigued and nervous. I agreed to come over.

Two hours later, after meeting with a woman I was mentoring, I stopped by Cap's house, an older, quaint little beach cottage—a fire burned in the fireplace. Cap and I sat on the couch and talked for a while before lapsing into a comfortable silence. Then, Cap reached over and took my hand. Everything he had said and done since I met him in the office was straight out of my letter to God.

"This feels so different to me," he said, chuckling.

I was thinking the same thing.

When I was ready to leave, he walked me to my car to say goodnight. It had been a long time since I had even thought about being with anyone. I had remained committed and faithful to my marriage to God. But with this man, everything seemed so special and ordained that it was almost unbelievable.

On Monday, I attended the Drug and Alcohol luncheon. I greeted everybody at the door and handed out the information that Cap wanted to be distributed. There were a lot of business people and community leaders there; some I knew, some I didn't. I admired Cap's efforts to pull together different aspects of the recovery community to discuss, network, and better address the needs of the addicted, the homeless, and victims of domestic violence in the county. It was an amazing privilege to see the kind of man I had described to Ruth, and that, it seemed, God was bringing into my life. I thought, *Only time will tell if this is real.*

22

Staying True

Ruth taught me that God goes ahead of us and works on our behalf before we even know what we need. She referred to it as *Prevenient Grace*. I could see how God had been preparing me in ways I hadn't even suspected for meeting Cap. I mean, He placed me in the commissioner's office, apparently knowing our suitability before either of us realized it. Then, I thought of all the times my recovery friend had invited me onto the riverboat and had insisted on familiarizing me with marine duties only a few weeks earlier. Now I wished I'd paid more attention to my friend when she tried to show me the rope knots!

The weather was perfect on the morning of our first official date. I arrived at the dock a few minutes early and looked around, wondering what kind of boat we would be traveling on. Then I saw Cap waving me down the dock to where he stood before a huge luxury yacht. Amazed, I followed him on board. The boat had four levels with two baths, three bedrooms, a living room, a dining room, and a large deck. At the bow was a walk plank with metal rails, just like in the movie *Titanic*.

Cap introduced me to the owner, who had hired him to transport the yacht to a Jacksonville marina, and to his good friend, Captain John, who would serve as first mate on the cruise down. After we got underway, I stepped to the bow and walked out on the *Titanic*-looking plank. I held the guard rails and felt the rushing wind wash over me as the boat plowed through the water. Looking straight ahead at the open expanse of ocean, I forgot about the boat and the crew and imagined I was flying over the water. It was invigorating. I felt nature wash over me and cleanse my spirit of years of stress with its surges of wind.

Captivated by this experience, I couldn't bring myself to leave. After an hour and a half, Cap came out and asked if he could get me anything. I thanked him but said no, then asked if it was okay if I stayed out there. I told him I'd never had such a wonderful feeling and apologized for being so self-indulgent. He assured me it was okay to keep enjoying myself there, and he went back up to the helm to drive the boat.

I learned later that Cap told Captain John, while pointing to me, "If you had a bunch of women on a boat, you'd want to pay attention to the one who goes out to the bow. That's the woman with passion. That's the one you might want to marry."

When we neared Jacksonville after four hours, I was still standing at the bow. I'd never moved. Captain John turned to Cap and said, "Looks like you've found the right one; she's got passion and staying power!"

After the boat ride, we rented a car, drove back to Cap's house, and made dinner. Cap told me he was impressed that I'd followed my heart's desire by staying on the bow the entire trip.

At the end of what was a perfect evening, Cap walked me to my car and kissed me.

The following night, he called after his commission meeting. I told him our cruise was the best date I had ever been on. He said he felt that way, too. We talked a bit longer, and then he said he would be in Savannah for the St. Patrick's Day weekend, running his tour boats.

He called me every day. When he returned, we spent the afternoon walking on the beach and talking. He said he was glad I was taking the time to get to know him better. It was refreshing to have somebody who appreciated my process.

On our second official date, he took me out on a smaller boat he owned. We docked at a waterfront restaurant and had a nice romantic dinner. He knew lots of people in the restaurant and exchanged many cordial greetings and pleasantries. I was proud to be with him. I liked how he carried himself, which was a new feeling for me.

When we returned to the boat to leave, Cap gave me a twenty-dollar bill. "Could you run back and get us cups of coffee with some Kahlua in it?" he asked.

At the word *Kahlua*, an alarm bell went off for me, bringing back memories of getting drunk on Kahlua. Right there on the dock, and for the first time in years, I had a powerful urge to drink again. Thoughts raced through my mind, like, *Wouldn't it be fun to drink again? Could I get away with it now? Maybe I could finally control my drinking!*

I froze. I didn't know what to say. During our brief time together, the subject of alcohol had not come up. I wondered what Cap would think of me if I told him I was a recovered alcoholic. I was no longer ashamed of that, but I knew that, for some people, it still carried a stigma. Would my alcoholism threaten my new relationship, or would my new relationship threaten my sobriety?

I knew that to maintain my sobriety I needed to keep my recovery as my primary goal, which meant always doing what was right for me. I had to be honest with Cap. I would not buy the Kahlua for the coffee and would tell him I was a recovering alcoholic and that, for my well-being, I could not date someone who drank. I liked Cap, but I knew who to put first this time. In the past, I would not have spoken up. I would have lost myself again and sealed the fate of another relationship gone wrong. Could I have a relationship and remain true to myself? This was the test.

So, I purchased plain coffee and went back to the boat.

"I'm a recovered alcoholic," I said as I handed him the coffee.

He gave me a nod in response to my unexpected confession.

"And if you want to continue dating me, then I have to ask you not to drink alcohol. I understand if you don't want to give up social drinking, but if that's your choice, we can still be friends." I tried to appear calm as I spoke, but my heart was racing.

Cap didn't respond at first. He started the boat, and we rode in silence for a little while. I was expecting the worst.

After a few more long minutes, he turned to me and said, "Well, then, I won't drink. I'll make a pledge to you and God not to drink even when you're not with me."

I let out a sigh of relief and smiled at him. He put his arm around me, and we drove the boat back home.

I could hear Ruth's words in my mind: *What you allow, you encourage! We set the future stage by what we accept in the present.*

That evening, we relaxed in front of the fire. When Cap walked me to my car, we kissed. It was like magic.

Cap and I saw each other regularly each week. We met for lunch, went boating, and attended commission functions together. Cap was always very attentive to me.

The first major holiday we spent together was Easter. He invited me to his parent's house to meet the rest of his family; besides his parents, there were three brothers and their wives, and nine nieces and nephews.

I also noticed no alcohol was being served. Everyone seemed to feel relaxed and at ease around one another without drinking. I was not used to this kind of family setting. It seemed as surreal as that first lunch I had had with Cap. Maybe there was a correlation between the changes happening within me and finding a connection with a healthy family like this one.

Everyone contributed dishes in the potluck style to create an extravagant feast from old family recipes or previously acknowledged favorites. Just before we ate, Cap's father, Neal, gathered us into a circle, and everyone held hands. He said a beautiful blessing over the food, this day of celebration, and the family. As he concluded, I noticed he wiped a tear from his eye as Neal thanked God for being blessed with such a family. Then, the sound of laughter and talking filled the room again as everyone got in line to fill their plates. The buffet spread consisted of honey-baked ham, homemade macaroni and cheese, Waldorf salad, bacon and baked beans, asparagus and cheese casserole, creamed corn, deviled eggs, and homemade biscuits.

After an incredible meal, a few of the older nieces and nephews went outside to hide the Easter eggs. Soon, all the younger children were given baskets for the egg hunt. The kids scampered about looking for eggs. If one of them lagged behind, the others helped them make more finds. When the hunt was over, all the children sat together and inventoried the treasures inside the plastic eggs.

Meanwhile, the adults gathered around the dining table to enjoy their coffee and a variety of homemade desserts, including cakes, pies, and cookies. Everyone caught each other up on the news in their lives. I watched them laugh and reminisce as they shared their stories. Throughout the afternoon, each of them took a few minutes to get to know me. They all said they were happy that Cap had found someone special.

I watched as the three youngest little girls jumped onto Cap's lap and asked him for a ride on his back. He got on the floor, and all of them climbed onto his back. At three and four years old, they reminded me of little lion cubs as they giggled and wrestled to stay on his back as he crawled about. It was adorable. The children obviously loved him, and he loved being Uncle Cap in return.

Then, I noticed one of the teenage girls sitting next to her dad, Cap's brother. She leaned her head on his shoulder as she cuddled beside him. He lovingly put his arm around her and smiled. I instantly hurt for all the love and family fellowship I never knew growing up, for the sweet and innocent affection I'd witnessed between a father and his daughter that I had missed out on, for the experience I would never have snuggling up next to my dad and laying my head on his shoulder, for never having felt that deep sense of connection with a father.

Several times, I had to push down a lump in my throat. I attempted to hide my self-consciousness and ignore thoughts in my head, like, *if they really knew who I was, they'd know I didn't belong here.* All the doubts I used to feel as a kid came flooding back. All the progress I thought I had made seemed to disappear.

When it was time to leave, there were warm goodbyes and lots of hugs. Cap walked me to my car and, in the few moments I had alone with him, I said, "I've never seen such a big family seem to like each other and get along so well. Is your family for real?"

Cap assured me they were. "My grandmother had a rule that lives on to this day: If you have anything bad to say about anyone in the family, then you need to bring it right to that person directly," he explained. "She never allowed any of us to say negative things about each other behind our backs."

I was impressed with the principles they lived by.

I thanked Cap and said good night. As soon as I drove away, the tears came. By the time I returned home, I still could not stop crying.

At the end of this day, I mourned for being unable to reminisce about good times gone by and for not having a sweet sense of emotional history with my family. I cried for the death of a dream and all the experiences I had so desperately wanted as a little girl and never got. I cried hard that evening over the stark reality of the love I had never had in my life.

23

A New Life

Cap and I had been dating for eight months. We spent a lot of time getting to know each other and developing a solid friendship. I insisted on taking it slow because getting sexually and emotionally invested in someone too soon had clouded my perception and made it difficult to see the reality of that person. It seemed God had brought us together, and Cap felt right for me.

Then 911 happened. Cap and I, along with the rest of the country, watched on television as the Twin Towers fell and thousands of innocent people of all ages died at the hands of terrorists. Life had drastically changed that morning for millions of people. Thousands of people had gone to work in the Twin Towers that day, placing great importance on their work—sending a fax, returning a phone call, finishing a financial report—only to find that none of that was important as they lost their lives in the next hour. Seconds before the collapse of the buildings and their imminent deaths, the one thing on most of their minds was letting loved ones know how much they loved them.

That attack and the deaths of those innocent people affected Cap and me profoundly. A month after 911, he took me to a little Italian restaurant for dinner. We ordered a pizza with everything on it.

"Will you marry me?" Cap proposed to me right then and there.

THE FATHER NOBODY KNOWS

I looked down at the pizza, completely caught off guard. I didn't expect this proposal so soon and didn't say anything. I froze. Even though it was what I thought I wanted, I couldn't say yes immediately. The thought of adding any more failed relationships to my sordid record or getting hurt again terrified me.

Cap and I continued to talk about it. I felt stuck. "You don't have to be afraid of me doing something to hurt you. I wouldn't because I'm afraid of your Father," he said.

"Afraid of my *Father*?" I asked, really confused. My father had been one of the worst culprits for abusing me emotionally and mentally, so I couldn't understand Cap's reasoning. "How was that supposed to comfort me?" I asked, feeling perplexed.

"Not your earthly father, your Heavenly Father, because I know how much He loves you. I know that, since your spiritual realignment, He wouldn't stand for anyone hurting His daughter." When I heard Cap's explanation, weeks of fear instantly disappeared.

He said, "Since 911, I can't stop thinking about how important it is to appreciate the love in your life. I think we need to celebrate our lives and get married. I don't want to pass on this opportunity to be together completely."

"That's beautiful, Cap. I just need to think about this," I answered gently.

"I thought this was what you wanted," Cap said, looking puzzled.

"I did, too. I'm sorry, but I really need some time." I couldn't believe my response, either. In my old life, I impulsively jumped into marriages with the wrong people without any thought at all. Now, I was doing everything right *with* Mr. Right, and I couldn't say yes because I was scared to death! I was so afraid of getting hurt again.

A NEW LIFE

One day, I decided to write a list of our similarities and differences. Our similarities list was short but essential. We both loved God and believed in family, commitment, and hard work.

The differences list caught my attention. It was long. We were opposites in our personalities, backgrounds, and preferences.

Cap grew up with three younger brothers and a family that was active in community functions, family gatherings, dinners, and barbecues. This included holiday celebrations: Easter egg hunts, Fourth of July fireworks, Thanksgiving Day feasts, and Christmas dinners, which were times to enjoy his aunts, uncles, cousins, siblings, parents, and grandparents in a small-knit island community with no crime.

I grew up in a home with an alcoholic mom and a raging dad, filled with dark family secrets, blacked-out windows, fighting, chaos, daily abuse, and New York City crime, where I learned to be streetwise.

Cap's family's legacy includes many contributions to society and the community in which they lived. They started churches, libraries, and many businesses. Some became politicians, lawyers, doctors, realtors, harbor pilots, entrepreneurs, writers, and artists.

My family's legacy was one of ill-fated journeys, choices, outcomes, and conditions, including poverty, divorce, affairs, swindling, embezzlement, and alcoholism.

Cap's family helped settle St. Simon's Island, and he has lived on the island his whole life.

My parents moved far from their birthplaces, settling in New York City. I lived all over the country and knew very little about my relatives besides my parents.

Cap never did drugs or smoked cigarettes. I looked for relief and escape through drugs and alcohol.

Cap likes to be spontaneous and loves surprises. I like structure, routine, and predictability.

Cap scatters piles of papers on his workspace and likes a *disorganized approach to organization*. I put everything in its proper place and love my space to be simple and clutter-free.

Cap is a multitasker. I am a single-focused person.

Cap likes busyness, people, and activities around him. I love solitude, peace, and simplicity.

Cap is a night person. You guessed it: I am a morning person.

It was apparent: God had sent me a man who was as different from me as night from day. Despite our opposite childhoods and lifestyles, we still shared the most crucial thing in common: our love for God and each other. We both put God in the center of our lives with great passion and cared deeply for each other.

I knew all too well that people are fallible. But when I entrust the people in my life to God, that act not only relieves my fears but also takes the pressure off others to maintain my serenity.

So, I accepted Cap's proposal with joy and peace in my heart.

I agreed with Cap's idea about having a surprise wedding on Thanksgiving Day at the family gathering. We made our marriage plans without telling anyone. We bought secret wedding attire consisting of a white baseball hat with a white bridal veil attached for me and a black baseball hat with the word "*Groom*" embroidered on it for Cap. We decided that when the time was right after dinner, we'd pull out our hats to mark the change of venue for the gathering.

Cap and I had agreed not to tell any family members beforehand. We got our rings and a bouquet of flowers. We had specially ordered wedding favors: twenty-five key rings engraved with the

American flag and our wedding date, sparkling apple cider, and plastic champagne glasses for the toast.

Our wedding plan was the most stress-free way to get married. If anything went wrong, there was no time to get upset or disappointed about it. Cap and I were the only ones who could have expectations since no one knew about the wedding. We decided to keep those expectations to a minimum so that we could focus on the joy of the event.

The morning of Thanksgiving Day, we loaded the trunk of my car with the instant-wedding paraphernalia and went to Cap's parents' house. No one had a clue. After everyone finished the first round of the Thanksgiving feast, there was a knock at the door. It was the pastor. As it turned out, he was an old family friend, so no one thought anything of his stopping in to say hello.

After a few minutes of general conversation, Cap stood up and asked for everyone's attention. When all eyes were on him, he announced that we were getting married. Everyone clapped with genuine joy. They thought we were announcing our engagement. Grinning, Cap explained that the pastor was actually here to perform the ceremony and that we were having a surprise wedding, right here and now, and everyone at this Thanksgiving feast would become the wedding party.

It took everybody by surprise and caused a great stir of excitement. Everything was perfect, including having the pastor perform the ceremony and give his special blessing. It was the most meaningful, inexpensive, and fun wedding we could have imagined.

That night, we drove to Cap's marina, where we went aboard his boat, named the *Catfen,* docked on Jekyll Island. It was incredibly romantic and meaningful. We were the best of friends who had made a lifetime commitment in front of God, family, friends, and the community to love one another through both good and hard times, until death would part us.

To celebrate our first day as husband and wife, we packed a picnic lunch the next morning and set out to sea. We spent the day fishing, sunbathing, and following dolphins as they trailed a shrimp boat that had just finished dragging its nets. That evening, we dressed up and ate dinner at *Latitude 31*, a favorite restaurant overlooking the water. After dinner, we strolled around the historic district of Jekyll Island, which was all lit up for Christmas.

Life felt surreal. Everything had worked out—no dramas and mishaps. There was a cosmic order to things as they fell into place. I felt safe by Cap's side. I was happy and elated. It was one of the most beautiful days of my life. Human logic defied the probability that I should be in this situation, having this experience with Cap. It was a testament to the miracle-working power of God.

Two days later, a small article about our wedding was published in the local newspaper. That my marrying someone was newsworthy in a positive light was another miracle!

The first few months of our marriage were like an extended honeymoon. Everything continued to fall into place. I was overcome by all the thoughtful and romantic surprises Cap had in store for me. I had never given much thought to occasions like my birthday, so I didn't expect anything when mine came around. When I woke up that morning, Cap gave me a beautiful card and made me breakfast. I was touched and thought that would be the end of it. But my phone started ringing off the hook with acquaintances, friends, and my new family all calling me to wish me a happy birthday. I couldn't understand how so many people could possibly have known about it.

A NEW LIFE

Then, Cap insisted I go for a ride with him, and we drove to the end of the causeway, where his family had a large electronic billboard. I looked up and saw the sign alight with big letters:

HAPPY BIRTHDAY, CATHERINE. WE LOVE YOU!

I was embarrassed and deeply moved at the same time. Cap handed me a newspaper. He said to open it to page two. I did, and again, to my surprise, on the bottom third of the page, just on the other side of the front page, were displayed two pictures of us, one at the Governor's Ball, the other of us on our honeymoon. Under the photos, it said:

> 'Happy Birthday, Catherine.' Catherine is my love and partner. She always encourages the best out of me as a commissioner and an individual. She makes the sacrifice in seeing her husband serve. Today is her birthday, and I hope her friends will call her and wish her a good day. Catherine, thank you for being selfless to the community. I love you and happy birthday, Your Cap.

Now I understood how people knew it was my birthday and why they called. You couldn't have missed it if you tried! Cap had literally put out a news bulletin to the whole community.

Later that evening, he gave me a surprise birthday party on the boat at the marina to which he had secretly invited my close friends. It touched my heart. I could recall many times in my youth spending my birthdays alone and feeling that no one cared about it. When it came to my birthday, I had to shut down emotionally rather than cope with the pain of the past. But Cap had created a wonderful new birthday memory that fulfilled my childhood longing to feel special on the day I was born.

Cap never hesitated to honor and acknowledge me publicly. When a local magazine wrote an article on Cap, he insisted that I be photographed with him. The caption under the photo reads:

> *Glynn County Commissioner Cap Fendig considers his wife, Catherine, to be his reward for serving the citizens of the community. They met one day when Catherine Fendig was working as a temporary staffer in the County office.*

When I saw the article, the photograph, and the caption, I thought that perhaps my Heavenly Husband was using my earthly husband to restore honor in my life. Suddenly 1 Samuel 2:30 popped into my mind:

> *"... the LORD says: 'Far be it from Me; for those who honor Me I will honor...'";* followed by Isaiah 61:7: *"... Instead of your shame you shall have double honor..."*

That was just the beginning of many new memories and feelings Cap would help create for me over time. Almost daily, I would come home and find messages from him written on the chalkboard in the kitchen, messages like:

> Your husband loves you!
> I am so proud of you!
> You are fantastic!
> Thank you for the way you love me!
> You are a great wife!

A NEW LIFE

I will love you always

—Cap!

Over the next few years, life remained busy. Each Christmas, Cap and I hosted the family-Christmas buffet in our little beach cottage. One year, in the middle of our gathering, I stepped out on our front porch to close the screen door. I turned around and looked through the window at the festivities inside our cottage. There were soft, glowing lights from the Christmas tree, decorations spread throughout the room, and the fireplace burning bright. Adults were scurrying around, getting plates of food and sitting in chairs lined up around the living room, while the children found places to sit. It looked warm, cozy, and informal. Christmas music was playing softly in the background. It looked like a hallmark scene of the perfect family Christmas, straight out of a Charles Dickens holiday story.

I had decided to pack up and put away my past. It was no longer relevant to who I was. I had felt it, made peace with it, and now wanted it to disappear into a storage box. People didn't need to know about it, and I could be someone different. I had a new name, identity, role, and environment. I lived two different lives, the one I had before I married Cap and the one I have now. Maybe I was finally living a normal-looking life.

24

The DNA Test

In the coming years, I came to know my husband's family, which was huge: grandparents, parents, brothers, sisters, great-aunts, great-uncles, aunts, uncles, cousins, second cousins, and third cousins. There were a few hundred family members in the local area alone.

This got me thinking that I must have relatives I don't even know about. My father was Greek and a first-generation immigrant. He came from a long lineage of Greeks from a small mountain village in Greece. I was told his family name was well-known in the village where his forefathers lived. On my mother's side, I didn't know anything about her father (my grandfather) and his family. There also had to be some distant relatives on my mother's side. Just because my parents had no contact with their extended family didn't mean they didn't exist. I started to plan a trip to Greece to search for my relatives. Cap liked the idea of a trip abroad, whether we found relatives or not.

I also wondered why I had such a passion for spirituality and God. I grew up in an atheist home, yet I sensed God existed. I had read how Christian family members in the past prayed for future generations to come to serve and know God. Maybe an ancestor prayed for our descendants' spirituality. Perhaps it was a distant relative who would never know me, or would I know them, but I was the recipient of their prayers for future generations yet to be born.

THE FATHER NOBODY KNOWS

It had been a few years since my mother and father passed. I still had questions. Did I have any living relatives I didn't know about? Who were my ancestors beyond my grandparents?

I had always believed in a Higher Power, one I call God. I had no exposure to religion at an early age that would influence me to acknowledge the existence of God. Throughout my adult life, I have been on a spiritual quest, always consumed with seeking to understand spiritual matters above all other interests. From a young age, I sensed God, and through my pursuits, I learned that He has saved and healed me. So, who in my ancestry line prayed for my redemption before I was born? Who came before me and prayed for their future, unknown generations to know God? There had to be someone.

Then, an online ad for a free two-week trial from a genealogy search site caught my attention. I used the service for two weeks to see if I could discover some of my ancestors.

I turned my attention to my mother's side. I knew that my mother's mother was a descendant of Daniel Boone's sister, Sarah Boone, which is why my mother is certified as a Daughter of the American Revolution (DAR). But I did not know anything about my grandfather's ancestors. His name was Clyde S., a farmer in Michigan. He married my grandmother from the Deep South as a mail-order bride. So, I enrolled in the free trial and started researching my grandfather's family line.

I typed in his name and found his birth date, marriage certificate to my grandmother, and papers from his military service in World War 1. He lived a whole lifetime, and I only knew his name and when he died. I did find the location of the farm he had owned. I Googled it, but it was no longer a farm. I found the names of my grandfather Clyde's parents and his three siblings.

THE DNA TEST

This meant that if Clyde's siblings had children, their offspring would be my second cousins. So, I might have some relatives. I printed out the search record.

Then I clicked on Clyde's father's box, and his parents' names showed up in two boxes connected to each of their siblings with lines appropriately connecting them. I printed this out. My great-grandfather's name was William S., born in New York in 1835. Then I found his father, Isaac S., my great-great-grandfather, born in 1805.

I continued to print out these pages with their boxes, lines, and statistics on the individual, including their birthdate, location, parents' names, siblings, and date of death. It started to get complicated, so I taped each printout of another ancestor on the wall in my office to see the continuum of relatives and who begat whom.

As I dug further, I discovered that Jan Wybesse S. was a Dutch Church Reformer and came from a long line of ministers. I had my answer: My 10th great-grandfather Jan Wybesse S. (who immigrated from the Netherlands in 1662) and his wife are the ancestors who must have prayed to God for me and the generations to come.

I was fortunate to have made it this far in my ancestral search, and I could have continued, as church records in Europe were kept for centuries. Instead, I stopped the search and was satisfied with the data I discovered. I knew there had to be a line of people in my ancestry who were focused spiritually on God. So, I concluded my free trial with the genealogy app.

I left the printouts taped to my office wall for a while. When I went into my office and sat in my chair, I thought about the lives that came before mine, people I would not get to meet. What hardships had they endured? What were their families like? What were their childhoods like? What did they do for a living? What about their deaths? Who did they fall in love with? What dreams did they have? Except for occasionally imagining these people's circumstances, I let go of my interest in my ancestors. I did not find any leads to unknown family members in this era. I had a brother, adult children, and grandchildren, and my husband had a large family.

A few weeks later, I took down all the printouts and made a file folder to pass on to the next generation one day. After putting away the file, I sat in my meditation chair. Within a few minutes of sitting quietly, I received a clear message: *Take a DNA test.* I recognized this as an inner directive. I discovered that such a DNA test would cost $100 and would reveal my ethnicity and genealogy. I shrugged it off because I had just researched my genealogy and knew my ethnicity: my mother's background was English and Dutch, and my father's ethnicity was 100% Greek. I could not see spending the money to learn what I already knew.

This inner intuitive directive persisted. I continued to resist its appeal for a few weeks, but it would not go away. Whenever I trusted my inner promptings from previous experiences, the affirmative outcomes taught me to follow my gut feelings. Although this directive seemed unnecessary, I paid the fee and ordered a DNA test.

A few days later, I received the package in the mail. It was a simple saliva test, an autosomal DNA test, which examines 700,000 DNA markers to identify your genetic ethnicity going back multiple generations. The results also compared yours to a database of other people's DNA, and a list of relationships is generated as your DNA matches. Often, unknown relatives can be discovered on this list. People can use a code name rather than their birth name to remain anonymous. The DNA will also show distant ancestors, their ethnicity, and the current family's ethnicity. The accuracy rate

THE DNA TEST

is over 99%. Besides the geographical ethnicity, it shows the percentage of shared common DNA results with grandparents, aunts, cousins, and siblings.

The directions said not to eat, drink, smoke, or chew gum for 30 minutes before giving the saliva. I filled the test tube with my saliva and mailed it in a prepaid mailer back to the genealogy company. The results will be sent back online in 6-8 weeks. I didn't think about it again.

A few weeks later, I was notified of the results. On my mother's side, it was precisely as I predicted. On my father's side, the test revealed I had zero Greek and one hundred percent Jewish (Ashkenazi) DNA. I looked at the paper blankly. How was that possible?

There must be a mistake, so I called the company. "Is the DNA of Greeks and Jews so similar that it can be mistaken?" I asked. Growing up in the ethnic blend of New York City, this seemed reasonable and possible.

"No, in the DNA world, that is like comparing apples and oranges. I'm sorry, you are not the first person to ask such a question!" the company representative replied.

"What does that mean?" My head was spinning just thinking about the implications.

"It means you do not have any DNA relating to a Greek ethnicity; it is Ashkenazi Jewish that makes up half your DNA. You show a few hundred family DNA matches, as well!" I ended the call, went back on their website, and saw well over two hundred people tagged as related to me, all Jewish. I didn't recognize any of the names. It revealed their ethnicity and the extent of our shared DNA. Based on the DNA match percentage, it estimated the type of relative, like first or second cousins. How could I be related to so many people I had never heard of and who weren't Greek or English?

I immediately called my brother, who was ten years older than me. Steve had been married, gone through a divorce, and had three grown children. Everything changed with his divorce, as he told me. Instead of living with a lot of stress and discord, Steve had chosen a simpler path and was much happier. He had a new job in sales and was in a new relationship with someone with the same values. Steve had been a high-powered executive but had now opted out for simplicity and peace of mind. After explaining my DNA results, he said he had goosebumps on his arms. "I remember something I had not thought about since I was ten years old. When Mom became pregnant with you, she and Dad started fighting all the time. I remember Dad having long bouts of rage, accusing Mom of being with another man."

"What? Dad may not be my biological father?" I was stunned.

"I'm just telling you what I remember," Steve said.

"I want you to take a DNA test to see if this test was mistaken," I insisted.

My brother agreed to take one.

The continued conversation revealed that, at that time, my parents lived in a small one-bedroom apartment in the Bronx. My brother slept on a sofa in the living room. The walls were thin, and there was no escaping the constant bickering between my parents. My father had been diagnosed with cancer and had his leg amputated just before my conception, and his cancer treatment had apparently left him infertile. There were undoubtedly suspicious and extenuating circumstances regarding my entry into this world.

I got off the phone and ordered another DNA test to send to my brother directly. This time, I didn't give a second thought to spending $100 on it. But now I was anxious about the results.

My reference points for knowing where I stood in the world had dissolved. It was like driving on unfamiliar backroads in the mountains when suddenly your GPS goes out, and you have no idea how to proceed or which road to turn on. Suddenly, my location in life was unclear. Who was I, and how did I get here?

25

Who's Your Daddy?

Sometimes, unexpected turns can lead to unimagined places that unfold our destiny. A few weeks later, my brother's DNA test results came in. He was a full-blooded Greek on his father's side. I called my brother. He sounded relieved because he still knew who his father was and that he was of Greek heritage.

"I started this search to find more relatives, not decrease them. Now my only brother has become my half-brother," I said, complaining to Steve.

"I will always be your full brother. It doesn't matter what the DNA says," Steve said reassuringly.

Sadly, we missed out on a relationship for most of our lives. Steve was ten years older and left home as a teenager. My dad treated my brother well. I used to think it was because Greeks culturally revered men over women. Looking back, it may have been our bloodlines that decided my father's attitude toward us. He would speak badly of me to my brother and vice versa. My brother and I only became close after my mother had a stroke, and I had to care for our father. And over the years, we have become very close. Steve wanted me to keep him updated about my heritage search so he could hear the latest developments. I promised to do that.

There was one blaring conclusion to draw: *my father was not my biological father!* I had spent decades in recovery programs helping young women, some of whom would say, "I don't know who the baby's daddy is." I used to think my father was awful to me, but at least I thought I knew *who* he was. Now, that was unknown to me, too.

With one question answered, many new ones popped up that I needed to figure out. Did my Greek dad know I was another man's child? Was this why he had raged at me from the time I was a small child? Whenever I came into a room, my presence would spark anger in him that he could not contain. Whatever I did to try to win his approval, his heart seemed impenetrable to me until the end of his life.

I could only conclude that something was unacceptable and wrong with me that I didn't know about, or at least until now. I assume he knew I was another man's child. Were my Greek father's unresolved feelings of betrayal and heartache the source of his anger and rejection of me? I had suffered tremendous guilt and shame for a lifetime, with no explanation for why. Was this even mine to carry?

I felt powerless and overwhelmed. So, I went to the refrigerator and took out my anger by throwing out the feta cheese and Kalamata olives. My identity as a Greek woman was over. It had all been a lie. It was not who I was. I decided I would not rest until I found my birth father, a biological family of origin, and my real identity.

It felt like the ultimate betrayal by my mother. My father was not the person I believed him to be, and my mother led a life full of secrets. How could my mother not have told me who my father was? If she hadn't lost her ability to speak and write due to the stroke, would she have shared that information with me?

That night, I sat up in bed and updated Cap. "My DNA test shows I have a zero percent Greek ethnicity and that half of my

DNA is of Ashkenazi Jewish ancestry. My father wasn't my father," I blurted out to Cap. I was still dazed and overwhelmed by my mistaken identity and the lifelong shame I absorbed from the misplaced anger focused on me.

"Does that mean we are going to Russia or the Ukraine instead of the Greek Isles?" he asked. "You know, I'm a southern boy and don't like the cold," he added, trying to lighten the mood.

I smiled. "I think New York City is a better bet. Tomorrow, I start my search through the genealogy matches to find out who my father is. I have to find him," I said, kissing my husband and turning out the light.

The following morning, I went into my office with a resolve to search for my father. My dad had brainwashed me into believing that being Greek was the most desirable identity you could have and that I was lucky to be Greek. I desperately wanted to know my family of origin because I felt disconnected from anyone as a child. Instead, I felt ashamed and had no sense of my self-identity. I was proud and excited when I discovered my Jewish heritage because I had always related to it in others. Now, I know it is not some random feeling; instead, it is based on DNA passed down through generations.

Growing up with Jewish friends in Jewish households on Long Island, I wanted to be like them. They were part of a community, and I was often included in their activities. Sometimes, I was even invited to the Passover Seder. I loved their traditions and family alliances. I wanted to be Jewish growing up, and ironically, I was.

As an adult, when I moved from New York, I used to say, "I feel Jewish." When I met Jewish people on my travels, I often felt at home, like a second tuning fork vibrating near the first one. Later, as I studied the early books of the Bible, the first five of which originated from the Torah, I related to the Jewish plight depicted there. They were often persecuted for who they were but kept God enshrined in their hearts as they searched for their homeland. I loved that it was so important to them as a people to be hospitable and to make a difference in people's lives.

I knew I needed to find out who my birth father was. The problem was that both my parents had passed, and I had no real clues regarding who my mother's love interest might have been back then. I did have a few hundred new Jewish cousins, most of whom were distant relatives, listed as DNA matches on my account. Almost all of them did not list their names but were identified with a code for privacy.

I narrowed the search to my closest DNA match, a second cousin whose code name was Adrienne. I sent my first message to the mysterious and unidentified relative. It was a delicate situation. I carefully worded my message since I was unsure whether my father was alive and how he was related to Adrienne. I did not want to say I was looking for my father because I just found out I am his secret love child from an affair with my mother, and you are my closest DNA match. So, instead, I sent the following message:

> Hi!
>
> It looks like our DNA matches closely. I would welcome the opportunity to talk about it. My email is catherine@............com. I look forward to hearing from you.
>
> Thank you,
>
> Catherine Fendig

A few days later, Adrienne wrote back:

I'm sorry, your name is unfamiliar. Can you give me some names of your relatives that we may have in common?

Adrienne

After several more polite emails, I did not hear back from Adrienne. So, I sent another message with more of the story:

Dear Adrienne,

I think you may need more information to help me. Recently, when I took a DNA test, I discovered my father was not my father. Before he died, he tried to tell me, but I thought it was his dementia and another made-up story. I had this further confirmed when I had my brother's DNA tested.

My mother's name is Frances Lake. At the time of my conception, she worked in Manhattan for a cancer research fundraising organization that partnered with selling Broadway tickets.

I want to find my father's name and my roots. I am looking to find out who my biological family is. I will remain respectful of this unusual situation. It would mean a lot if you would assist me with the discovery of my new Jewish family tree.

It is my understanding that you and I may share the same great-grandparents. This is what brought me to contact you. I have a good life today. I am married to a good man with a good family. I am still hoping you might respond.

Catherine

Then the dreaded message came back from Adrienne:

Given your and your mother's names, dates, and ages, I found no relatives that I am aware of who might assist in your search. Keep looking. I'm sorry, I cannot help you any further.

Best wishes,

Adrienne

Adrienne was my last hope and the only solid connection I had to my mysterious, unknown father and family. A sense of hopelessness washed over me. I had done everything I could to expose and identify myself. Why was Adrienne not revealing anything about her identity? I knew I had to let go of this search since I had no other leads. I had tried messaging other distant matches, but no one responded.

That evening, I got into bed. "Adrienne is not going to be able to help me. It's over. I have no more leads," I told Cap and cried into my pillow.

"Would you give me permission to write to Adrienne tomorrow?" He asked.

I agreed. What could it hurt?

The following day, Cap wrote this message to Adrienne, and I sent it:

> Hello, this is Catherine's husband. She just shared your last e-mail with me. Thank you for your responses. As you can imagine, after 59 years, she has found out her father was not her father but someone else. The DNA clearly established this fact.
>
> The match she has with you is the highest match outside of her brother, and it represents a definite biological link. We know you have a direct connection to Catherine, and she is family. For Catherine to obtain the identity of her true father, only you can provide that link. We request that you contact Catherine so that she can further search out her roots. I am sure you understand this need by now.
>
> Your further assistance would be greatly helpful.
>
> Catherine's husband,
>
> Cap Fendig

Surprisingly, Adrienne responded immediately, offering to contact me at the end of the month after visiting Connecticut for a Bar mitzvah.

26

The Davidic Dynasty

After weeks passed, I became anxious again about not knowing who my father was. What if Adrienne didn't get back to me? What if she did, and we still couldn't figure out our connection? I had too many "What ifs . . ." circling in my mind.

How do you find people using DNA? I was clueless and had no experience. However, I have an innate investigative side and know how to listen to and follow my Higher Power's direction. With that realization, I was confident that, in time, I would find my father.

I went to my meditation chair and sat quietly. "God, you revealed this to me, so please help me find my father!" Then, I had a fleeting thought: *if a new person closely related to my father took a DNA test and remained anonymous, I would have a new closer link to explore.* I got excited at the prospect and felt hopeful. I continued with my meditation and ended with a simple prayer request for a new DNA test of an identifiable relative.

Later that afternoon, I returned to my computer and checked the genealogy app. A new relative had popped up on my matches chart that was just as close to Adrienne. It listed her real name as Wendy H..., but at least I could reach out to speak with her. I messaged her right away. She messaged me back, giving me her phone number, and agreed to talk with me the following day.

Then I called my brother and told him about Wendy. "Can you recall any names of people Mom knew when I was small who could have been my father?" I asked, grasping at straws.

"I have been thinking about it, and I remember her talking about a friend named Dr. L . . . or maybe it was Mr. L . . .," Steve said.

"Yes! I remember her bringing me home a collectible coin every few weeks. She would tell me it was from Mr. L . . . I collected the coins and ended up with a shoebox full of them. They were varied, either small, big, silver, gold, foreign, or domestic. I loved the coins because someone I had never met regularly sent me presents. Mom always seemed happy when she had lunch with Mr. L . . . in Manhattan. I do remember mom telling me not to show them to my dad. Funny, I never thought about it further until now. Could Mr. L . . ., who sent me those coins, have been my dad?" I asked. It was the only tangible name I had now.

"Maybe? It was a memorable name in her vocabulary. You'll figure it out," Steve added.

When I got off the phone with my brother, I Googled Mr. L . . . in Manhattan. Yes, you guessed it. There were too many to count. I might as well be looking for Mr. Smith in Anytown, USA. Besides, I didn't know if it was him or another man who was my father.

Wendy and I finally talked the following evening. I was always mindful that I was the product of an affair, so if my father were alive, I didn't know if I was talking to his children or grandchildren, who did not know of my existence. I didn't want to disturb or upset an entire family. I introduced myself, gave her my age, my maiden name, where I grew up, and told her I wanted to know more about my family members. I told her my mother had passed.

Wendy told me she lived in Florida, was eleven years younger than me, and was a counselor and a professor. Her father had passed away six years earlier. He would have been close to my age. "My father grew up in New York. Maybe we are related through my grandfather, Macy L . . .," Wendy shared.

She said the name Mr. L . . .! It felt like I had been fishing all day in still waters without even a nibble, and then suddenly, the fishing pole was bent over by a big fish on the line.

"Wendy, that is the last name I heard my mother talk about when I was little," I shared excitedly. I felt safer now in revealing my quest to find my father.

"It is a big family. My mother was divorced when I was young. I haven't spoken to anyone in a while. I have wanted to learn more about my father's side of the family. My Uncle Lance, who everyone called *Lanny*. He might be able to help you. Tell him I say hi if you talk to him," Wendy said.

"I will. Thank you," I said gratefully.

"My mom knew all of them. I will see if she can call you. Send me a picture so I can see who you look like," Wendy said. We ended the phone call and agreed to stay in touch.

I texted her a picture of myself. She texted right back. *You definitely are a L . . . You look like them. You'll see!*

A few days later, Wendy called back. She said she had sat down with her mom and got me some names for me to follow up on. "My grandfather, Macy, who could be your potential father, had two brothers, Bucky and Irving, who also fit the age range. So technically, either of them could be your father," Wendy explained.

"Are any of the brothers alive?" I asked, hoping they were.

"No, I'm sorry," Wendy said.

For a moment, I felt a gut punch. I knew the chances of finding my father alive would be slim because he would be in his nineties at best. I still held out hope, though, until now. There was a reasonable probability that one of the three brothers was my father, but now I had to accept that I could not meet him in this life and would only get to know him through the people he left behind.

I had done more research and discovered that DNA tests only show degrees of relatedness and are defined as first cousins, second cousins, third cousins, and so forth. The more DNA you share with someone, the closer the relationship and the fewer degrees of relatedness you have. The degrees and the amount of DNA you share can predict whether you are siblings, cousins, parents, grandparents, great-grandparents, aunts, great-aunts, etc. However, the test doesn't define it except for degrees and labeling the potential relationships.

Suddenly, I was looking at a new mountain to climb. Since the three brothers were deceased and I could not get their DNA to test, I would need to find the offspring of each of the brothers to discover if they were my 1st cousins or my half-siblings.

I wrote down the names Wendy gave me when I talked with her mom. Here were my potential fathers and siblings:

Psychiatrist, Dr. Bucky L., whose five children included a set of triplets.

Police Officer, Macy L., who had four children.

Lawyer, Irving L., who had four children.

Then, I printed out a page for each brother and taped it to my office wall, where I had previously tracked my maternal grandfather's lineage. Next, I printed out a page for each of the offspring to keep track of what I found. I noted that the first brother was Dr. L., a name my brother recalled. The second brother was Mr. L., and I remembered hearing my mother say that name. Since I had their adult children's names, I decided to focus on contacting them first. If it were Dr. L., I would only need one contact with one offspring to identify my father and would only need to make one awkward request in a phone call.

This was quite fortuitous, so I sat in my meditation chair and asked God for a closer DNA contact and a clue. The first relative who spoke with me was Wendy, whose grandfather's last name is L . . . Now, I was on the verge of discovering who my father was. God had to be orchestrating this search. How else could I explain the synchronicity of asking God for a new DNA test result identifying a closer relative, and Wendy's latest arrival on my list of closest relatives matched through our DNA?

At this point, I wondered if I should stop my search. Maybe I was searching for a family that would rather not know I existed. Could I handle more rejection? Would the risk be worth it? On the other hand, what if it was a close and kind family? What if I experienced a strong family connection and healing through this search?

I played through these two potential outcomes. I told myself that I had experienced a lot of rejection in my life and still survived. But here was a chance for a different result. Maybe the odds were not stacked in my favor for a positive outcome, but I was guaranteed nothing if I stayed still, stagnant, and safe. Besides, I wanted to know who my father was. Didn't I deserve that?

That evening, I got into bed with Cap. "I think I'm getting closer. My father may be one of three L . . . brothers: Bucky, a psychiatrist; Macy, a police officer; or Irving, an attorney. I feel like I am in the game show *To Tell the Truth*, where they ask *if the real one will please stand up*. Only no one is alive to do so," I explained.

"Then how will you find out who your father is?" Cap asked.

"I will need to contact their adult children and ask for a DNA test," I said, taking a deep breath.

"That could be tricky. Are you up for that?" Cap asked.

"It's the only way to find out," I said, kissing him goodnight, turning out the light, and trying to forget about it.

The following afternoon, I turned my attention back to Adrienne. I knew she would be contacting me any day now. I sensed she had been uncomfortable about interacting with me, a stranger. I wanted to let her off the hook so she wouldn't feel obligated. I messaged Adrienne, letting her know I had found another close DNA match named Wendy, who got me closer to figuring out who my father was. She sent the following message back:

Hi Catherine,

Interesting! Wendy has shown up on my list of DNA connections, and I have no idea who she is, either. I will call you tomorrow evening.

Regards,

Adrienne

Instead of giving up on my mystery search, Adrienne reiterated that they would be in touch, which further stirred my curiosity. Who was Adrienne? Thanks to Wendy, I knew it was a potential second cousin.

In the meantime, I felt dazed and disconnected from everyday conversations with people and normal activities in the first few months of my DNA search. It took a lot of effort to focus while I handled reservation calls for our business. I was constantly preoccupied with questions I had about who I was, and had lost interest in everyday routine activities. I looked at other older men on the street and realized anyone could be my father, but I would not know it. Everything I thought I knew about my genealogy was a lie. My historical reference to my familiar identity had been wiped out, as amnesia does to our memory.

Finally, at the proposed time that evening, my phone rang, showing a California phone number. It was Adrienne. When I answered, I was greeted by a friendly, upbeat male voice. He introduced himself as Steve; Adrienne was his wife, who oversees the account. Steve was a retired surgeon and Corporate Medical Director after leaving his practice, and they lived in Beverly Hills. He apologized for being so mysterious, but was only being cautious. I assured him it was perfectly understandable.

I reported my findings from my contact with Wendy. This immediately gave Steve the missing piece to our puzzle. He knew of the brothers but was closer to the psychiatrist, Dr. Bucky L. Steve admitted he had also lost touch with Bucky. He said the last time he saw Bucky was when he and his wife had the triplets. Maida and Indie were two of the triplets.

"Bucky's mother would be your grandmother, a sister to my grandmother. They were very close throughout their life. That's how we are 2nd cousins," Steve explained.

"I'm so excited to learn this. What was my grandmother like?" I asked.

"Your grandmother was a bit of a socialite in the Manhattan scene back in the day! I have some glamorous pictures I will send to you. Her sister was a well-known midwife in Brooklyn and assisted in thousands of deliveries over many years. There is a lot more I can fill you in on, but I have to eat dinner," Steve said before ending the call.

"This means so much to me. Thank you," I said gratefully.

"Okay, Cuz! I'll call you again to see how your search is coming," Steve said.

I looked at the time. It was 11:00 pm. Two hours had just flown by. Steve had been so easy to talk with. It warmed my heart when he casually said, "Okay, Cuz." I didn't take that for granted. It was an acknowledgment of my legitimacy.

I was wide awake from the phone call. When I entered the bedroom, Cap was just starting to drift off to sleep. I gently nudged him. "Are you awake?" I asked.

"Now I am. What's up?" Cap asked.

"I met Adrienne, who is actually Steve, my cousin. His wife Adrienne set up his account. Steve is a retired surgeon in Beverly Hills. Our grandmothers are sisters, and he called me Cuz!" I said.

"I'm glad for you. That's great," Cap said as he drifted back to sleep.

I turned off the light, pulled the comforter around my neck, and stared at the ceiling. The moonlight was coming through the partially opened blinds. Relief settled over me. I now had two positive alignments with two new biological family members, Wendy and Steve. The following afternoon, I planned to look up one of the triplets; they would be potential father # 1, Dr. Bucky's kids, and my potential sisters. Sadly, I learned that their triplet brother, Jared, had passed away. I chose Maida because that was the name of my mother's best friend back then. I knew it was not her, but maybe this was a sign.

I searched for her home phone and found it under her husband's name.

I keyed in the numbers and stared at the phone. I felt my heart racing—the "What ifs" started circling my mind. I didn't want to upset someone by telling them about me with the implications about their father if he was married when I was conceived. So, I put the phone down. I went back to my work. Later that evening, I tried to make the call again. Fear got the best of me whenever I picked up the cell phone. The following day, I had the same experience. If I could just make myself call her, I would not have to think about it again. I couldn't push myself over my threshold of fear.

Then that evening, at 9 pm, cousin Steve from Beverly Hills called. "How is it going?" he asked.

"I found one of the triplets' phone number, Maida," I said.

"And what did she say?" Steve asked with his upbeat energy.

"I just can't seem to make the call. I hate coming into this family through lies and betrayal," I admitted, holding back my tears.

"Would you like me to tell you something so you'll never have to feel bad about yourself again?" he asked.

"Yes, I would," I responded eagerly.

"A few years ago, I hired a well-known genealogist to extensively research our family lineage. He discovered our great-grandparents were directly linked to a well-studied Rabbi from the 1400s. During the time of King David, God promised the King that He would never forsake his descendants. From that time until the 1400s, rabbis kept records of the different family lines from King David. Rabbi Meir was a direct descendant, and you, my dear, are a direct descendant of Rabbi Meir, making you related to King David and a part of the Davidic Dynasty," Steve explained.

"That is mind-blowing," I said.

"Whatever happened to make you feel so bad about yourself, now you know of your royal lineage. King David was one of history's most iconic kings. But he was guilty of infidelity and had to turn back to God for forgiveness. There were consequences to his actions, but God still loved him. Now, make that phone call tomorrow because your family needs to know their ancestral history, too. You could be their messenger, as well," Steve explained.

"That's amazing," I said, feeling at a loss for words.

"You even have a family crest, which I will send you. Now make that call," Steve said as he ended the phone. It was a few minutes past 11:00 pm. I felt dazed.

I went to the bedroom to tell Cap. He was already asleep. I shook him. "Can you wake up?" I asked.

"Yes. What's up?" Cap answered. He was groggy, and his eyes were still shut.

"Cap, I'm related to King David! I know we are all related spiritually, but genetically, my DNA is traced back to my great-grandparents through Rabbi Meir and from him to King David. Present-day descendants are part of the Davidic Dynasty," I explained.

"That's great," Cap said. His eyes were still shut, and I could tell he had fallen into a deep sleep.

I slipped into bed and turned the lights out but was wide awake. One of the reasons I started this search was because I was convinced that some ancestor along the way must have known God and prayed for me, even though I did not exist at the time, and they would never meet me. So, finding out my lineage validates that genetics and spirituality can play an important role in potential, regardless of the environment. Did my lineage now explain my lifelong spiritual search and my always seeking a personal, intimate relationship with God?

I had read and studied the Bible many times. Now, I wanted to go back and reread about King David's life. So, I quietly got out of bed, grabbed my Bible, and went into my office. I got comfortable in my meditation chair and started reading about King David in 1st Samuel.

King David Reigned from 1000 to 962 BC. Much of his story is told in the 1st and 2nd Samuel books in the Old Testament. He wrote many psalms and was a poet, harpist, and hymnist. He was the second king of ancient Israel and is known to have united all the tribes of Israel. His son Solomon succeeded him and expanded the empire that David had built.

King David was known for being persecuted unfairly for years by King Saul. He was a skillful warrior, and when Goliath, a Philistine giant, challenged King Saul to send a man to fight him, no one volunteered. David, armed only with a slingshot and stones, volunteered to face Goliath. With only one shot to the forehead, David killed him.

King David was also known for his successful rule, had tremendous faith, and continuously looked to God for direction. He also succumbed to temptation and had an affair with Bathsheba, but he later turned back to God. God's promise to him regarding his descendants was that they would not be forsaken: "Your house and your kingdom will endure forever before me; your throne will be established forever." 2nd Samuel 7:16 (NIV).

Joseph was one of King David's descendants whose immediate family had betrayed him. Despite many hardships, Joseph never lost faith, and eventually, he went from prison to the palace. The story of Joseph and his family's betrayal gives us hope that God can use what was meant for harm to us for good.

Since I liked deciphering signs, I looked up the word royalty. In Hebrew, royalty refers to reign and power over. The lives of King David and Joseph reminded me that we can reign over our challenges and circumstances. We all have that capability through our spiritual DNA.

The following evening, I received an email from cousin Steve. He had sent a picture of my grandmother and his grandmother, both dressed beautifully from 1932. There was another picture of the three brothers, my potential fathers at a wedding in 1961. It was the first time I saw the three men. One of them was my father, and the others were my uncles. I studied the faces in the picture for a while. I could see my physical features in the brothers. Steve also sent a photo of the family crest. I added the pictures to the papers I had taped on the wall in my office, tracking relatives I was finding and their relation to each other.

I knew it was time to call Maida. I keyed in the number. It started ringing. My heart raced. Then I heard a soft female voice answer the phone. "Hello," she said. It was Maida.

"Hi. My name is Catherine, and I recently took a DNA test. I found out my father wasn't my father. I also discovered that you and I have the same grandparents, which means I am closely related to your father and his brothers. It also means you could be my sister," I explained nervously.

"Whaaatt," Maida said, stretching out the word 'what' with a slight but familiar New York accent.

"I know this sounds strange and coming out of the blue, but if you could take a DNA test, I could find out who my father is, and we could learn how we are related," I said, feeling extremely awkward.

"Could you hold on? Let me put my husband on. He knows about this stuff," Maida responded.

I took a deep breath. When he got on the phone, I explained how the DNA search came about. Lucky for me, Maida's husband was well-versed in genealogy and was in the middle of conducting such a search of his own. After a lengthy conversation, I offered to pay for Maida's DNA test, which they would have sole access to. Then, they could share the results with me if they so choose. Of course, I hoped they would, but I wanted them to know this was not some scam, and I respected their privacy.

They agreed to help me by having Maida take the DNA test. We exchanged addresses and emails. They were lovely. Maida got back on the phone. I told her I had a nice picture of our grandmother from 1932 and would send it. She said she had very few photos of her and would be happy to receive them.

When I got off the phone, I ordered my third DNA test for $100 and had it sent directly to Maida. Now the wait began to see who my father was . . .

27

Cousins or Siblings

The following day, after the shock had worn off, Maida called me. "You could be my sister," she said.

"Or your 1st cousin," I added. "Is your mother alive?"

"No, she passed away. I can't imagine my father having an affair with your mother, but you sound nice," Maida said.

"I understand that feeling. We don't know whether your father did yet," I reiterated.

Maida said she had lost track of her cousins, and it had been nearly thirty years since they had spoken. "Everyone got along; we just went our own ways and lost touch," she explained.

"Well, if this test shows we're 1st cousins, I will contact Lance next."

"I'm going to call my sister Indie today. I'm not sure what she will think of all this," Maida said. Then she shared that she and her sister Indie were very close. Maida let me know she would welcome having another sister or cousin.

Maida and I spoke for a while, sharing details about our lives, including work, school, children, and marriage. Nothing deeply personal was said. We just gave each other a snapshot of our lives. Before we ended the call, Maida said she would tell her sister Indie about me and our DNA connection.

"Please feel free to give Indie my phone number if she wants to talk," I said with some concern. I considered the kindness I received from Maida, Wendy, and Steve my good fortune. But my upbringing had taught me to expect the other shoe to drop. I hoped that wouldn't happen.

I used my energy the rest of the day to focus on the menial tasks. Being so preoccupied with finding my father, I was past due for food shopping and rushed off to the grocery store. It was busy with locals and tourists stocking up for the weekend. When I got to the bread aisle, my phone rang. It was Cap telling me our first mate for the Dolphin boat tour was called away by a family emergency.

"You want me to mate this afternoon?" I asked. Cap replied that he did.

"Okay, I'll mate with you in an hour. I love you," I said, ending the call.

An older woman was standing in front of my grocery cart. She had silver, tightly permed, teased short hair, glasses, and pink lipstick. She was wearing baby-blue polyester pants and an oversized floral cotton blouse. The woman was holding a loaf of bread and staring at me with disapproval. I realized she heard only my end of the phone call about "mating."

"On a boat. I'm a first mate on a boat," I explained.

I could see by her expression that she had been aghast, thinking I was talking out loud about having sex that afternoon. She nodded, showing some relief, and gave me an embarrassed smile as she put the bread in her shopping cart and scurried away. This was life on a small island.

After grocery shopping, I went home and slipped on my boating clothes. I went to the marina and checked in the twenty-two passengers of one extended family for our dolphin tour. The boat trip was a private party, a family reunion. They had brought sandwiches and drinks. It would be a leisurely excursion with this family engrossed in visiting each other. I untied the lines and lifted the fenders off the boat's sides.

Once we left the dock, I moved to the front of the boat and sat down. The wind blew through my hair and seemed to rinse the stress of my family search off me. Then, I started scanning the horizon for dolphins. "Dolphins to the right at 2:00," I shouted to the group. Everyone stood up and looked for them. Cap steered the boat toward the pod. Within minutes, we were surrounded by a family of dolphins swimming toward the boat and under it. Then, they would surface in the back, front, or on either side. It was a game of hide and seek. Everyone loved watching them. The dolphins were like magical pranksters.

"Oh look, a baby dolphin with its mom," said one of the passengers. Everyone ooed and awhhhed. When they swam away, we continued with the tour, and the family went back to eating and visiting with one another. I took my seat back at the front of the boat and continued to let the wind blow over me.

I felt myself move back into the present moment. Over the last few months of searching for my family heritage, I have spent most of my waking moments reviewing the past. But it was the present where I usually found the most safety and peace. I was grateful our first mate was called away. I needed to step outside myself for ninety minutes and feel back in the flow of nature. I felt renewed when we returned to the dock.

That evening, after dinner, Maida's sister Indie called. We introduced ourselves to each other. Indie was happily married, and they had three grown sons. She was a trained therapist and an artist. Her husband is a clinical forensic Freudian psychiatrist and an author.

Indie's three sons were doctors. I told Indie that raising three doctors was impressive.

"Yes, it was a busy time, but we're a close family," Indie added.

"When Maida and I, our husbands, sons, their wives, girlfriends, and children get together on holidays, we have a big crew," Indie said. I learned that Maida also went to school to be a therapist. She had two sons, one in real estate banking and the other an attorney.

I went over my DNA search with Indie. "Do you know anything about your ancestral lineage on your great-grandmother's side?" I asked.

"No, I don't. I am interested. What did you find out?" Indie asked.

"Steve, our cousin in California, hired a prominent genealogist who discovered our great-grandmother is a direct descendant of Rabbi Meir from the 1400s, and he is a direct descendant of King David. So, your family is a part of the Davidic Dynasty. Steve is sending me his records," I explained.

"Whaaatt . . .," Indie said.

"You sound like Maida when you say *Whaaatt*," I said, reminding me of Maida's response to these findings.

"My son is studying Rabbi Meir's teachings right now! He will find this fascinating," Indie responded. "I'm going to take a DNA test, too!"

I gave Indie the information regarding the test and the company I used. Before we ended the call, we agreed to stay in touch and share our findings. I now had two new cousins, part of the triplets, with whom I had much in common and felt a strong connection.

COUSINS OR SIBLINGS

As I spoke with each biological relative, I was struck by the similarities we shared and how well our energies matched. I recognized I had the same interests and drives in many respects as my biological family—spirituality, education, therapy, entertainment, and writing. I wondered where those interests had come from because they were not modeled or supported while growing up. I always needed more confidence and the resources to follow through and accomplish my dreams.

A few more weeks passed, but I thought about Maida's DNA test every day and what the results would yield. One of the happiest times of my life was waiting for a pregnancy test that revealed my daughter was on her way. I was elated, finally having a family member I could love. If my life were a tapestry, my daughter's story would be one of the most beautiful threads. However, this part of the weave focuses not on her but on repairing the thread that frayed long before her arrival.

Then, I thought about my mother when she found out about her pregnancy. Each night as a child, I remember my mother would come home from work, have a few strong drinks, and then sit on the edge of my bed. I can still hear the ice cubes clinking in her glass as she drank and told me about being pregnant with me. My Mother said some people she knew pleaded with her to get an abortion. They were illegal at that time. She told me that the only reason I was alive was because she wouldn't listen to them. So, if it weren't for her, I wouldn't be alive. It was a strange story to tell a child. I never got the impression of being warmly wanted and welcomed into the world. I never understood why until now, given that her husband wasn't the father.

Six weeks later, the DNA test came back. Maida and her husband called, and I put it on my speakerphone. "You and Maida are related," he said. "Bucky is not your dad but your uncle, making you, Maida, and Indie first cousins. Welcome to the family."

"Thank you, and I'm glad to have you and Indie as my new cousins!" I said. While I was glad to have identified our family connection, I was disappointed that I still didn't know who my father was. I went to the papers taped to my office wall. That left two brothers for my search: police officer Macy and attorney Irving L. I would focus on potential father # 2, Macy, next.

Wendy had given me two of Macy's sons' names. I randomly picked Lance and did a Google search on him. I discovered his life and professional medical career had inspired two popular TV series of the 80s, *St. Elsewhere* and *Northern Exposure*. When Lance was interning at the Cleveland Clinic, he arranged for the creator and producer of what was to become the TV series St. Elsewhere to do rounds in the hospital as research for the TV show. When Lance finished his first-year residency, he took a hiatus and left the Cleveland Clinic to become the first physician to become a New York City police officer. He was currently the Vice President and Chief Medical Officer of an integrated healthcare system. Looking at his accomplishments and current positions, I figured the chances of him taking my call would be slim.

I found his office number. When I called, I noticed my heart wasn't racing, figuring a secretary would probably answer. I left a message, giving my name and phone number, and said this wasn't a medical matter but a personal matter regarding family heritage. I hoped I wouldn't come to a dead end here, but I was prepared for the worst.

I did not expect to hear from him anytime soon. To my surprise, he called me back in fifteen minutes. "This is Dr. L. How can I help you?" he asked.

"Yes, thank you for returning my call so promptly," I said, taking a deep breath. Now, my heart was racing.

"My name is Catherine. This is a little awkward and a bit uncomfortable, but six months ago, I found out that my dad wasn't my biological father and that my mother had an affair. It looks like my father might have been either your father, Macy, or his brother Irving.

"Wait a minute. How did you jump to those conclusions?" Lance asked.

I filled him in on my DNA search and journey through the cousins thus far, which led me to Steve, Wendy, Maida, Indie, and now him. I told him I first checked Bucky's family DNA, and he is my uncle. "Your niece Wendy says, 'Hi *Lanny,* and sends her regards," I told him.

I heard Lance chuckle. "*Lanny* was my nickname! Is Wendy okay?"

"Yes, she is. Maida and Indie also send their regards," I added.

"Ah, my cousins! I haven't talked with them in a long time. How are they?" he asked.

I updated him on their lives and their adult children. Then Lance asked me about dates regarding my conception and my mother's location. He told me his dad was a NYC cop, and they lived in the city at that time. I hoped my dad was potential father #3, Irving, so he didn't have to consider that his father had an affair. Both his parents were deceased.

He told me his Uncle Irving, back then, had just married his third wife, a blonde bombshell who had a successful career as a Broadway actress. "How did you come up with the name L . . . to search?" he asked.

"My mother would routinely have lunch in Manhattan with a Mr. L . . . and he would send something home for me each time through my mother," I explained. "Would you consider taking a DNA test so I can find out if your father, Macy, is my father or uncle, and if you are my cousin or half-brother?" I asked, covering the phone receiver as I took another deep breath. I could feel butterflies in the pit of my stomach. "Of course, I will pay for it," I added.

There was an understandably long silence on the other end of the phone, which felt like an eternity to me.

"You obviously know some of my family. You sound legit. Let me mull this over, discuss it with my wife, and I promise to call you back tomorrow."

I thanked him for considering the test. Like the other cousins, it had been easy to talk with him.

That evening, I called my cousin Wendy and told her Lance had said hi. She was excited to hear I had talked with him. I called Maida and Indie and let them know about Lance. Lastly, I called Steve in California with the three-hour time difference. Steve was thrilled to hear about Lance possibly taking the DNA test. "This means a great deal to us and those in our family whom we have lost contact with over the years. Keep it going, Catherine," Steve said encouragingly.

When I finished updating my cousins, I felt like God was using me in some strange way to bring members of this massive family back into touch with each other. I washed my face and got ready for bed. It was 11:15 pm. Cap was already in bed and reading something on his phone. He put it down. "Well, what's the latest?" he asked.

"Bucky is not my father but my uncle. I spoke with Macy's son, Lance, a doctor and a medical director like Steve. He will call me back tomorrow after he talks with his wife about the DNA test," I explained.

"I'm proud of you," Cap said as he squeezed my hand.

"Thanks for being supportive and understanding." I turned out the light and kissed him goodnight.

The following evening, Lance called. "I spoke to my wife, and I'll help you. Text me the info on getting the test, and I'll pay for it," he said.

"Thank you so much. This means a lot to me," I said.

"It'll be interesting to see how this pans out. I'll be in touch when I get the results," Lance added before ending the call.

I quickly texted him the company name, website, and phone number so he could order the DNA test. I also texted him my email address, cell phone number, and home address, along with a picture of his grandmother, father, and his uncles and their wives at a wedding they attended.

This was now the fourth DNA test I would be waiting for. I hoped the next six weeks would go by quickly. I was on the verge of finding out who my father was.

28

Finding my Father

I tried to focus on catching up with menial chores like business filings and paperwork that I had neglected. Three weeks into the DNA test wait, I spoke to Wendy, and she discovered she had breast cancer. I contacted Lance and gave him Wendy's phone number and email address. He provided information and connections to Wendy regarding her medical concerns.

Finally, six weeks passed, and Lance called. I was in my office.

"I got the test results. It would have been cool to have a half-sister, but we are cousins, and it looks like Irving is your dad," Lance said.

"You would've been a nice half-brother, but I'm glad we are at least cousins," I said. I told Lance about his Davidic ancestral lineage and promised to send him a notebook when I put one together. He had two grown sons who might be interested in learning about their ancestors, so they would pass it down to their children.

"Do you know the names of Irving's grown children?" I asked.

"You need to talk with my brother Jeffry. He was very close to Uncle Irving. Let me talk with him and have him call you," Lance offered.

So, I got off the phone with Lance and updated all my cousins. When I got into bed, I then updated Cap. "Looks like Irving is my dad. I don't know much about him, but Lance's brother was close to Irving. I will talk with Jeffry and learn about my father," I said.

I said goodnight to Cap and turned the light out. I thanked God for having brought me this far and for helping me identify who my father is. I looked forward to getting to know Irving through Jeffry.

A few days later, Lance texted me Jeffry's cell phone number. He was a psychologist. Lance said Jeffry was one of Irving's favorite relatives and that he would know a lot about him. Lance had filled Jeffry in on my search and suggested I call him.

Once again, I had to call a new relative, introduce myself, and ask questions. I felt the adrenaline surge through my body, and my heart rate sped up. It was a familiar feeling. I felt like I was on the edge of a swimming pool, wanting to jump in and escape the day's heat but fearful, anticipating the initial shock from the cold water. I decided to dip my foot in.

I texted Jeffry:

Hi! I'm Catherine, your new cousin! Would it be all right if I called you in 15 minutes?

Jeffry texted back:

Yes.

So, I waited fifteen minutes and made the call.
"Hello, this is Jeffry . . .," Jeffry answered.
"Hi! I'm Catherine and . . ."
"Yes, my brother Lance filled me in," Jeffry said. I was glad he interrupted me and steered our conversation. When I'm nervous, I

can be too talkative and take too much time to get to the point. He did read people for a living.

"Okay, thanks. I would like to know about Irving, my father," I said, feeling more grounded.

"Irving's first wife (I will call her wife #1) came from a family that owned a famous bakery company, which later became *Wonder Bread*. He worked for them briefly, and then Irving started his own law practice," he said.

"My dad was married to the Wonder Bread family?" I asked.

"Yes, and they had two children, a girl named Skippy whose married name escapes me, and a boy, Robert L., who became a theatrical director, changed his name to Bob Livingston, and went on to win a Tony Award," Jeffry added.

"I have a sister and a brother, and my brother won a Tony Award on Broadway?" I asked, feeling stunned.

"Yes. As a family, we have all lost touch. Irving's only sister had three children. One of them is very famous, Joel. He created the music festival Woodstock in upstate New York with two partners in 1969."

"Really? I wanted to go to that event so badly but was too young. To think it was created by my first cousin!" I said, getting surprises around every branch of my family tree.

"Irving divorced wife #1 and married his second wife (I will call her wife #2). Shortly afterward, they adopted Michael, and right after that, she got pregnant with Gail," Jeffry said.

"Another brother and sister," I observed, excited to meet them one day.

"Yes, and then they moved to the South Shore of Long Island. Then, when Gail was 2 1/2 years old and her brother Michael was

3, their mother committed suicide, leaving Irving to raise two small children," Jeffry explained.

"Oh no, how sad," I said, empathizing with the tragedy Irving faced. "What did he do?"

"He had to hire full-time live-in nannies because he worked long hours in Manhattan."

"Then what happened?" I asked.

"Irving had a flashy lifestyle. He dated a lot and was once involved with one of the McGuire sisters."

"Was he a ladies' man?" I asked.

"Irving liked an exotic female look, and to a Jewish man, no offense, it could mean a Shiksha—a Christian woman with blond hair," Jeffry added.

"You just described my mom's look, except she wasn't a Christian."

"Then, in early 1954, Irving married wife #3. She sang at your cousin Joel's bar mitzvah. Shortly after, Irving and his wife moved to Roslyn Estates."

"Roslyn is where I grew up. I had friends in Roslyn Estates," I said excitedly. I could have played on the street where Irving lived. I wondered if Irving knew I lived within a mile or two of him. Or was it Irving that made it possible for my parents to move from a one-bedroom apartment in the Bronx to buying a house in Roslyn while barely making ends meet on one meager secretary's salary?

"Irving did extremely well for an attorney with offices in the Empire State Building. He was very connected to the political and social circles of Manhattan. Irving met people for lunch meetings and networked with his connections all the time," Jeffry said.

The cover image of my first book, *Linking Up,* flashed across my mind. I wrote about my extensive networking in Virginia Beach, where I became well-connected regarding spiritual issues and projects. I met people regularly at the Jewish Mother restaurant to help them find the resources they needed and network with others. Had I been following in my father's footsteps without knowing it? Was his DNA imprint for networking born into my genes like the story of the two sets of twins switched at birth, with similar inclinations? No one had taught me how to network and connect with people, yet it was as natural as breathing for me.

"He was a regular at Lindy's, the famous restaurant known for their cheesecake. He even had his own table with a little bronze plaque with his name engraved on it," Jeffry said, not knowing the reverie and insight his tales were sparking in me.

"My mother regularly met Mr. L . . . for lunch in the city. I knew Lindy's restaurant and remember going there with her to eat lunch and cheesecake numerous times," I told Jeffry. Was that where my mother met my father for their lunches together? Had I sat at and eaten at my father's table with her? I had never met him, but had he seen me there as a child with my mother? The puzzle pieces were now fitting together.

"Irving was also the attorney for the Damon Runyon fund," Jeffry said. Another bell rang off inside me.

"That is where my mother worked when I was conceived," I said, barely keeping up with the insights spurred by his information. That must have been where they would meet, and it started their relationship.

"Irving was a nice guy, but tough. He was gregarious and charming and was very generous."

"I need to ask you, did Irving have a coin collection?"

"I don't know about Irving, but my father did. Irving and him were very tight. They each had their own side of the street. One had a criminal law practice briefly, then became a police officer, and Irving was a probate lawyer. Irving was a giving person, often giving gifts and collectible coins to people he cared about," Jeffry said.

I told him about my coin collection and how it was linked to Mr. L . . . It had been my only clue about my father. "I never met him, but Mr. L . . . would send home an unusual gold or silver collectible coin for me every time my mother met him for lunch. I collected them as a young child. I had a full shoebox of coins by the time I was six years old. That was a lot of lunches," I said.

"I felt some affection for this mysterious Mr. L . . . because no one ever gave me gifts or thought of me as worthy of them," I admitted.

Jeffry had a wealth of information for me. I was able to take a walk through my father's life with his stories. I thanked him, but the words seemed a pale expression of what it meant to hear these details of Irving's life. I was overwhelmed with emotions. It felt like my brain was shutting down, and I could not think straight. I got off the phone and cried. The tears were a mixture of gratitude and grief. I was grateful to get a glimpse of who my father was and saddened that I would never get to see him, talk with him, go to lunch with him, or even hug him in this life.

For a few days, I processed a lot of emotions concerning the discovery of my father and made a few phone calls to my other cousins, updating them on Jeffry and Lance. One of them suggested I try to contact Joel. When I discovered Joel had been one of the creators of the Woodstock Rock Festival, a defining event and pivotal moment in music history, I thought it would be worth the effort. I tried looking for his number but failed to find it. My husband suggested I call 411.

"A public figure like Joel will not be listed in 411," I argued.

"You have nothing to lose. Try it," Cap suggested.

So, I called 411 and was given a phone number for Joel. I figured it was an old number, but I called it anyway. It rang and a man answered, "Hello."

"Is Joel there?" I asked, not expecting it to be him.

"This is him," Joel responded.

My mouth dropped. "It's Joel," I whispered to Cap.

"Hi, this is Catherine Fendig . . ." I explained my story to him and named the cousins I had been in touch with: Steve, Maida, Indie, Lance, and Jeffry.

"This is so interesting. It's not your usual call! I think you're legit because you have just named all my cousins," Joel said.

"I would love to hear what you knew about my dad. I know this is a lot to take in on a phone call. I could send you an email with family pictures and my information to verify my claim and for you to consider," I suggested.

"I'd like that. I'll give you my email address," Joel said.

"Thank you again. I'll send this off to you now," I said.

"Great! I'll get back to you," Joel said before ending the call.

I was impressed with how cordial he was on the phone. I have been so fortunate with each new family encounter, as unusual as they were at first.

That evening, I emailed him details about myself and information about his ancestral genealogy that I had received from Steven.

The following morning, I received a lengthy, detailed email from Joel. He shared that my father's third wife (whom I will refer to as wife #3) gave him his first guitar as a teenager. This started him on a lifelong journey into the music world that eventually led to conceiving and producing the Woodstock Festival.

We exchanged a few more emails over the next few months. Joel told me about his sister and brother, and I was able to have a few exchanges with his sister as well.

Had I finished my DNA search? Not at all! I wanted to find my two brothers and two sisters next, and I was eager to meet my cousins in person.

29

Brothers and Sisters

This year, Hanukkah took place in mid-December for eight days. Six days afterward was Christmas. Hanukkah falls on different dates each year based on the Hebrew calendar. It always falls on the 25th day of Kislev, the ninth month of the Hebrew calendar. Hanukkah can fall between late November and late December on the Gregorian calendar, which is what we use to mark the date to celebrate Christmas on December 25th.

I had always celebrated Christmas to remember the birth of Jesus. It is a time to give thanks for the love, hope, and joy found in Christ. There are many different traditions created around Christmas. For most people, it is getting a tree, decorating it, and buying gifts to exchange with family and friends on Christmas Day. The remarkable miracle Christmas celebrates is that God sent an angel, Gabriel, to Mary, a virgin engaged to Joseph. The angel told her she would become pregnant through the Holy Spirit, not needing a human father to propagate. The baby would be Jesus and God's manifestation in human form. He would grow up to provide great teachings to mankind.

Growing up in a predominantly Jewish community on Long Island, I observed my friends celebrating Hanukkah each year. It is known as the Festival of Lights and lasts eight days. Hanukkah commemorates the rededication of the Jewish temple after the Jews defeated the Syrian army. They needed oil to light the temple lamps to rededicate the temple, but they only had enough oil for one night. Miraculously, the oil lasted for eight nights. The holiday is a celebration of resilience, hope, and faith, as well as a remembrance of how the Jews did not turn away from God and their faith during difficult times but stood by their beliefs.

It is celebrated with a nightly menorah lighting. This is a nine-branched candlestick holder with a central flame that is higher than the four flames on each side. A new candle is lit each night, and by the eighth night, all candles are lit. Prayers may be said, reciting a blessing or scripture reading of some of the Psalms while lighting the candles. After the candles are lit, there can be singing of special hymns and eating traditional foods. I remember eating latkes (fried potato pancakes), Challah (a braided Jewish bread), Brisket (a simmered seasoned beef roast), and Matzo ball soup. Then, for dessert, rugelach (a pastry filled with nuts, dried fruit, or chocolate) or Kugel (a sweet casserole baked with egg noodles, sugar, eggs, raisins, and sour cream). Some families give each other a small gift each night.

This year, I celebrated Hanukkah to honor my Jewish heritage. I bought a menorah and candles. I also celebrated Christmas to honor my Christian heritage. My granddaughter was visiting us during Hanukkah, so I explained the story behind the menorah and told her I would give her a gift each evening after we lit the candles. She loved this tradition, and the period between Hanukkah and Christmas became her favorite time of the year.

Whether Jewish or Christian, it is a season to celebrate and acknowledge miracles. Over the past year, I have had a number of personal miracles to celebrate and be grateful for. The biggest one was family.

It was the eighth day of Hanukkah. I lit the candles as the sun went down, which was early in the winter. I said a prayer for my cousins and one for my siblings, whom I hoped to meet soon.

The following morning, I devoted the day to searching for Irving's grown children. He had two children from his first marriage, Bob and Skippy, and two from his second marriage, Michael and Gail. I printed a paper for each one and taped it to my office wall, adding to its growing collection of family members. Finding a sibling raised by my father would be the next closest thing to meeting him.

I chose to start with the oldest, Skippy. She was the firstborn and would know the most. I got my half-sister's married name and phone number through new family connections. Most of my cousins knew of Skippy but had not spoken to her in a long time. I did an internet search and found out she was married to the vice president of a multinational mass media and entertainment company. Her mother came from a family that created one of the major food chains responsible for *Wonder Bread*.

I was not stalking anyone, but doing these searches before I made an introductory call left me feeling like I was invading someone's privacy or personal space. The listing was on the internet, so it was public information. Still, I felt intimidated by her husband's level of achievement and that her family was so well-known. I refocused on my goal, which was to learn more about my father and to share the ancestry information with Skippy for her children and grandchildren. Of course, despite the twenty years between us, I was excited to connect with my sister.

I called her and introduced myself. I told Skippy about my search and all the circumstances and numerous DNA tests pointing

THE FATHER NOBODY KNOWS

to Irving as my father. "That would make us sisters. I would love to meet you," I said.

"How did you get my phone number?" Skippy asked.

"Through a cousin who knew your married name," I answered.

Skippy asked me a lot of questions and recognized I had been talking to members of the family she knew but had not stayed connected with. "I've had a good life. I'm married to a good man and have four grown children and ten grandchildren. I was not talking to Irving when he died," Skippy said.

"I'm sorry. That must have been difficult," I said.

"Why don't you come to my home for lunch next Sunday. I will call you during the week," Skippy said. She sounded open to meeting me. I accepted the invitation and was grateful to finally meet my half-sister. So, I planned to fly to New York for an overnight trip.

Two days later, Skippy called, "I've thought about it and don't want to visit the past. I'm sorry this happened to you. But I don't want any part of this. I wish you luck, but please don't call here again," Skippy said before the call disconnected. I didn't call her back to try again. I wanted to respect her privacy and this request. I knew that ruled out asking her for a DNA test.

Her words were sharp and stung me. I had gotten used to the kindness and open-mindedness shown to me by my cousins. I went to my meditation chair to reset my thoughts. It had become my safe place. I felt the residual pangs of shame caused by such rejections for something I had not done, which I first felt in my childhood. Jeffry said Irving's first marriage had ended in a nasty divorce. Maybe Skippy was reacting to wounds that had nothing to do with me. Hadn't I learned that lesson well from my Greek father and his anger toward me as a child for something I could not understand? I reminded myself that everything was okay and I had not caused her dismissive response. I was not guilty of some unknown infraction and could just let the shame wash off me. I surrendered the outcomes of this journey to my Higher Power, trusting God and reminding myself that what was best for all of us would unfold.

I wanted to feel good about myself and recognize that I had value. When I thought I was Greek, I tried to feel like how they responded to other Greeks, as if they were long-lost brothers. When I went into a Greek restaurant, I always shared that I was of Greek descent. The owner, cook, or waiter always asked where my relatives came from. Were they Spartans or from Athens? Were they from the North or South? In those moments, I felt like I mattered. It was a connection with strangers, even though it was small and fleeting; it felt good to have a national identity. I just wish my father had been proud to have a Greek daughter.

I was grateful to have found three more siblings. I decided to start with the two younger ones from Irving's second marriage. Maybe they would be more open to talking to me since Irving's marriage to their mother ended through death and not divorce. Then, I could come back to find my brother, Skippy's sibling, from Irving's first broken marriage.

I sat in my meditation chair quietly, reflecting on the importance of finding my sister, Gail. I prayed for help locating her and kindness and care in our future exchanges. I made a cup of coffee and then sat down at my computer. I began my search for Gail L . . . in New York. The first two entries that popped up were obituary notices. I read through them. One was Gail's because her parents were listed as Irving and his wife. The notice reported that she died surrounded by loving family and friends after a heartbreaking battle with breast cancer. She was only eight years older than I. I felt my heart sink. I was not going to get to know her. Our life paths had missed each other by only one year. I had to catch my breath. I had not expected to see her obituary.

After I stared at my ancestry wall, stunned, I took a deep breath and read through the rest of the obituary. Gail had attended my High School, if not in the same years. Then, she got a BS degree in Sociology and worked at the AA headquarters in Manhattan. Gail returned to school for graduate studies in Holistic Health with a certification in psychology. She was a therapist, channeled teachings from an ascended master, and was an author. She was happily married and left behind a stepson, a soul daughter, her brother Michael L . . . and his wife, longtime soul sisters, and countless other cherished friends and students.

In this snapshot view of her life, it looked like she was happy and loved. Friends and sisterhood were vital to her. We had shared some apparent parallels and common interests: counseling, AA, the supernatural, writing, teaching, learning, and reaching out to others. What would it have been like to meet her and talk? Why had our lives just missed intersecting by months? Were our life paths and interests inherited? Were they locked away in our gene pool? It certainly seemed that way.

I read over her obituary again. She was an author, and I immediately searched for her online. I saw she had written an autobiographical story of her soul alignment process. I zoomed in on the cover. There was a picture of her sitting in a chair. I could see the similarities in our facial features: nose, forehead, eyes, and smile. I ordered a copy online. As an author, I was grateful she had left her insights and story behind for others to read.

I did not look for my brother that day. I saw in her obituary that she had left behind her brother, Michael. I decided not to think about him for the rest of the day. This discovery had been emotionally draining. At least I now knew more about Gail when I found Michael.

The following morning, I woke up early. I went down to the beach for a walk to greet the sunrise. I loved the early morning dawn because very few people were out. The air was fresh and cool. As I walked along, I felt my anticipation of the sun just beginning to peek over the horizon. Slowly, it moved up, exposing more of its light and bright fiery colors, until it surfaced in full glory like an orchestra crescendo.

Years earlier, a friend told me how, one evening, he answered the door. Two policemen informed him that his parents' private plane had just crashed, and they had lost their lives. My friend was close to his parents. Friends and family began to fill the house. He said it was one of his life's longest and worst nights. "How did you make it through?" I had asked him.

"A funny thing happened the next morning. The sun came up," he said assuredly.

I always remembered his story. That is what a sunrise does for you. Life continues despite its heartaches.

I had experienced a sad and disappointing start to finding my siblings, but the sun rose this morning. I decided to look for my brother Michael. He had been close to Gail.

Michael was my adopted brother from Irving's second marriage. I knew his mother passed away when he was only a toddler. We were not genetically connected, but Irving raised him, and I hoped he would tell me more about my father and my sister Gail's life. I sat at my computer to search for Michael L. from New York. The first entry that popped up was an obituary notice. My heart stopped. I held my breath. "Please don't let this be my brother," I whispered. I read through it. It listed my father and his second wife as his parents. He was 67 when he passed, only six months after my sister Gail died and six months before my first DNA test and my family discovery. He had been a social worker, a musician, a songwriter, and a performer. He had been married and had children and stepchildren. It looked like he had lived a good life. I was stunned and saddened. Death was so final. At least with Skippy, there was still a slim chance that we could meet and talk one day. There was no chance I could meet my father, sister, and brother.

A few days after I found that both Michael and Gail had passed away shortly before I could find them, I saw an episode in the docuseries *Long Lost Family* entitled, *If I Had Only Known About Her*. It was about a woman who longs to meet her biological father, a man she credits for saving her life during an emotionally turbulent childhood, even though they never met. I was in tears watching the story unfold, thinking about my father and siblings who had passed before I had a chance to talk with them.

I was sure I grew up in a home in Roslyn and attended one of the top ten high schools in New York State, thanks to Irving's generosity. I knew financially that my parents could not afford to buy that house and give me that school experience, which I think saved me. It was so ironic to realize I went to the same high school as my brother and sister, if eight and nine years apart. But if we had been closer in age, we could have been in the same class and not known we were siblings. I could have become friends with Gail, gone to her house, and not known we were sisters.

Once again, I put down my search for my siblings. It had been painful. After a few days, I woke up early and headed to the beach for my sunrise walk. It was overcast and cooler than usual. There weren't many birds out either. As I walked, I kept looking for the sun. I knew it was behind the clouds, and I just couldn't see it. It was how I felt about my sibling search. As I was finishing my walk, I saw a few rays of sunshine stream through a hole in the cloud cover above the horizon. It was mystical and magical, providing confirmation that the sun was still rising and giving me hope. Then, the ray vanished behind the clouds. I drove home.

30

My Father's Ring

I had one older brother left to track down. I had heard that he had some success with Broadway musicals during the 70s. I hoped it would be easy to find him. He was my last chance to connect with a sibling.

Once again, I started a search on the internet and put his name in Bob Livingston, New York. There were numerous entries for his name. Reading the first one, I found that my brother had been involved in the theatre and TV as a playwright and director. He received two Tony Award nominations for a Broadway musical, one of which won the best Broadway musical award one year. The title was *The Me Nobody Knows*! My heart skipped a beat. I felt like *The Me Nobody Knows*.

Did he know about the affair? I quickly looked up the storyline and found the Broadway show was a musical that explores the fears and aspirations of a multiracial group of young people from low-income neighborhoods in New York over a single day.

I then returned to my original search for Bob and was excited about what he had written for TV. I saw some familiar shows he had worked on, such as *Maude* and *All in the Family*. One article described him as a force of nature—a complicated and charming man with a big personality and multiple talents.

Then I clicked on what was an obituary. I took a deep breath and held it. Was this some cosmic joke? How could everyone have passed away just before I arrived? He died only a year and a half before I took my DNA test. I walked away from the computer. This wasn't fair. I sat in my meditation chair and cried. Why?

My search for my siblings came to an abrupt stop. Where was my ray of sunshine and the hope I placed in this search? I felt like the *The Me Nobody Knows* title ironically described my past place in the family as the product of an affair.

Over the next few days, I practiced acceptance of the outcome of the sibling search. Recovery taught me my peace lay in the practice of acceptance. I never got to meet my siblings, and I never got to meet my father. That was reality. Or, as some say, *It is what it is*.

I wanted something to make me feel connected to my father. I wanted a piece of jewelry, something I could wear to remind me that our connection was real. I wanted a ring, maybe one with his birthstone in it.

It was three weeks before Christmas. My Christmas present to myself would be a ring in remembrance of my Father. I had a budget of $300. It's not enough for a new or elaborate ring, but maybe I could find a second-hand one on eBay. I began searching and found one I liked. I put a bid for as high as I could afford. I watched it—no other bids. Anticipating acquiring my new piece of jewelry, I watched the last two minutes of the bidding countdown. Thirty seconds to go, and the ring was mine. Then, moments before the bidding ended, a higher one flashed across the screen, and then it closed. I lost the ring. It was more than a ring. It had become a symbol connecting me to the Father I never had. I felt that old, familiar emptiness in the pit of my stomach. Finally, I surrendered to the inevitable and turned the computer off.

Alone in my office, the following evening, I prayed and talked with God. "Maybe that was not the ring you had intended for me . . . But it feels important to have something that can symbolize a relationship with my father. Dear God, you know my heart. Could you lead me to the perfect ring? Thank you!"

Once again, I scrolled through the rings offered for sale on eBay. In only a few minutes, I found another acceptable ring. I put my bid in. A few nights later, I sat and watched the last few minutes of bidding. This time, I saved my highest bid for the last minute. There had been no activity all day on it. I knew I had it this time, and I got excited, finally, to have my ring in honor of my Father! I pushed enter for my last and final bid with only seconds to go. Immediately after, a higher offer was received and flashed across the screen, and the window closed. Sold to the highest bidder, and it was not me! Disappointment washed over me. I shut the computer and went to bed.

"Why can't I get a ring to remember my dad by?" I asked God, trying to resist having a spiritual temper tantrum. After all, I already felt shortchanged in many areas of my life. I didn't hear any response from above, so I decided to continue searching for the elusive ring on eBay. Over the next few weeks, the same bidding scenario repeated. Finally, I realized that God was not interested in me finding a memorial ring; hence, there was no grace, special favor, or blessings on this pursuit. I just had to go it alone. Christmas came and passed, no ring, no father memento! I had to resist feeling bad for myself. It was just a ring.

I sat in my meditation chair. It was time to talk with my Higher Power. "What is up?" I asked. I started to cry. "I can't meet any of my brothers and sisters. Why would you let me know about my DNA right after all three of them passed away? It felt bad enough that I couldn't meet my father. On top of that, I can't even successfully bid on a little remembrance ring for him," I blurted out through my tears.

After I cried it out, I sat quietly with my eyes closed. It felt good to cry and empty my heart. I listened in the silence, but I didn't hear anything. Was anyone listening? It didn't feel like it.

The day after Christmas, an unexpected miracle occurred. Just when I thought it would be impossible to connect with my brother since he had passed away, I had a strong feeling to look at Bob's obituary. I never finished reading it that day. There, I saw that he left behind a wife of 27 years. His wife's name was listed. What if I could find her? What if she could share things with me about my brother? She would be the perfect person to tell me about my brother's life and Irving's.

Using some of my newfound investigative people-finder skills, I located Ruth. After I told her about the journey that led me to her, I sent her the DNA test results of my connection to his family. "Maybe Bob or Irving led you to me," Ruth said. We both got the chills and goosebumps.

I learned she also had a strong spiritual side, so the goosebumps would become a regular occurrence in conversations about our connection. Ruth was a psychologist with a private practice. She lived off Times Square in an apartment she and Bob had had for years.

I knew she was the closest person to my brother, and if she was open to seeing me, I could get to know my brother through her. So, she invited me to lunch at her place in Manhattan. I wanted to go as soon as possible so she wouldn't change her mind. I booked a flight for January 4th, the anniversary of Bob's death.

On the morning of my flight, it was snowing heavily in New York. Many flights were canceled, but not mine. I was eager to meet

Ruth. I arrived and took a cab directly to her apartment. She was beautiful and greeted me warmly, which helped ease my nerves. She had made a lovely salad for lunch, topped with chunks of baked salmon.

After she talked about my brother for some time, Ruth stopped mid-sentence and excused herself from the table. Then, she left the room and returned with a little gift box. "This is something for you!" she said as she handed it to me.

As I unwrapped it, she explained, "Friends of mine tried to talk me out of giving this to you, but I felt guided."

What could be in the box? Then I saw it—a beautiful gold ring with a diamond on it.

"That's your father's ring!" she explained. "It was given to him on his Bar Mitzvah when he was 13 by his parents, your grandparents. By the diamond are his initials. When he grew older, he wore it as a pinkie ring. Then he gave it to your brother. When we married, your brother gave it to me as an engagement ring, and I wore it for 27 years until his death."

"But how could you know about me wanting a ring? I've been trying to buy a ring in memory of my Father for weeks!" I was baffled.

She gasped! "I woke up one morning last week with a clear, intuitive directive to give you your father's ring!"

We both sat in silence, staring at the ring. I put it on, and it fit perfectly. Indeed, my prayers had been heard. Had the reason for my numerous unsuccessful attempts at bidding to secure an eBay ring been because God had my Father's "real ring" laid aside for me? Had Heaven's Gate brought us together on the anniversary of my brother's passing to feel the love that continues after death?

THE FATHER NOBODY KNOWS

Meeting my brother's wife and receiving my father's ring gave me a new awareness of an old principle of living.

Things are not always what they seem!

"Do you know what the symbolism of a ring is?" Ruth asked.

"What does it stand for?" I asked.

"It is a symbol of love and affection, but also of eternity. A ring is an unbroken circle without a beginning or end. Your story comes full circle with love," she explained.

"I can't thank you enough," I said, wiping my tears away.

"I'm so happy you have your ring, and we are in each other's lives. You have helped me lift some of my grief. Thank you," Ruth said as she squeezed my hand.

We spent the rest of the afternoon looking at pictures of my brother, his childhood, my father, Ruth, Bob's wedding, and the celebration service of Bob's life. Ruth gave me a lot of pictures to take home, especially of my father.

We had spent hours sitting at the kitchen table, intimately sharing our thoughts and feelings with each other. We both felt like we were not the only ones in the room and that the unseen forces of love had brought us together to help fill an empty space in our hearts. Before I left, we cried again and had spiritually confirming goosebumps. "Bob would have loved to have you for a sister, and you would have loved him," Ruth said, wiping tears from her eyes. "It's as if you've brought Bob back to me, or perhaps he brought me to you, or you to me. Either way, we live on through each other. Which is so comforting," she said as we hugged, promising to keep in touch. I was so blown away by the day.

Before I left for the airport the following afternoon, I looked up the address of Lindy's restaurant. Sadly, the one where Irving had a private table had closed in 1969.

Even with me having four siblings, I could not get a DNA test regarding my father. I would never meet my two brothers and sister, who had passed away just before I discovered them. Nor would my older sister take a test since she did not want to talk about her past.

The miracle of having my father's actual ring was more powerful than any DNA test result. I looked at my hand with awe and wondered how my father's bar mitzvah ring from 1923 was now on my finger. Do I need more proof of who my father was?

When I got home, I checked my DNA match list one more time. There was a new and close DNA match. It was Skippy's granddaughter. Did she look at my name with curiosity? Did she wonder *how a perfect stranger was so closely related to her?* Unless Skippy had a change of heart, I would remain unknown in her family for now.

31

Rabbi Rachel

The cousins in New York were now communicating on a group email thread, which included me. There was talk of holding a reunion weekend in New York. Friday night would be a small gathering of the first cousins, their spouses, and me. Cap could not come due to our business and his commissioner's duties. The reunion would serve two purposes: I could meet them, and they could all see each other after a long absence—forty years for some—from their lives. We all set a date for two months. One cousin made a joke that I was the Shiksa who brought the family together again.

I remember hearing Jeffry telling me that Irving liked blond Shiksas. I Googled the name for more clarity and found that it referred to a gentile woman or a Jewish woman who does not follow Orthodox religious teachings and rules. Fair enough, I thought. I was happy to be the Shiksa that brought the family back together again.

I felt compelled to call Rabbi Rachel from our local Temple Beth Tefilloh. I met her briefly during a community leadership meeting on the homeless issue with my husband, Cap. In a town with churches of all sizes on every street corner, Rabbi Rachel was often lovingly called the *Chief Rabbi* of the County because she was the *only* one. Outside our area, the closest Jewish communities were an hour north or south of us. Rabbi Rachel often spoke to other faith groups, offering her understanding of the Jewish framework for dialoguing and connecting people of different faiths. I respected her for reaching out and forming an alliance with the pastors of other churches to better our community. I thought she represented the temple well. When I met her, I was drawn to her energy. She had her feet well planted on the ground, was a visionary, and could also talk about issues of the heart.

When I called the rabbi and told her I had something personal to discuss, she suggested we meet at a local cafe. I shared about finding my biological Jewish family, and she expressed genuine interest and was supportive. We discussed my spiritual journey of being raised in an abusive atheist home, studying Eastern philosophies, the New Age, and the supernatural. I shared having numerous prophetic dreams in my twenties, and then I moved to Georgia, where I first read the Bible and joined a Recovery Bible study group for many years. Then, I studied under internationally known evangelists. I told the rabbi I was dedicated to whatever approach to God I was learning.

Rabbi Rachel said, "Yours is a story about Joseph. He had to endure many hardships until he found his place and purpose. I'm glad you're going to meet your Jewish family. You can call me while you are gone if you need to talk. Otherwise, when you return, we will get together to process your feelings and see where you want to go from there."

My search for God continued to take me to unexpected places.

Cousin Steve (listed at Adrienne) from California emailed me with news about a new family member. He recently met another cousin who did a TV commercial for Ancestry. He sent me her picture, and we looked just like sisters. The resemblance was uncanny.

Whenever we found another family member, it felt like a new baby was born, even though many of us were in our 50s, 60s, and 70s. "What a story! Now we have a cousin in TV commercials for Ancestry," Steve said enthusiastically.

I filled him in on the plight of my brothers and my sister, Skippy, and Ruth's gift of my father's ring. "You've done well. I'm proud of how you are bringing this family together," Steve said.

"I couldn't have done it without you!" I said gratefully.

"We've come a long way. When you first contacted me, I was very suspicious. I even contacted my sister, a lawyer in the attorney general's office," Steve said, laughing.

"I'm glad you finally came to trust me," I said.

"You can thank Cap; his letter gave us a broader perspective," Steve said.

"Yes, my husband really came through for me."

"Here's the big question. Adrienne, our grandson, and I want to visit you on St. Simons Island for a week. Are you ready to meet your cousins?" Steve asked.

"Yes! Please come! When?" I answered excitedly.

"Is next week too soon?" Steve asked.

"Tomorrow isn't even too soon!" I answered. We both laughed.

We talked about their travel plans. Their grandson, Tyler, was 13 years old. He loved golfing, and so did Cap, so we added that to their itinerary. We have some of Georgia's best golf courses. They would fly into our local airport in Brunswick. "How will I recognize you at the airport?" Steve asked.

"I'll be the only one standing at the one gate," I said, laughing. I heard Steve laugh at that. He was used to flying out of Los Angeles International Airport, which had nine terminals and 146 gates.

THE FATHER NOBODY KNOWS

The following week, I was waiting at the gate for my cousins. It was the only flight due in, and they arrived on time. We greeted each other and hugged. I was elated to have my family visit me. This was a new experience. We walked them over to the baggage pick-up, where there was one small luggage go-round, and there was only one on it. We had another laugh.

When we arrived at our home, Steve's wife, Adrienne, noticed my dog statue near the door when we walked onto the front porch. It was a peculiar possession I acquired a year ago. A friend who was selling her house had this dog statue. She wasn't sure if she wanted to keep it. I became obsessed with wanting to buy it from her. I don't know why I felt compelled to get it. It was of a tall, slim greyhound dog sitting at attention. It was painted solid black.

"Look at the dog statue," Adrienne said with some surprise, pointing it out to Steve.

"You like it?" I asked.

"I love it! We have the same statue at our home. We named it Lurch. Maybe they are cousins, too," Adrienne exclaimed. Was that why I was obsessed with acquiring that dog statue? Nonetheless, I treasured showing my new family around my now small southern hometown.

We went inside and met Cap. They were impressed with his southern accent and warm hospitality. I showed them around our old southern beach cottage, and then we sat down to breakfast. I served assorted bagels, lox, vegetable cream cheese, capers, onions, tomatoes, an assorted fruit tray, and coffee. It was so easy to talk with them, and Steve had the same weird sense of humor as I did. We all laughed throughout our breakfast.

Then we took them on one of our Trolley history tours of the island and had lunch in the village by the pier. Steve and Adrienne loved the small-town feel of the island as we later walked along the street and perused the little tourist shops. We chose one of the sweet shops to sample homemade chocolates, settling on a scoop of homemade ice cream.

"This place feels like a throwback in time," Steve observed as two little boys rode by us on their bicycles.

"Yes, very different than growing up in Brooklyn and the City," I said.

We filled each day with tours, activities, golf, good meals, laughter, and sharing stories. On our last day together, I called Rabbi Rachel and told her my cousins were visiting from California. "I would love to meet them. Would you like to bring them to the temple?" she asked. I excitedly accepted her kind invitation.

After lunch, we drove to Temple Beth Tefilloh in Brunswick. The rabbi met us there and took us on a temple tour. "This temple is the center of our Jewish community here and is 127 years old. It was established in 1886. The name of our temple means House of Prayer," Rabbi Rachel explained. We all looked up at the soaring ceiling and admired the elaborate molding design and the warmth of the native pine wood used, darkened with age from its protective shellac coating. The sun lit up the colorful stained glass used throughout the temple.

Then Rabbi Rachel showed us the temple's Torah scrolls. One of the scrolls was 150 years old. "I discovered that when they built the temple 130 years ago, they buried a time capsule in the Tabby wall. It is to be opened when it is 250 years old. That leaves only 120 years to go," Rabbi Rachel told us. "Remember to tell your children to tell their children so they can see what's in the time capsule!"

"That may happen, knowing this family," Steve responded. We all smiled at each other.

It was fascinating to think that information and historical items can be passed through the generations of time, but we only get to meet three or four generations during our lives, if we are lucky. Yet weren't our DNA, our genes, also like time capsules? Didn't they hold secrets from our ancient history, only to be revealed long after our ancestors were gone? Steve then shared with Rabbi Rachel the genealogist's findings regarding our connection to King David through Rabbi Meir and our lineage to him, which led to a more interesting conversation.

"I'm hoping some cellular memory will kick in when I take the rabbi's Judaism 101 class," I added. I noticed Steve nod at the rabbi. We all smiled.

We thanked the rabbi and told her I would see her again when I returned from New York.

But it was time to take them to the airport. Their time here had ended. I picked them up at the hotel and drove them to the airport. "You don't have to go through the hassle of parking; you can just drop us off," Steve offered.

While he was talking, I pulled into a parking space adjacent to the entrance with no parking fees. "You're still in Brunswick. It's easy," I said. We all laughed again.

After we checked their bags through, I walked them to the gate. Boarding had begun. I felt a pang in my heart as I hugged each of them goodbye. I didn't want them to leave. They felt like real family, my family, and the whole week had been so positive. It was a new experience for me—something most people have throughout their lives. My heart was filled, but I held back my tears. I was not good at saying goodbye. I gave Steve the last hug. I noticed he wiped a tear from each eye. I did the same. "We'll call you when we get in," Steve said.

"Thank you for coming. It was amazing," I said, and my cousins smiled and walked through the gate.

I walked back to my car alone. I started to drive down the road and pulled the car over. I didn't need to hold back the tears any longer. I already missed them. As a child, I felt starved from a lack of family and connection. I knew this existed, saw it in my friends' families, and longed for it. I felt a genuine family connection with Steve and his family, which wasn't based on sharing a history over time; it was just there.

A few weeks later, I received a self-published book from their visit, along with pictures from our escapades, and a warm thank-you note. I wrote back to express how I felt and what they meant to me.

My next family outing would be with my cousins and their spouses from New York, coming to Indie's to see each other after 40 years of losing touch for some of them. It was a big family reunion and an opportunity for me to meet some of them for the first time.

32

A Shiksa Reunites the Family

Finally, I got a taxi that could take me to Indie's. It was raining, and there was a lot of traffic. I was nervous. The Jamaican taxi driver started a conversation that led to my story coming out. As we arrived at my destination, I was a bit calmer. It helped to tell the taxi driver the details of my DNA search that led to this reunion.

"Everything is gonna be okay," he reassured me.

We pulled up to a beautiful new building on the waterfront with lights from the New York City Skyline in full view. There was valet parking. I handed the driver a big tip, although you couldn't put a price tag on the comfort he gave me. "Go along. Go discova ya family. They goin' to love you," he said as I stepped out of the cab.

The doorman escorted me into the lobby, where there was a security check and ID clearance. I took the elevator and got off at the tenth floor. My family would be on the other side of the next door I walked through. Would I be facing another rejection like how my father treated me my entire life, or would they accept me as family? I took a step forward and opened the door.

Indie met me and gave me a big hug. "I can't believe you're here! My new cousin," she said as I followed her into the living room, where the other cousins were gathered.

THE FATHER NOBODY KNOWS

I saw Maida, Indie's sister, whom I had talked to on the phone. We gave each other a big hug. "It's really you!" Maida said with excitement.

"Yup, she's Irving's! Look at the resemblance," Jeffry said, coming over to give me another hug. I then met their spouses, who were just as kind and welcoming. I was grateful that my biological family did not make me feel any less legitimate, given I was Irving's child through an affair.

We all sat down on the couch and chairs around the coffee table. Indie had made a festive charcuterie board filled with cheeses, hummus, dips, nuts, and an array of colorful cut-up vegetables. I sat on the couch facing a breathtaking view of the New York City skyline seen through floor-to-ceiling glass walls.

We started recounting my first phone call to each cousin. We were all laughing at how we felt on both sides of the call. "I was so nervous," I admitted.

"I was confused and speechless and had to hand the phone to my husband," Maida said with a chuckle.

"I would have been okay with having a new sister," Jeffry said.

There was so much good energy behind the reminiscing and laughter. I felt an instant connection with my cousins. It was unexpected and magical at the same time. It was like we recognized each other on a deeper level.

Then Jeffry brought out his bar mitzvah photo album, and we all gathered around him. Page by page, they identified relatives and retold their childhood memories. It was fun to see all of them rekindle their memories of when they were young.

"Remember Irving's beautiful winged yellow Cadillac convertible?" Jeffry asked.

"I remember going to his house in Roslyn and swimming in that big built-in pool," Indie said.

"He gave my parents his wrought iron and glass patio table from that house," I said, describing it in detail, "but I never got to meet him."

"I remember that table and eating at it after swimming," Maida said enthusiastically.

How was it possible that we never knew each other, but the table they ate at as children made it to my house when I was six?

Jeffry turned to Maida. "Your dad, Bucky, went to Cornell along with Macy and her dad, Irving."

"I didn't know they all went to Cornell," Indie said.

The lively conversation continued as they compared childhood memories. We all had a similar sense of humor, and as I experienced with my cousin Steve from California, we laughed a lot.

"But why haven't any of us kept in touch?" Indie asked.

"Well, it took a Shiksa to bring us back together," Jeffry said as he raised his wine glass.

Two hours of storytelling just flew by. We then sat down at the dining room table. Indie had prepared a five-star, mouthwatering dinner of filet mignon, salmon with a pesto garnish, sauteed asparagus, broccoli, sourdough bread, and a couscous and tomato dish.

After dinner, I gave each cousin an ancestral packet I made of the research Steve had found through his genealogist. We discussed the ancestry findings over coffee and chocolate truffles.

"Have your beliefs changed after finding out about being Jewish?" Indie asked.

"Being Jewish can be your race or religion, or both," Maida's husband explained.

"I'm proud of my heritage. I have often said to my husband and friends, 'I feel Jewish,' and grew up with Jewish friends in Roslyn. Maybe I had a psychic sense about that. It makes sense because I've always had a strong passion for God. While I believe in Christ, I want to explore this new part of my spiritual life with Rabbi Rachel when I get home," I shared.

"Well, I never had a bat mitzvah," Maida admitted.

"Maybe we can have one together!" I said. We all laughed.

After discussing our King David heritage, we took pictures together and said goodnight. One of the cousins was staying in a hotel in Manhattan and offered to drive me to my hotel.

The following afternoon, Cousin Jeffry and his wife picked me up, and we went to Maida's home for a barbecue. Their grown children, spouses, girlfriends and boyfriends, and extended family, including Ruth (my brother Bob's widow), were coming. Maida's suburban house was large enough to accommodate all of us.

We all arrived at nearly the same time. Soon, the house was filled with introductions, conversations, and much laughter. Maida's house was a split-level, so different groups gathered on each floor level. Salads, casserole dishes, and desserts were brought and placed on the long outdoor table on the back porch to accommodate everyone for a sit-down meal.

As I walked from one room to the next, I saw one of the adult children, who was Orthodox, wrap a thin black leather strap around his uncle's left arm. I learned this is *Tefillin*, worn for daily morning prayers. It is put on the weaker of one's two arms to show that we cannot overcome our adversaries without the grace of God. I liked what the practice represented. There was so much I did not know about Judaism. What I did know was that God was leading me step by step to find my Jewish family.

A SHIKSA REUNITES THE FAMILY

When the food was ready, we all sat down at the patio table. The table was filled with family, spanning three generations. Everyone I met was engaging, kind, and respectful. During the meal, I found that one of my cousins and I had many parallel experiences, including broken ankles, cancer, and angel encounters. She gave me the book *Toward a Meaningful Life* by Rebbe Menachem Mendel Schneerson.

Another cousin gave me our grandmother's recipe for pot roast, a family favorite. I soaked in the deep feelings of family ties that I had longed for my entire life. How was it possible at fifty-nine that this was my first experience of this feeling?

After we finished our meal, we took a group picture. I remembered the Easter dinner I had attended when I first met Cap's family. There were twenty-three of us in their family photo that day. Back then, I thought about how I missed having relatives who could make up a large family resembling Cap's. I now marveled at how God had created an equally large family for me. It seemed an impossible dream I had forgotten a long time ago. Besides Cap's, I had friends who had family photos with lots of relatives in them. Now, I had one of my own. I looked at the pictures on my phone in amazement. I looked like my cousins. This was my family.

The day before I left, Indie, Maida, and their husbands drove us to Roslyn, Long Island, to visit Irving's home. My biological father lived only two miles from the house where I grew up. I recognized it immediately as we drove down his street. I had friends from school in that neighborhood, and when I played there, little did I know I was near my father's home.

We drove up a large circular drive. The front entrance was impressive, with four white two-story columns lining the portico. On either side of the front entrance were the original ornate cement statues sculpted into the wall. It reminded me of a senator's or high-ranking official's home. It was so beautiful that it was once featured in *Architectural Digest* magazine.

Before I came to New York for the cousins' reunion, I looked up the address of my father's home. He had not lived there in decades. I found the present owner and contacted her to see if I could see the inside of her house. I had become very proficient at finding people.

I told her my story, and she said her best friend had just had a similar experience after taking her DNA test. I wondered how many secret affairs from the 50s, 60s, and 70s were now being brought to light. Because of the owner's personal experience of her friend's DNA search, she agreed to let me see the house the day we visited Roslyn. Even though she would not be there, the woman allowed us to walk around the property and look in the windows. She let her maid know to expect us.

Inside, the house had retained its original splendor with high ceilings, intricate moldings, and stunning wood floors. It was decorated in period pieces from the 1920s. There was a grand dining room with a table that seated twenty. There was a library, a parlor, and a large living room with a piano. The backyard's landscaping resembled an English courtyard surrounding a large built-in pool. Suddenly, I remembered my parents going to Mr. L.'s house to pick up furniture. My brother and I were not allowed to go. But I knew it was the nice man who gave me those coins over the years. I wondered why we couldn't go. They returned with a beautiful glass, wrought iron dining set and six chairs. It was an outdoor set, but my parents were so broke that it became a prized possession and was used as our dinner table. My Greek father kept it until just before he died, and I sold it. I was looking at the spot that was the original placement for my father's poolside dining table. I felt complete seeing the home he lived in, even though I had lost the table.

When I described the table and chairs, they remembered them. Indie and Maida reminisced about swimming in the pool while their father talked with their uncle Irving. They remembered wife #3 as being beautiful, but she spent more time indoors while they were there.

The day before I returned from New York, I met a childhood friend, Linda, who lived in Queens. I had told her I thought I had found Irving's gravesite. Eight months earlier, I had unsuccessfully tried to find online where Irving was buried.

Then, a few days before I left for New York, Irving's name and grave locator popped up on my genealogy app. It was Irving's birth name and death date. I thought I had finally found his burial site. I looked up the cemetery and found it was in Queens, only a mile from where my childhood friend Linda lived. She offered to pick me up from the train station and take me to the cemetery before I flew home.

We went to the beautiful Mount Carmel Cemetery. In the new section, people's faces were imprinted on the headstones. We drove to the older section and found the listed block number. I immediately noticed that the headstone was a double marker. The name on the attached headstone was Sarah, his beloved wife. I thought, who's Sarah? I hoped it was not another disappointment. Then I saw Irving's name wasn't spelled right, and this man was nineteen years older than Irving when he died.

Linda came up behind me and asked who Sarah was. I came all this way to pay homage to my father, but found that this man wasn't my father, Irving. I did discover that my grandparents were buried in an even older section of the cemetery, but unfortunately, it was an abandoned and uncared-for section behind locked gates. I found a picture of their tombstones online. We walked around the cemetery a little bit longer. Linda and I had grown up playing in the Roslyn Cemetery since our houses were next to it. The cemetery always seemed quiet and magical to us as 6-year-olds.

We both came from very abusive homes, so we spent most of our free time on the street or in the cemetery playing. Linda's father worked for Bob Hope, Sid Ceaser, and Red Skelton. They had two baby grand pianos in the living room of an immaculate house that we were never allowed inside. The stepmother kept all their food under lock and key. Linda would get random beatings or groundings depending on her stepmother's mood.

"How did we survive?" I asked her.

"Did we have a choice?" she responded.

We walked along in silence. I could sense she was reflecting on her life then and now, just as I was. "When you saw your father's mini-estate only two miles from where you lived, did you resent him for not doing more for you as a child?" Linda asked in a more somber tone.

"Honestly, I don't. I never met or knew my biological father. We kept our home life a secret. How could I expect him to know how bad it was? I never felt like I deserved more. It was all I knew," I answered Linda.

"But did you miss not getting to live the lifestyle your biological father had?" Linda asked.

"As a child, how can you miss what you never had or even knew about?" I said.

"That's true," Linda said thoughtfully.

"I know he contributed to my upbringing because we lived in a neighborhood with some of the best schools in the country that my parents couldn't afford. I'm grateful for that, and he left me with some nice cousins. Besides, if it weren't for Irving, we would not be friends," I said.

I hugged Linda and thanked her for going with me to look for Irving's gravesite. We went to her favorite pizzeria for a slice. Nothing beats New York pizza! Then, Linda drove me to the airport.

I planned to continue my search for his resting place.

33

The Closest Link

After the cousins' reunion, I kept thinking about Irving and his third wife. When I was six, I stopped hearing about my mother meeting Mr. L. for lunch, and the coin gifts also stopped coming. This was when Irving and his wife sold their house in Roslyn and moved to the city. Had wife #3 found out about me back then and stopped Irving's further contact with my mother? Or had she known all along about me and my mother?

Irving and his wife were together until he died. My cousins told me she was younger than he. Wife #3 was a Broadway star when I was conceived. What was she like? What happened to her after Irving's death? Had she continued her career on Broadway? Did she leave New York? Was she close to my sister and brother, Gail and Michael, who were young children when she married Irving?

Curiosity reigned, and I sat at my computer to discover what happened to wife #3. I did an internet search and found she was alive and living in Michigan. There was a picture of her and an article describing her as a former opera singer holding a signed Salvador Dali program. Then I saw an article reporting about wife #3 as an actress, singer, and dancer playing various leading roles in Michigan's theatre circles with a lengthy performance resume. They listed her accomplishments as being in several Broadway productions during the 1950s and even performing alongside Jackie

Gleason and Phil Silvers. The article mentioned her traveling worldwide, marrying, and helping to raise her husband's two small children.

Then, with a few more clicks, I found her home address and phone number.

I still had more questions about my father. How did he die? Where was he buried? No one seemed to know, and my attempts at locating his tombstone were futile.

It had been forty-seven years since Irving's passing, and his wife would have many answers. I know that she knew of my mother and Greek father. As I said earlier, Irving gave them a glass and wrought iron patio set before they moved from Long Island to Manhattan. I kept the patio set until my parents passed. I would have kept it if I had known it had belonged to my biological father.

There were no more lunch meetings after Irving left Roslyn and moved to Manhattan. My mother no longer worked in the city, and Irving didn't live in Roslyn. Had his wife known about me and made Irving cut all associations with my mother once and for all? Or were the timing and events of his move and absence all purely coincidental?

I wanted to reach out to wife #3. She would know my father well. They were in love and had been married for years. She was married to him when he died. She would know where he was buried and how he died. If she knew, I reasoned, the wound of his infidelity would not be as severe as it was when it first happened. Or would it? If she didn't know, how much pain would I cause now by her finding out about me?

It was a moral dilemma. In recovery, when doing the ninth step to make amends to people, the guideline suggests that making direct amends should be avoided if it can create new harm.

Recovery protocol also teaches us to examine our motives when considering taking any action. Are we considering the well-being of the other person? I sought spiritual counsel and made another appointment to meet with Rabbi Rachel.

I called the rabbi. We agreed to meet at the local cafe again for another update. I shared with her about meeting my biological family. "This is a beautiful story and experience you are having. It touches my heart. How can I help you?" Rabbi Rachel asked.

"Rabbi, I believe in Christ, but I also believe in God and love," I explained.

"How do you feel about discovering your Jewish roots?" she asked, looking me directly in the eyes warmly. I felt seen by her.

"I keep thinking of what a Jewish guide in Israel said. He had served as a guide for many Christian groups exploring Jerusalem and had many conversations with Christians, believing that Jesus was the Messiah and was returning one day. The guide shared that from a Jewish perspective, he does not believe the Messiah has come. The guide said, 'One day, when the Messiah comes, I will have one question for him. Have you been here before?'"

Rabbi Rachel said, "That is an important question, highlighting the difference between Christians and Jews on the issue of waiting for the Messiah. If you want to know more about the Jewish framework of precepts, consider attending our temple and one of my Torah classes." She gave me the schedule; I accepted the invite and marked my calendar.

"Rabbi, I have a pressing dilemma. Can I seek your counsel?" I asked.

"Please," she said, adjusting her posture in her chair.

"I've found my father's widow, and she is alive. He passed almost fifty years ago, but I'm sure she knew about me back then.

I want to reach out to her because I have questions only she can answer. What if my contacting her stirs up old wounds? I asked myself, is fifty years enough time to recover from infidelity and a secret love child? Is it wrong for me to try to reach out to her? What do I do?" I asked, letting out a deep breath.

"I can't tell you what to do. I can suggest you search and follow your heart," Rabbi Rachel said with a smile.

I was grateful Rabbi Rachel had come to oversee the Brunswick temple. I felt a genuine connection with her and looked forward to learning more about Judaism from her. I knew that female rabbis were rare. I never saw one growing up. I learned that the first woman to receive rabbinic ordination was in 1972. The rabbi had only been in Georgia for a few years. It felt like it was a divine orchestration to cross paths with her at this critical juncture in my life.

After considerable thought, I decided to follow my heart and reach out to Irving's wife. I called her phone number. It was a landline with a recorded message identifying her by name. I left a general message: *"Hi, this is Catherine Lake Fendig. I have recently talked with Maida, Indie, Lance, Ruth, and Joel. I discovered Irving is a close relative through a DNA test. I would welcome the opportunity to talk with you anytime. My phone number is 912 . . . . Thank you!"*

When I hung up, I felt my heart racing. What if she had answered the phone?

After a few days had passed, I tried again, leaving a phone message. No one returned my call. I made one more attempt to contact Irving's wife by writing a letter. I included pictures and background information on myself. I hoped to ease her concerns regarding my legitimacy and that I was who I said I was.

A month went by, and there was no response. There could be many reasons why she did not respond, ranging from poor health, travel, and lack of knowledge of who I was to total disinterest. I was disappointed and puzzled, but once again, I knew I had to release it.

Then, a few weeks later, I went to the mailbox and retrieved a package. I opened it to find my sister Gail's autobiography. Gail was an author and a counselor, and I wish I could have met her before she passed away. I made a cup of coffee and immediately went to my meditation chair to read it. When I opened the book to the first page, I found it was signed by her and said *Blessings!* It was the most significant author's signature I could have on my bookshelf.

Gail shared that since her father and stepmother were career-driven and worked long hours commuting to Manhattan, nannies were hired to care for her and her brother. Then, later, I read that after her father had passed away, her relationship with her stepmother became strained. I read that Gail and her stepmother had a dispute over Gail's inheritance, which ended up in court with an award made to Gail.

Could that be why wife #3 was not responding to my attempts to contact her? If she knew I was Irving's daughter, did she think I was trying to get money from her? I hoped not because I wasn't. On the other hand, maybe she knew about me and, like Skippy, did not want to talk about the past.

Irving's wife was the last and closest link to my father's past. Would I meet my stepmother? Where was my father buried, and what caused his death? I knew God had been orchestrating this search from the beginning. It seemed that an in-person meeting with her would be inevitable one day. But since she lived over 1,000 miles away, a fifteen-hour drive, and in a state I had no connection to, I wondered if this meeting would ever occur.

34

Somewhere in Time

Our tourist business is seasonal, with the busiest month of the year being July. There are no days off, and Cap compares it to being a farmer: "You have to bring in the harvest when the plants are ripe." So, if we do something for my birthday, we do it in the fall.

We were only a month away from the start of the next tourist season when Cap handed me an envelope with a bow. "It is an early birthday present, but we need to use it now," Cap said.

I opened the envelope. Inside were tickets to spend a long weekend on Mackinac Island, Michigan. It was a place Cap had visited in his youth and had always wanted to take me there. "What a surprise! Why now?" I asked, thinking he had forgotten about going back. It had been years since we had talked about it.

"It's time we took a little vacation that doesn't have to do with work, politics, or DNA. You've worked hard and have been supportive on all fronts," Cap said.

I happily accepted the gift. I had taken a lot of trips to New York without Cap because of our business and his commissioner's obligations. I had plans to take our granddaughter to California and the Grand Canyon next month as a gift for her graduation from elementary school.

Mackinac Island, 4.5 square miles, was noted for taking people on a passage back in time, being vehicle-free, with horse and buggy as the only mode of transportation. It became a tourist attraction and summer colony in the late 19th century. We were going to stay at the Grand Hotel, known for having the world's longest porch at 660 feet and for being where the movie *Somewhere in Time* was filmed. The movie was about playwright Richard Collier in 1972. While staying at the Grand Hotel, he becomes enamored with a photo of a turn-of-the-century stage actress. He discovers that by using self-hypnosis, he can will himself back in time to 1912, where he met with her in the hotel and fell in love with her.

I watched the movie. It is a fascinating romance about time travel and destiny. I felt like I was time-traveling by putting together the pieces of my mother's past affair and Irving's life half a century ago. The movie also made me think of wife #3, the Broadway stage actress, just like in the film. If only I could just talk with her. She would be my link to the past, like Richard Collier visiting the turn-of-the-century actress in the Grand Hotel.

It had been six months since I had thought about Irving's wife and a year since I tried to contact her through letters and voicemail. Suddenly, I remembered her last known address was in Michigan. I pulled up Google Maps and saw that she lived on the way to Mackinac Island. We were to fly into Detroit and rent a car to drive to the island ferry. This was my opportunity to find her.

I never identified myself as Irving's daughter; I was only a relation. But she knew who I was. I could feel it. Irving's affair with my mother must have been painful for her. It was not her fault or mine. But we were the only two left alive now from that triangle. Irving died when I was only 13 years old. She was the person closest to Irving before he died. If I could meet her, it might be like meeting him, even for a brief moment. Like in the movie *Somewhere in Time*, I fantasized about revisiting the past during the time of his affair and my childhood. There were two ways I could time travel: by talking with Irving's wife or staying in the Grand Hotel and trying to hypnotize myself back in time as Collier did in the movie. Neither way held much promise, but talking with her seemed my best option.

I needed to talk with Cap. "Irving's wife lives on the way to Mackinac," I told Cap when we got ready for bed that night. I gave him a moment to think about it. I was like the fast-moving rabbit, and Cap was more like the tortoise, slow and steady. It made for a good team when we worked on projects together.

"I had given up on that opportunity, but here it is again. It may be my last chance. She is 90. Could we drive to her home and let me knock on her door?" I asked, hoping Cap would understand.

Cap had forgotten Irving's wife lived in Michigan. His surprise vacation trip to get me away from everything brought me directly to the most challenging part of my search. "Okay, I will drive you to her door, but whatever happens, we go on to Mackinac and relax. Deal?" Cap replied.

"Deal!" I said, and I gave him a big hug.

We landed in Detroit and rented a car. The first stop was a florist. In case I found Irving's wife at home, I got a large bouquet. We drove to the address. I took a deep breath, got out of the car, and knocked on her door. Moments later, the door opened slowly. It was her.

"Hi, I'm Catherine Lake," I said, giving her the flowers. "I'm traveling to Mackinac Island for a vacation. I discovered I was closely related to Irving through a DNA test. I've found the rest of the family and the cousins. I just wanted to say hello and ask you a few questions."

My heart was racing. The little girl in me was scared.

"Irving is not your father," she said immediately, in a cold, stern voice, pointing her finger at me.

I felt her words pierce my heart as they diminished my self-proclaimed legitimacy. I had never mentioned Irving as my father to her. She had to have recognized my name.

"I know," I said, quickly agreeing with her and glossing over the truth. Her response showed that she knew who I was but didn't want to acknowledge me, so I changed the subject. She wanted me to remain the secret nobody knew, even if it was a little late for that.

I told her how each of the cousins was doing, filling her in on their marriages, children, and professions. "We all went to visit your home in Roslyn," I said, redirecting the conversation and hoping to dissipate her anger. I was hoping she would invite me in, but talking with her on the front steps was as welcoming as she could be.

"You know I made that kitchen lavender. It was lovely," she said, responding more calmly.

"Yes, the house was beautiful," I said.

"I helped Bob produce his musical, and I talked with him just before he passed," she said.

"I met with his wife, and she sends you her good wishes," I said, noticing wife #3 smiling as she looked up toward the ceiling in thought.

"None of the cousins could remember what Irving died from and where he's buried. Could you tell us?" I asked. I felt shaky, hoping my referencing Irving would not get her mad at me again.

"That's because Irving wasn't buried anywhere; he was cremated, and he died of cancer," she informed me.

"Thank you. The cousins will be happy to know what happened," I responded, again fighting off the feeling of not belonging.

"Be sure to send them my greetings," she said. "It's funny. I never answer my door or phone. I just happened to be walking by it when you knocked."

"I'm glad you answered it," I said, wishing her well as I left.

Irving's wife said, closing the door, "Thank you for the flowers; they are lovely. Enjoy Mackinac. It's a beautiful place."

I got back in the car. "Looks like it went well. You both talked for a while," Cap observed.

"Yes, when I introduced myself, she sternly informed me that Irving was not my father before I shared anything. It was clear she would not acknowledge me, so I kept the conversation about the cousins," I said.

"Are you okay?" Cap asked.

I nodded. "Let's go to Mackinac. Maybe I will have more luck with time traveling at the Grand Hotel," I said with a smile.

Cap added, "But only if you come back to me." I reached over and took his hand.

That night, her words kept replaying, "Irving is not your father." For a moment, it felt like I was back to being the me nobody knows. I wanted to feel like "I am enough. Why isn't who I am enough?"

Who am I? What was I looking for? Validation? Identity? Early in life, my difficulties and low self-esteem came from overidentifying with my father. Am I now seeking my identity through my biological father and his family? Was I still trying to find my worth in my relationship with others? My identity had to lie elsewhere. It had to be more profound, stable, and permanent. There had to be a place where I felt I belonged and was connected that wasn't defined by other people.

My husband felt confident and secure in himself. He said it came from his faith in God, not people. I had felt that in the rooms of recovery. I looked at many of those I met there as family. What joined us? Alcoholism? Or was it a common bond from seeking our true spiritual nature and a desire to live surrendered to a Higher Power? From that stance, wasn't it easier to see our relatedness to everyone?

I knew the answers would come, but for now, I needed to continue to shake off the shame I felt from wife #3's denial of Irving being my father.

I rode my bicycle around the 8-mile bicycle path on Mackinac Island, seeing Arch Rock, the picturesque harbor, and Fort Holmes. The aqua-colored water reminded me of the Virgin Islands, but this was an ocean-sized lake in the cold northern states.

The Victorian architecture and historical buildings on Mackinac Island have been preserved so that the restaurants and storefronts resemble those of the 19th century. Life seemed so much simpler then. The background sounds of the horses and their buggies riding through town supported that imaginary passage back in time.

While Cap went to play nine holes of golf, I walked down to the lobby and onto the porch. It was wide, and both sides were lined with white wicker couches, chairs, and side tables dating from the 1920s. Second and third-floor hotel room balconies inside the porch faced a long row of large white columns supporting the 660-foot-long veranda. I sat in a white wicker rocker, looking out past the columns at the front of the hotel to a view of the lush green acreage.

I kept thinking about my father, Irving. What would it be like to sit with him on this porch in this glamorous place? Since so much of his life touched the New York entertainment world through his wife, the Broadway actress, and his son, the Broadway playwright and director, he would feel right at home here. I closed my eyes and rocked gently. It was peaceful and quiet. I envisioned the pictures I had of him from around the time I was born. He always dressed impeccably in a tailored suit and tie. I wished I could travel back in time to meet him. Had he been to this hotel? His wife certainly knew about it and grew up near here. In my mind's eye, I saw him walking down the porch toward me. Then he took a seat in the rocker next to me and smiled. I returned the smile. After a few minutes, I slightly opened my eyes to peek at the rocker beside me. The chair was empty now. But he had been here; I could feel it.

For the next few days, Cap and I played tourist and relaxed for the first time in years. I sensed being on the verge of starting the next chapter of my life. I felt like I had been on a trip back in time for years.

35

DNA and Memoir Writing

I was in the habit of checking my DNA matches to see if I had any new and close relatives. I sensed that my time checking for DNA matches was nearing its end. I met many beautiful people whom I can proudly call my relatives. Still, I once again checked for any DNA matches.

A new cousin named Meredith showed up. She was a memoir writer of 12 nonfiction books (several San Francisco Chronicle best-sellers). Could memoir writing be in our DNA? Even my sister wrote a memoir. Meredith was also a book critic for *The New York Times*, *The Los Angeles Times*, *The Boston Globe*, and *The Chicago Tribune*. Her most recent release was *The New Old Me*. Another title I could relate to. I contacted her with my usual introduction. After she checked me out online and looked at my website, she responded with warmth and humor. "Can cousins date?" she asked.

"Do you mean kissing cousins?" I replied pertly. She was evidently gay, and I was straight, but we had fun with our play on words. We both shared a love of telling stories and a passion for recovery. To find our family connection, we enlisted the help of her mother. As we compared notes, we discovered that we had the same great-grandparents. She shared that her father had been a Pepsi Company vice president, and her mother was a researcher on human rights and racism at the University of California, Berkeley.

On the one hand, I was continually amazed at the accomplishments of the people I was related to, while at the same time, it challenged my insecurities. I kept telling myself, "I was good enough regardless of the environment I was raised in."

I was excited by the title of her last book, *The New Old Me: My Late-Life Reinvention*. It described the metamorphosis I was going through. I told Meredith about my upcoming trip out West with my granddaughter.

"Let's get together for lunch when you come to L.A.," Meredith suggested.

I accepted.

I planned to meet Meredith on the last part of our trip. My granddaughter Kayla was twelve, and I was eager to show her places important to me as a young adult. We flew into Phoenix, Arizona, rented a car, and drove to Sedona. We stayed at Sky Ranch Lodge, which had great *Red Rock* views and was near a sizable Native American medicine wheel. We hiked to it. It was the same one I had hiked to thirty years ago—a large circle with four quadrants outlined in stone.

"What is the purpose of a Medicine Wheel?" Kayla asked.

"It is a symbol of hope and healing. It represents the four elements of the Earth: Air, Water, Earth, and Fire, and it can teach us about the four aspects of ourselves: the physical, mental, emotional, and spiritual. It can also represent the four directions: North, South, East, and West," I explained. "It is a place I visited that reminds me of our connectedness to each other and the World."

Then, we drove over the Hoover Dam to the South Rim of the Grand Canyon and stayed at the Yavapai Lodge. We woke up early and went to the canyon to watch the sunrise. It was so quiet and still as we watched the sun peek over the canyon rim, slowly rising to its full exposure and starting the day. We were startled when a large Elk crossed our path as we walked back down the trail away from the canyon. "That was a good sign," I said, pointing to the Elk.

"What is it a sign of?" Kayla asked.

"Elks can be a symbol of protection and guidance. It can be a message to stay on course and see things through," I explained. "God can use nature to talk to us through signs and symbols. You just have to listen to them when they catch your attention."

We left the Grand Canyon and drove to Las Vegas. I wanted to take my granddaughter to see the Pyramids in Egypt, but couldn't, so we stayed at the Luxor Hotel, which featured an ancient Egyptian theme and resembled a thirty-story-high pyramid.

"Why did you want to stay in the Pyramid Hotel?" Kayla asked.

I told Kayla about my trip to the Great Pyramid when I was 26 years old. I took my phone out and showed her photos of the Great Pyramid of Giza. "The Pyramid is made of more than 2,300,000 limestone and granite blocks, weighing an average of 2.5 tons each. It is still a great mystery how it was built so long ago," I explained. "As you get older, check out the hidden mysteries. Life is full of them."

"Do you mean like when you met with the Professors in Peru who talked with the UFO man?" Kayla asked.

"Yes, exactly!" I answered, impressed with her attentiveness and inquisitive nature.

"Do you think the UFOs had something to do with building the Pyramid?"

"I don't know. Anything is possible, but that is what makes it a mystery, or until we find the answer," I told Kayla. Like me, she was fascinated with the stars, space, science, and mysteries.

Then, we drove through the desert to California. When we arrived at the Pacific Coast Highway in Malibu, I parked the car on the side of the road. "Let's go walk in the Pacific Ocean."

"Now?" Kayla asked.

"No better time than now when the opportunity presents itself!"

We walked down a long flight of wooden stairs to the beach. Kayla and I ran into the water and stopped before we reached the breaking waves. "It's colder than the Atlantic Ocean," Kayla noted.

"Are you sure?" I asked, splashing more cold water on her.

We sat on the beach for a while and then drove to a little hotel in Santa Monica. The following day, we drove to La Jolla to see the seals in their natural habitat. While swimming in the ocean, one of the seals came close to Kayla. It was scary and fun at the same time.

We returned to Santa Monica and drove to Hollywood the following day. We took pictures in front of Grauman's Chinese Theater and walked the Hollywood Walk of Fame. It consists of 2,783 five-pointed terrazzo-and-brass stars embedded in 15 blocks of sidewalk.

Kayla recognized a few actors and actresses from movies and TV shows she had seen.

When I saw Shirley MacLaine's star, we stopped. "I used to work for her," I said.

"Really! Who is she?" Kayla asked.

"She's a famous actress and author," I said.

"How did you get that job?"

"I followed my intuition, moved to Virginia Beach, and got a job working at a psychic institute. Then, one of my new friends I met there was hired to run Shirley's seminar tour and offered me a position working for her," I explained.

DNA AND MEMOIR WRITING

"Wow! I didn't know that," Kayla said, looking down at Shirley's star.

"It's important to listen to those gentle intuitions because they can lead you to miracles you would never have imagined possible," I explained.

"You mean like your DNA test and finding your dad?"

"Exactly!"

We returned to Santa Monica and, the next day, drove to the Hollywood Hills to meet Cousin Meredith. We walked into the coffee shop and spotted her already at a table. We ordered coffee, and a soda, and a blueberry muffin for Kayla. We took a few pictures for the new family photo album.

"I saw that you write memoirs; I do, too," I told Meredith.

"Do you think memoir writing is in our DNA?" she asked.

"My half-sister also was an author and wrote an autobiography," I shared.

"What did your mother think when you told her about me?" I asked, remembering that Meredith had gone to see if her mother could help figure out our connecting relative, making us second cousins.

"Yes, as I wrote to you, we might be related through our great-grandmothers, who were sisters," Meredith said.

"That is what I thought when I traced it back through our grandparents," I said, showing her some of our family lineage charts.

"Wow, you're going back over 1,000 years. I can't even remember what I did a year ago," Meredith joked. We both laughed. She was quick-witted, and there was no shortage of humor in this family line.

"Imagine if all of humanity found out we are genetically linked; peace might take on a new look," Meredith commented.

That was a profound thought.

Kayla and I shared about our recent travels to the Medicine Wheel in Sedona, the Grand Canyon, the Pyramid in Las Vegas, the seals in La Jolla, and the Hollywood Walk of Fame. Meredith included Kayla in our conversation and asked what she liked on our trip.

We discussed many things over coffee. I filled Meredith in on the other cousins I had met. I enjoyed conversing with Meredith and admired her confidence. At the end of our meeting, we got up from the table. I told her I was heading to Beverly Hills to see another cousin.

"What do you have plans to do with them?" she asked as we walked out.

"We are going to visit the Reagan Library in Simi Valley since one of them is on the board," I answered.

Meredith stopped abruptly and turned back to me. "Are you a Republican?" she asked.

"Yes," I answered hesitantly.

She cupped her hand over her mouth, and her eyes opened wide. "I can't believe I am related to a Republican!"

"It's not that bad," I said, not wanting our meeting to get derailed. "Half of our cousins are Democrats, and half are Republicans. Even the twin cousins are divided on politics. We all agree to disagree."

I thanked Meredith for taking the time to meet us, and we gave each other a goodbye hug. The politics within our family of cousins was just a microcosm of the division in politics in our country. Relationships with people I cared about were more critical than having angry political debates. I was glad Meredith and I could keep our focus on getting to know each other.

I sensed the winds of change were coming into my life. I also sensed that my search for new DNA family members was nearing completion. After meeting Irving's third wife, I had gotten some of my most challenging questions answered. I had time-traveled through the memories of the kind and willing family members, my cousins. Meeting Meredith, author of *The New Old Me: My Late-Life Reinvention,* became a sign for me to think about remaking my own life going forward with all I knew.

36

The Cousin's Table

Over the next year, I met Rabbi Rachel for coffee, attended the temple, and took Torah classes. The Rabbi was concerned about the increase in antisemitism and hate crimes. She offered a six-week class on Mussar, a Jewish spiritual practice that gives concrete instruction on how to live a meaningful and ethical life. The practice relates to moral conduct, discipline, and learning appropriate behavior and balance through spiritual work on our character traits. There were similarities between the Rabbi's course and recovery principles. The Rabbi encouraged honest and difficult conversations, worked with people who might not understand one another, and helped them come together.

I took a class led by the Rabbi called *Judaism 101*. She gave us an overview of Jewish history, holidays, calendars, Shabbat, Israel, prayer, and the Jewish life cycle of birth, Bar Mitzvah, confirmation, marriage, divorce, and death. The last class was a closing dinner celebration at her home. She had a gift for affirming people.

When we studied the Torah, the Rabbi emphasized, "The goal is to look at the Torah as an inner guide to becoming a better person. It is essential to develop humility and empathy, which require selflessness."

I made new friends in the classes and at the potluck gatherings. One woman named Edna was very friendly to me at the potlucks.

I was alone, and she always put out food, utensils, and drinks. I offered to help. I could have candid conversations with her and ask questions about Jewish beliefs and traditions. "Who is Jesus to you?" I asked as we sat down to drink some coffee.

"Jesus was born, lived, and died a Jew. I can feel proud of that. For me, God alone is Lord, so the significance of Jesus is to be found in his life, not his death. I see Jesus as one who lived a life of faith in God, but he is not God," Edna replied.

"What does Judaism believe about the Holy Spirit since Christianity regards it as part of the Trinity of God, the Father, Son, and the Holy Ghost?" I asked.

"In Judaism, we think of divine force, God's influence over the whole universe," Edna explained.

"Judaism and Christianity have a lot in common, and they also have some major differences," I said, grateful to have such an open talk.

"Well, most of the New Testament was written by men like Paul who were born and raised as Jews," Edna said.

"Christians pray to Jesus, who do Jews pray to, and how do they address God in prayer?" I asked.

"The name of God used most in our Hebrew Bible is YHWH, and it is common to pronounce this as Adonai, which means *My Lord*," Edna explained. Our conversation ended when we heard the Rabbi start to make an announcement.

Having learned more about Judaism through the Rabbi's classes, attending the temple, and conversing with Edna, I celebrated some Jewish holidays with new meaning and understanding. As we approached Rosh Hashanah, I learned that it is the anniversary of the day God created Adam and Eve and is therefore celebrated as the head of the Jewish New Year; thus, our actions now set the tone for the year to come. It is a two-day holiday on the first and second days of the Hebrew month of Tishrei and usually occurs in September.

Rosh Hashanah is also considered a time of judgment as each person passes before God, who decrees their rise or fall, enrichment or impoverishment, and life or death for the coming year. It is a time of asking God for forgiveness for what we have done wrong during the past year and to remind ourselves not to repeat the same mistakes in the year to come.

The first observance is to hear the shofar on the first morning. It symbolizes the trumpet blast at a King's coronation and is considered a call to repentance. On Rosh Hashanah, prayers are read daily, asking the Creator for a year of peace, prosperity, and blessings in the coming new year.

On the first day of Rosh Hashanah, a custom is to go to a body of water and cast your sins into the water. This is known as the Tashlich ceremony, and to say the verse "And you shall cast their sins into the depths of the sea." I thought of my trip to Israel and being baptized in the River Jordan. That was a symbolic way of washing away our sins and beginning anew.

I wrote a list of them on a small rock that I wanted to cast away, as a way to repent to God, so I could go forward with a fresh start. I went to our dock and walked down to the water's edge. The tide was moving swiftly. I threw the rock in the water. "I cast my sins to the depths of the sea," I proclaimed aloud as the rock sank. I exhaled, feeling a little freer, releasing my sin to YHWH. I learned there is a holiday prayer book called *A Machzor*. I spent some time in the temple, and then that evening, I attended the gathering for the holiday feast.

The kiddush was recited over wine, and then a blessing was said over the bread (round challah loaves), which were then dipped in honey to express the wish for a sweet year, with an apple slice dipped in honey, pomegranates, and dates. The desserts included a honey cake that tasted like Baklava (which I was pretty familiar with), Taygalach (Ashkenazi-soaked dough balls), which were also sweetened with honey, and Halvah, which had nuts, tahini, and honey in it. I also learned to say the greeting "Shanah Tovah," which means "Good year." It was a small temple. Some people who attended knew my story and reached out to help me feel comfortable and welcomed. The temple was a place to feel more authentic. I felt accepted for who I was and was no longer hiding out.

On Rosh Hashanah, we acknowledge that we are responsible for our actions. This day starts the ten days of atonement, ending on Yom Kippur, the Holiest Day of the year. During this time, we are encouraged to think of words or deeds that have hurt others, seek forgiveness, and make amends for our wrongdoings. God seals each person's fate for the coming year into the Book of Life on Yom Kippur.

Yom Kippur is a day of reflection, prayer, and fasting, and is a day of complete rest—no driving, work, etc. I observed Yom Kippur's fasting for 25 hours, starting at sundown and continuing until sundown the following day, as a day of atonement. I got an English copy of the *Al Chet*, a confession of sins and prayer. I wanted to connect spiritually with my ancestors by honoring their traditions.

Indie's son and future daughter-in-law were getting married in New Jersey. Their wedding would be a large gathering, and the first one where all the cousins would attend. After arriving in New

THE COUSIN'S TABLE

Jersey, we rented a car, drove to the hotel, unpacked, and settled into our room.

Later in the evening, we met with a few cousins and had dinner at the hotel restaurant. I was so glad and relieved to have my feet on the ground after the turbulent ride on the plane earlier. The restaurant had a cozy, candlelit, calming atmosphere with soft jazz music playing in the background.

Indie and her husband visited us at the table. She shared, "I have created a Cousins' Table at the wedding reception tomorrow."

"That's special," one cousin responded.

"This is the first event I will have a large extended family attend. I want to honor that," Indie said, exuding love and pride.

We all lifted a glass to toast the occasion. "L'chayim!"

The following afternoon, we attended the wedding, which took place in a courtyard. The couple was stunning. Since the bride wasn't Jewish, they chose to have a minister officiate the non-denominational service. They were married under a chuppah, a wedding canopy representing God's presence at the wedding and the new life that they would build together.

After they were pronounced man and wife, the groom kissed the bride and stomped on a glass to break it. This great Jewish tradition symbolically reminds us of the fragile nature of life. It reminds us that, like glass, our relationships must be treated with special care. Glass can be strong enough to hold our love yet fragile enough to break.

It was a beautiful service. We all moved into the ballroom, where we found our seating card for the *Cousins Table* no. 7. It had a dance floor in the center with a band to the side. The tables were tastefully decorated with white place settings, floral arrangements in the center, and candles on either side. At one end of the ballroom was a long rectangular table for the bridal party.

Cap and I took a seat at the Cousins' Table with all the cousins and their spouses. My brother's wife and her guest were there. Even though they were hosting the wedding, Indie and her husband sat at the table with us.

I pulled out the wedding invitation to review the details. A gold sticker of a hummingbird fell out of the card, and a little message accompanied it. This emblem reminded me of the supernatural occurrence with the gift of a hummingbird pin after my Greek father's death, and the healing that had occurred with him. This is what was on the message:

Legends say hummingbirds float free of time, carrying our hopes for love, joy, and celebration. The hummingbird's delicate grace reminds us that life is rich, beauty is everywhere, every personal connection has meaning, and laughter is life's sweetest creation.

I sensed my parents' presence at the wedding, watching over me. Was Mom celebrating me finding out the truth? Did my Greek dad appreciate the kindness this family has extended to me, just as I gave to him? Was Irving pleased to see such a family reunion with his daughter invited to sit at the cousins' table? Was my brother Bob glad to see his widow embracing life surrounded by his family and friends? Were my brother Michael and sister Gail happy to know our family had come together despite the challenges? Secrets were out in the open and healing with love.

As if reading my mind, one of the cousins made a joke, "Can't you see Bucky saying to Irving in Heaven, 'You won't believe this! Take a look at this *chatunah!*'" Everyone at the table laughed. Someone told me it means wedding in Hebrew.

I looked around the table. It was a miracle that I was included in this celebration of love with my biological family.

There was lots of dancing. Then, the band played Hava Nagila, a lively and traditional Jewish song about rejoicing. I knew every word of the song and the dance from my youth and the many bar and bat mitzvahs I attended. This time, I felt the energy of it pulse through me with new meaning. Everyone from our table got up and went to the dance floor.

Then, the Hora, or chair dance, was next. We all got into a circle and clapped as they raised the groom and the bride in a chair while the Hava Nagila played. There was more dancing and clapping. Then, each of the bride and groom's parents was lifted in the chairs, and the music played on. When it was over, we went back to our table. I felt exhilarated and connected to my ancestry, my tribe, and my family.

We had wedding cake and coffee, talked and laughed some more, and the music continued to play. People came and went on the dance floor.

Then, the song "We Are Family" by *Sly and the Family Stone* played. We all looked at each other and, without speaking, got up and danced. I can still hear the words. It felt like a scene in a movie. I couldn't have scripted this any better if I tried. It was the last dance of the evening, a celebration of love filled with joy. Little did I know that it also marked the end of one life cycle for me and the beginning of another.

37

No More Secrets

The morning after the wedding, the cousins met at a local diner for breakfast. We chose a long booth to fit into, and I first slid down the bench seat on one side. I was claustrophobic, and if I felt trapped, I could have a panic attack. After we were seated, I had to share about this tendency in case I suddenly needed to get out.

"Don't worry! You're seated at a table of psychiatrists, psychologists, and therapists! You'll be fine," cousin Indie said reassuringly. We all laughed. Knowing their professional orientation and understanding of my predicament, I remained seated throughout breakfast. The panic dissipated.

Interestingly, I have a lifelong passion for understanding human dynamics and counseling. I applied and tried to attend graduate school for clinical counseling years ago. In my Jewish family, I had an uncle who was a psychiatrist, a cousin who is a psychologist, another cousin who is a clinical forensic Freudian psychiatrist, three cousins who were therapists, and two half-siblings who were therapists. Was that inclination in my DNA? Then, I thought about my passion for writing memoirs. My first book was published when I was thirty, and I have been learning ever since. My cousin was a bestselling memoir writer, and my half-sister was also an author and memoir writer. Was that in my DNA, too? Then, I was also drawn to the entertainment field, working for Shirley MacLaine and others in the public eye. I often thought about TV stories and films, and loved the theatre. Growing up in New York, I often went to plays like some people go to movies. Then, I learned my half-brother was a director and playwright on Broadway. Another DNA match?

I had to wonder if our life orientation got passed on. Did such genetic potentials lie dormant, awaiting our discovery of them? What if our parents helped us find them and draw them out? I had walked through life blindfolded, stumbling around, trying to figure out what my gifts and calling were. When I looked around my childhood environment, nothing affirmed my intuitions, so I doubted my gut feelings and what I knew to be true deep down.

I compared myself to the story about my brother Bob's birth. When I had visited Ruth, my brother's widow, she told me how my father designed his birth announcement like a Broadway show playbill. The cast, synopsis, and three acts were listed with all the details about his birth. Bob grew up, became a playwright/director, and won a Tony Award for best Broadway musical. How prophetic was that? His gifts and their potential were recognized from birth. His stepmother was a Broadway actress, and his father was a lawyer and a proficient jazz pianist.

I couldn't help but wonder what my life would have been like had I grown up knowing my biological family.

After we finished breakfast, we said our goodbyes and returned home from the wedding. I was once again filled with a sense of family and belonging in a new way. I was so grateful for each family member I met and how they answered my questions, filled an empty place, and healed me. I wondered if I could ever convey my gratitude to them. Then, I received a box filled with a few dozen roses sent to me by my cousin. An attached note read:

"Dear Catherine and Cap, you are not the only grateful ones . . . thank you for all you have done for our family!"

I now knew more than ever the importance of finding my family. Finding my biological family gives me a feeling of *being a part of such family celebrations,* and *not being a part of them* at the same time. I am related to this family and share their DNA, so I am a part of them. But I do not share a history of memories or growing up with them, so I am not a part of it. I wish I had been, and I'm grateful I got to be today.

When I learned I was related to these relatives and that I shared a passion for writing, entertainment, and counseling, I decided to override negative childhood messages about being stupid and being a loser. I permitted myself to move forward with my dreams. I started believing in my potential and innate capacity.

I took on and practiced a different mindset. Instead of agreeing with the inner critic my Greek dad helped develop within me, I asked myself, "What can I do to accomplish this?" When frightened and wanting to shrink back, I said, "You can do this! You have what it takes!"

Who am I? I kept asking myself. I had to be more than where I came from or who I fit in with. I had to be more than beliefs and genetics. Where is my passion? What is my calling? What is true for me? What do I want? What is my path? Will I find it? Will I have the courage to express it? Can I be authentic without fear of repercussion for speaking my truth and being myself?

It was time to focus on my life going forward. The persecution from my childhood was long over. I was a different person. I had delved into my past and woven together a new history. I had a new story of who I am with an awareness of my true potential. I could feel my confidence and belief in myself growing. It was time to ask *what Catherine really wanted* and *who she was spiritually.*

I decided to try something I had wanted to do years ago but never persevered; I wanted to attend graduate school for clinical mental health counseling. It was a lot to take on full-time, especially at 60 years old. Could I do it? Would my brain still work well enough to write research papers, create presentations, learn statistics, and pass exams?

I was like an athlete signing up for a race I had to complete. I needed to know that I could do it. Could I push myself past the limits of what I thought I could achieve? I had hoped to return to writing one day, but this was always my second career goal.

How often had I told myself what I learned from my Greek father in his anger, "You don't have what it takes," "You'll never amount to anything!" I needed to prove something to myself and maybe to him. I kept telling myself, "I do have what it takes!" How many positive affirmations would it take to cancel out each negative one? I remember Dr. Phil saying, "We need 1,000 attaboys or attagirls to erase one big-time put down from a parent." In that case, I could not count how many attagirls I would need to erase a lifetime of all the put-downs from my rageful father.

One night, after an emotionally draining and exhausting day, I fell asleep at my desk while searching for colleges. I dreamed of walking down a street and turning the corner to find a large, beautiful lion with a full mane staring back at me. He moved slowly, so I ran back down the street and grabbed Cap. He had a key to an outdoor closet on the side of a nearby house. It was small, and as we closed the door to lock it, it turned into a flimsy shutter door. So, we waited. Outside the doors, I heard people gathering into two groups. Each group began singing to the other. I knew the lion was pleased, calm, and not harming anyone. Then, I turned and saw my mother standing there. She looked beautiful, in her 30s, and her eyes shone with light. "I've got so much to ask you. I know about Irving!"

She replied, "You were quite the little secret!"

I turned to Cap, and he wasn't even looking at us. I turned back to my Mom. I was eager to talk with her. "I like who my father is. It makes me proud!" She smiled. "How did you meet Irving?" I asked.

"A friend had me meet her at a restaurant, and he came," she told me. I was instantly transported to the front of the restaurant on the corner of a busy intersection in Manhattan. Then I was back there standing in front of my mother. I couldn't help but notice the growing light in her eyes and the warmth of her presence that drew me in. "Did Irving know?" I asked.

"Yes," she said.

"What about his wife?"

"Yes," Mom answered.

"Did you tell her?" I asked.

"I didn't have to. She looked at me and knew." Suddenly, I stood on the water's edge, and my mother was in a small rowboat. She looked at me with the bright light still emanating from her eyes. It was dusk, and what appeared to be static electricity was shooting through her body. She began fading in and out like the television cable lost its signal. Then she was gone. I wanted to swim to the boat and bring her back with me. I felt our love for one another in this life that had never been fully expressed. It was an intimate familiarity that I longed to have with her that was never fulfilled.

I woke up feeling disoriented. The dream seemed so real. Was it? My DNA search was complete. I had found the answers and my family. I discovered Irving and learned about my mother's life, secrets, and struggles. Had she been watching, helping, and guiding me through this journey? I remembered the hummingbird at the wedding. Had it been a sign that she was near in spirit? Maybe my search was part of her moving on from here with me to experience more freedom there. Through it, I sensed the healing and completion for my mother and me.

I was now celebrating holidays through both traditions. Passover celebrates the liberation of the Israelites from slavery in Egypt to their ultimate exodus to freedom, while Easter celebrates the resurrection of Jesus (Yeshua in Hebrew) from the dead after He was crucified. Both holidays come in the spring.

Passover is celebrated for eight days. It falls on the 15th day of Nisan, between March 26th and April 25th. Family and friends gather after sundown on the night before to recount the events of the Israelites' journey to freedom using food, wine, prayers, and songs to tell the story. Then, on the first night, the seder meal is held using foods of symbolic significance that honor the liberation, accompanied by prayers, traditional readings, and the retelling of the story of the Israelites in Egypt, read from a book called the *Haggadah*.

Eating unleavened bread during Passover commemorates the Israelites' quick departure from Egypt, as they didn't have time to let their bread rise. Matzah is a cracker-like unleavened bread eaten during Passover. Three pieces are placed on the table along with salt water to represent the tears of the slaves. I remember having matzah at the seder meals at my childhood friend's home. I never knew the significance of the traditions and observances of the holiday.

In the spring, Christians celebrate Easter on the first Sunday after the first full moon following the Spring Equinox, usually between March 22 and April 25. The key events of the resurrection were Jesus being arrested, condemned to death by crucifixion, and then placing his body in a tomb sealed with a large stone. On the third day, some of his followers went to the tomb to find it empty, with the stone rolled away. After several days, Jesus appeared to his followers in various places and times, confirming the promise of eternal life.

Easter is celebrated by attending church services, enjoying festive meals with family and friends, and having an Easter egg hunt. Hiding colorful eggs for the children to find symbolizes the story of the resurrection in which Christ's empty tomb was discovered.

Passover and Easter took on new meaning for me. They were personal now. Hadn't I been liberated from the slavery of my past thinking and beliefs? Could I now resurrect who I am into the fullness of life?

PART THREE

Spiritual Identity

Finding Me

There were two career paths I felt passionate about throughout my adult life: memoir writing and counseling. Memoir writing, reaching out to others through storytelling and experience, was first, and counseling was second. I had never followed through on furthering my education to become a licensed counselor. At sixty, I decided to challenge myself and apply to graduate school. Wherever that endeavor took me, it would also enhance my writing.

So, after discussing it with Cap and receiving his encouragement and support, I announced to my family and friends that I was enrolling in a full-time graduate program for my Master of Arts in Clinical Mental Health Counseling. "You'll be 62 when you graduate. Isn't that an age when most people plan for retirement?" Steve, my brother, asked. His life had gone more traditionally than mine.

"Yes, but I am just getting started," I answered.

"How are you going to pay for tuition? Student loans? Are you trying to 'keep up with the Joneses,' heredity-wise?" Steve asked, showing an older brother's concern.

"No, I am doing this for me. I had wanted to do this when I was younger, but never believed I could. And yes, I am taking out student loans because I'm going to see this through whatever challenges present themselves," I explained.

"Okay, just checking! I believe in you, too, Sis," Steve said encouragingly.

I had always wanted to learn more about mental health, having been personally challenged with depression, PTSD, and addiction. Through my DNA search, I gained more confidence in my own abilities. After discovering that many of my biological family members were not just involved in the treatment of mental health but were full-fledged psychologists and psychiatrists, it inspired me to follow through on this unfulfilled dream. I had tried to go back to school years earlier, but it did not work while I was taking care of my father. Looking back, I could see it was not the right time. I was overwhelmed with caring for two elderly parents. When I applied to my university of choice, I was accepted.

I needed to take an undergraduate statistics course offered at the local college. It was a condensed class offered over two months in the summer. I was grateful that after 18 years of working during our busy tourist season, we had hired employees to replace me. I had to pay for the class upfront, and if I didn't pass, I could not start the counseling program. A lot was riding on my successful completion of the course. In the first quarter, I scored a 90 on the quarterly exam. The next quarter was more difficult; I lost my grasp and understanding of the concepts and formulas being taught. It showed on my midterm exam when I scored a 50, a failing grade. After that test, half the class dropped out. We went from a class of 20 students to 10. After that, I saw the professor. She suggested tutoring. I met with a tutor in the library for a few hours each day. Ahmed was a senior math major receiving tuition credit in exchange for his tutoring services. When I was working with Ahmed, I felt like I understood the formulas, but when I was at home alone, I felt lost in the homework. In the third-quarter exam, I got a 44. That brought my grade average to 57, which was not passing. I couldn't start graduate school unless I passed this statistics class. Doubts and fear infiltrated my mind. I wanted to quit. Feeling distraught, I left the school building that night.

As I was walking to my car in the parking lot, a powerful lightning storm hit. I ran to my car. As I approached it, I punched the remote key but nothing happened. I looked inside the car; it was the make, model, and color, but not mine. Feeling disoriented, stressed out, discouraged, and frightened, I turned to look for my car. I saw another one that looked like mine a few lanes away. I was soaked by now and moving quickly, fearing a lightning strike. This car responded to my remote. But when I ran to it and got in, it was not my car, with men's running shoes in the front seat. I jumped out and hurried back to the building. Standing there, I had to wonder if this was a sign. I mean, I was trying to go to graduate school at 60. What was I trying to prove? Hadn't I missed this opportunity already?

I stayed under the portico and caught my breath. I spotted my car with its identifying sticker when I scanned the parking lot. I gathered my courage and ran to it after the next lightning bolt struck. I called Cap when I was safely inside my car. "Cap, what am I doing, melting down over a statistics course and dodging lightning bolts in a college parking lot at my age?"

"Stay in the middle of the channel," Cap said calmly. It was a seafaring term, which meant that once we set sail on a committed course, if we encountered challenges such as stormy seas, we stayed on track and in the middle of the channel. The term reminded me not to veer off course due to momentary emotional upsets and the fear of running aground.

"Okay, you are right. Thank you. I love you," I said. Cap was one of the steadiest and calmest people I knew, making him a good sea captain and, in this case, a life counselor.

"A plane experiences its greatest intense pressure on take-off, which is where you are in your flight. By the end of the day, this will all be okay," Cap said reassuringly.

I was resigned and told myself I wasn't going to quit statistics. Then, if I could not pass the class, I would take it as a sign and rethink my plan. Recovery had taught me to suit up and show up.

The last quarter of the class went quickly. In my free time, I lived in the library with the tutor. I took the final exam and did not feel good about it. When the final grades came out, I got a B+. The professor applied a slight curve to the grades of the few remaining students who had made every effort to learn this subject.

So, I was going to graduate school against all odds. A few weeks later, I ran into one of the former students from the statistics class who had dropped out early. I told her what happened. She was signed up again to take it. I suggested she do everything she could and stay with it, "Just don't quit. The teacher rewards good effort," I told her.

Succeeding in school was about discovering who I was created to be spiritually. But I wanted more than an identity as a counselor or an author, more than just a career path. I tried to align my life with my Creator to live the life I was meant to live. If I could find that, everything else would fall into place. I had acquired enough self-awareness not to sabotage myself as I pushed past my comfort level, and I had the love and support of family and recovery friends now to push me forward. So, I started graduate school.

I enrolled in a full-time, year-round, fully loaded schedule to graduate in two years. It was difficult, and I had some meltdown moments, but I didn't quit. Fortunately, my husband had devoted a lot of time to work and politics, so he understood the time I had to put into schoolwork for two years. I learned a lot about group counseling, individual counseling, theories, techniques, research, mental disorders, diagnosis, treatment, creating presentations, taking exams, and writing papers. In graduate school, the professors held us to a much higher writing standard, using proper citations, grammar, and content. Improving my writing skills was an unexpected benefit of returning to school.

To graduate, I needed to intern as a therapist at a psychiatric hospital for one year.

My intern hospital served as an emergency room for people who were either off their medication, having suicidal or homicidal ideations, detoxing from alcohol or drugs, or in need of stabilization from a mental disorder or a psychotic episode. During the interview, I shared that I had twenty-eight years in recovery. The director was pleased with my background and experience. Every day, I faced unpredictable and possibly dangerous situations with patients, some of whom became aggressive. At other times, I got to experience the pure joy of seeing patients gain awareness and insights that brought them peace and emotional release.

Each morning, I met with the other therapists and the director to find out my assignments for the day. Most required meeting with new patients for intakes or providing group therapy in either the Adult Psychiatric Unit or the Dual Diagnosis Unit for treating addiction.

Security and safety precautions were high, with all patient units on lockdown. I dealt with numerous threatening situations where patients became aggressive or showed potential for violent behavior. I did intakes for new patients who were experiencing suicidal ideations, homicidal ideations, paranoid delusions, detoxing off drugs, or having a psychotic break. I was taught not to show fear and to keep my voice tone and expressions neutral. My childhood and later caring for my father prepared me for this in some ways, but the most volatile situation came toward the end of my internship.

One day, I was conducting group therapy for the Adult Psychiatric Unit. The assisting nurse had been temporarily called out of the room. Every seat was filled except one. There was an empty chair between me and the door. As I started to go around the circle to check in with the patients, a large young man with the physique of a football player came in and sat next to me. I was taught not to have a patient sitting between me and the door in case of an emergency. I recognized him as the patient who had to be restrained earlier and locked up because of his attempted assault on a staff member.

When I looked at him, the room became silent. The other patients recognized him from this morning's incident.

"Do you know I could f**king kill you right now?" he asked, glaring directly into my eyes with his hand outstretched toward me.

"I bet you could," I said softly with a smile. My survival mechanism had kicked into play. "Excuse me for one second. I forgot to bring my group sign-in sheet," I said nonchalantly. I calmly walked past the patient threatening me and into the hallway. Out of the corner of my eye, I watched this patient just sitting there. I didn't give him the reaction he expected. Once in the hallway, I motioned to two strong-armed male staff members looking for this patient. They removed him from the room without further incident.

I resumed a check-in with my patients. Sheila raised her hand. "I was doing better until he came in. The way he acted scared me. I was afraid he would hit you like my father used to hit my mother. I wanted to run out of here," she shared.

"How do you feel now?" I asked.

"A little shaky but better," Sheila said, looking around the room. A few other patients nodded in agreement, showing they felt the same way as Sheila.

"What helped you?" I asked her.

"I took a few deep breaths. I told myself I would be okay, and you would get help," Sheila said.

I added, "The key to resolving such situations is not to overreact." Everyone nodded; lesson learned.

We spent the rest of the group's time talking about how past trauma can be reexperienced in the present time when something occurs that brings the past forward into our lives. We also looked at relaxation techniques and grounding exercises to regulate our triggered emotions, such as deep breathing, meditation, and practicing mindfulness (the 5-4-3-2-1 method) by naming five things you hear, four things you see, three things you can touch, two things you can smell, and one thing you can taste. We also discussed the importance of expressing your feelings as they surface and developing a support network after your stay here.

I completed the group therapy session. When the other patients left, I exhaled. I felt shaky. This patient's threat triggered memories of my past with a violent boyfriend. I had jumped at jarring sounds and sudden movements by other patients.

I hid my past from my coworkers and prayed my way through the times when those memories and feelings were triggered by patients showing aggression. Somehow, I made it through my year interning at the hospital.

39

Going Deeper

I took the college board exam and then a four-hour state board exam. I was 62 and older than the students and professors. It had been decades since I had to use my brain to study for such comprehensive tests with everything on the line. Even after having a 30-year-old (TBI) Traumatic Brain Injury from my car wreck in the mountains, I passed both boards with flying colors. I stayed in the moment, prayed, studied hard, used memory shortcuts, and relied on God's help and oversight.

After two and a half years and facing many challenges, I became a therapist in a counseling center with my own office, complete with a comfortable beige couch, two pale blue chairs, and a desk. The counseling center was tastefully decorated with soft, muted tones of beige and blue, creating a soothing and relaxing atmosphere. Now, I could see if being a therapist is what I was created to be.

I started seeing clients at the counseling center. I was grateful for my time at the hospital since it prepared me well. The clients I was seeing were mostly not in an extreme crisis mode. It was a different kind of crisis, an emergency without the same urgency. Instead of direct attention to mental disorders, there was more focus on addressing emotional, social, and spiritual issues. A patient's average stay at the hospital was three days to a week. Then, they were referred to the next phase of treatment with another provider, which could be inpatient or outpatient care. The clients I was now seeing were longer-term, allowing more time to discover and explore their thoughts, feelings, circumstances, and life choices.

At first, it felt natural since I had spent a few decades in recovery and sponsoring other women. I had spent years learning that I didn't need to have answers for people, only to help them find their own. It was an art and a science, asking the right questions, which could direct the client to new thoughts and perceptions that could lead to their growing awareness and healing. Having a safe place to explore and reconsider our thoughts and feelings was essential to therapy. An effective therapist can serve as a reflective tool for the client. Still, the therapist needed to be nonjudgmental and neutral.

As counselors, this meant we needed to clear out our stuff and be able to identify transference or countertransference. Transference is when clients project their feelings about someone else onto the therapist and then see them through that lens. Countertransference is when the therapist's feelings about someone or something are projected onto the client, and they consider the client through that lens.

As a new therapist, I had seen clients with addiction issues, mood disorders, depression, inner child issues, and various fears and anxieties. Then, something unusual happened. Almost every new client who came to me was dealing with infidelity. As they shared the details of discovering their mate's infidelity, I felt growing tension throughout my body and caught myself holding my breath. I was careful not to show the effects of hearing their experiences on me. I knew there were traumas in my own life I had chosen not to process, and I hoped I could just pretend the consequences away. I did not want to share these feelings with my supervisor. I had processed so much of my past that I tried to convince myself I could remain neutral for my clients.

Countertransference loomed heavy in the air for me as I continued to counsel clients who had suffered the pain of infidelity. I fought feelings that I was an impostor in the therapist's chair. The more I heard about the actual heartbreak these clients experienced, the more inadequate I felt to help them. I continued to bury my feelings and push through these sessions.

Then, on my birthday, I booked a new client who took being triggered by stories of infidelity dilemma to a new level. The last scheduled appointment I had was a two-hour intensive session. The client, Susan, had driven a long distance because she wanted to speak with a therapist who did not know her. She lived in a small town where everyone knew everyone.

Susan was an attractive married woman in her early fifties. She was a dance instructor and the director of her dance school for young girls. She had two grown stepchildren, whom she helped raise. Her husband was a young widower when they met. Susan had never wanted her own children, but took on the role of stepmother when she fell in love with her husband. She was supportive of her husband as he climbed the ladder of success. Susan loved reaching out to the young, underprivileged girls in her community by offering several scholarships to her dance studio each year. Susan professed she had a strong faith and belief in God.

From the intake questionnaire, I also saw that Susan reported she was overwhelmed with emotions due to the challenges in her marriage from infidelity.

She came into my office and sat on the couch facing me. She grabbed a bunch of tissues from the tissue box on the coffee table.

I introduced myself, sharing my professional background. "What brings you here today?" I asked.

"I need to tell someone what has happened to me. I don't know what to do. I've been hiding my real feelings for a while," Susan answered.

"This can be a safe place to explore what is on your mind," I said encouragingly.

She took a deep breath and wiped a few tears from her eyes. "My husband, Ed, had an affair. It hurts so much," Susan said, looking down and crying into the tissue.

"I understand how painful it is," I said softly.

"There's more," Susan continued, looking up at me. "A few years ago, Ed and I were both working long hours and barely saw each other. Money was never an issue for us because we both loved our work. He is a well-respected entrepreneur in our small town.

"He started going out a few nights a week and coming home drunk. He is not an alcoholic, but had taken to drinking. During that time, I found out he was having an affair with his secretary. She got pregnant and had his baby, a little girl," Susan said, crying harder.

"Take your time. Breathe," I said, trying to reassure her.

"I was devastated. So, I kicked Ed out of the house," Susan said. Then she explained that Ed had fired his mistress and that she went to work as a waitress. After a year of living in an efficiency apartment, Ed wanted to come home and work on their marriage. Susan agreed and told him that if he gave up all parental rights and had nothing to do with this woman, she would let him move back in.

"How did that work out?" I asked, noticing Susan was not teary-eyed.

"At first it was like a honeymoon. Ed and I had missed each other a lot. Then, one day, Ed told me the little girl's mother contacted him. She asked for help because she needed to go to rehab for her drinking problem. She had no family or resources and asked if Ed and I could take her daughter in while she was getting help, and for future visits. I told Ed an unequivocal no. Do you know what Ed had the nerve to say?" Susan asked. I noticed the tone in her voice had an edge.

"She's my daughter, too. I don't want to turn my back on her. We have so much to offer. That's what Ed said," Susan replied, enraged.

"What did that bring up for you, Susan?" I asked.

"Hate! I love kids, but I hate that little girl! I don't want her ever to set foot in my home. She is still wrecking my marriage and my life," Susan yelled out, shaking her head.

Suddenly, I was no longer a neutral therapist sitting in my chair. Susan became Irving's third wife, and my father rolled into one. Ed was Irving, the mistress was my drinking mother, and the little girl was an abandoned and neglected me. I felt a sword pierce my heart. I struggled and refrained from crying out, "Don't hate her. That little girl didn't do it!"

"Ed owned up to it, admitted everything, and apologized to me and our adult children. I am staying in the marriage for the sake of our family. My husband wants me to help him with this child and to have visitation. Ed told me we can't continue to move forward in our marriage if I keep hating this little girl," Susan explained.

"What do you want in this situation?" I asked Susan directly.

"I'm tired of living with secrets. I want to save my marriage, and I want to stop hating this little girl," Susan admitted, tears flowing down her face.

"Can I tell you a story about a little girl that might help you see this situation differently? One that might change your heart from hate to healing," I asked Susan.

"Yes, please," Susan said.

THE FATHER NOBODY KNOWS

"I was that little girl you won't let into your home," I said, taking a deep breath.

Susan looked confused. I told her about my father and his affair with my mother and what it felt like to be hated by my stepfather, never able to have a relationship with my birth father, and being raised in so much toxicity.

"You can choose how to look at that little girl. You can hate her for the betrayal, trauma, and pain she represents that your husband's poor choices created for you. Or you can see her as an opportunity to stretch the capacity to love an innocent child who, through no fault of her own, has been abandoned by her father and is living with a broken mother. How would you like to see her?" I asked Susan.

"I don't want to hate her. It's exhausting, and it's not me. It's not what God wants from me," Susan said with calm resignation.

"That little girl needs a hero, someone who can affirm that she is worthy by accepting her with love," I added.

"If I could rise up and be that to her, I would feel so much better about myself, and I know my marriage would heal," Susan said with new resolve.

"What was it about your husband that first drew you to fall in love with him?" I asked.

"I loved how caring and loyal he was to his children after being widowed," Susan answered without hesitation.

"We know he has made devastatingly painful mistakes in your marriage, but isn't that quality in him that you first fell in love with the same trait that motivates him to ask you to help him care for this little girl?" I asked Susan carefully.

"It is," Susan answered.

GOING DEEPER

"If you can get past the horrible mistakes and betrayal you have had to live through with Ed, you have a chance to help this innocent little girl," I blurted out.

"If I can't forgive my husband, I don't think we can repair our marriage. He has been doing everything he can to make it right for us. I have been stuck hating her," she explained.

"Do you want to forgive him?" I asked.

"Yes!" she said, and then she started crying. We talked about healing and forgiveness and what that might be like. I suggested she get marital counseling with her husband so they can work through these deep issues of the heart together. Before she left, she hugged me and thanked me for being so honest and vulnerable with her.

When she left, I closed my office door. I saw how my entire life led to that therapy session with Susan, where I could give a voice to that little girl who was set up to experience a lot of pain in her life. I had to ask myself, was the purpose of my whole DNA search to be uniquely positioned in this place and time, where I could have the divinely orchestrated privilege of speaking up for a child who couldn't? Do we get guided on a journey, thinking we know the destination, and then discover we land in a different place for a different purpose than expected? And yet, it is exactly the way it is supposed to be. Had we known where the real journey was taking us, would we have gone?

That day, I took my therapist hat off, knowing I had struggled through the ultimate experience in countertransference. I knew there was still something big I needed to heal. Speaking my truth and being authentic has been a challenge since childhood. I had always feared being myself. I also knew I could not continue to work as a therapist until I addressed a lingering issue, something I had hidden from others. As a therapist, your greatest tool is yourself. The more authentic, healed, and transparent you are mentally, emotionally, and spiritually, the more effective you can work with clients.

Practicing therapy shed a light on something I wanted to keep hidden. Maybe it was time to return to my first passion, writing.

40

The Haunted Cabin

I needed some time away from my life. The best way to process what I had learned about my identity search was to go away and write my story.

I met with my supervisor and then the director of the counseling center. For the first time in years, I shared the truth about myself and my past without shame. I was no longer ignoring my feelings. I shared that I needed to stop practicing therapy and find my own healing. I agreed to leave in a month and transfer my current clients to another on-staff therapist or bring closure to the clients if they chose that.

I decided to take three months to write. I packed my car and rented a cabin on a lake in the mountains.

The cabin was on the edge of the woods with lakefront footage in the backyard, even a dock to put a chair on and have coffee at sunrise or tea at sunset. I felt free for the first time in decades. There was no one to answer to except my notepad and computer. I unloaded the car, put on my bathing suit, and jumped into the lake. It was cold and refreshing. I wanted the cool, fresh water to rinse off the stress and struggles of the past years. I climbed back on the dock and lay on my back, soaking up the late afternoon rays of the sun. A tangible peace washed over my whole body. There are no time schedules, meals to prepare, or anyone to report to. I must have dozed off for a short time. I dried off and went back into the cabin.

I drove to the nearby grocery store and stocked up on food. It had been years since I had been absolutely alone. No children or grandchildren were vying for attention or making demands, and I was no longer caring for two terminally ill parents. With their passing and my adult children all moving away, it was the first time in years I was free from taking care of others.

As sunset approached, I went to the dock with my salad and tea. This was a touch of heaven.

As evening fell, I noticed how dark it was outside and how quiet it was inside the cabin. There was no cable. The initial excitement about my escape from my life turned into apprehension about being alone in the mountains, where I didn't know anyone. I spent the next few hours rearranging the cabin and setting up my writing station. I moved the kitchen table against the wall to be my writing desk, allowing plenty of room for my computer and note-taking.

When I finished unpacking my clothes in the first bedroom, I looked around the second one. I noticed an eerie painting of a young blond-headed girl over the bed, staring at me. Suddenly, I felt cold and uneasy and had chill bumps rising up and down my arms. Feeling spooked, I jolted out of the bedroom and shut the door.

When it was bedtime, I was afraid to turn the lights off, so I left them on. I had this strange sensation that I was not alone, and if I turned the lights off, whatever I sensed might appear. I was wide awake, so I started reading to distract myself from imagining what might lurk in the night! Finally, I must have passed out from exhaustion in the wee hours of the morning.

I awoke to the sun shining on a new day. I decided to blame my uneasiness the night before on fears of the dark I had since childhood, which I associated with my parents' nighttime scrabbles, and where there was no safe place to retreat. It had been a while since I had trouble falling asleep. I did not think of those fears surfacing in my writer's retreat. In the light of day, they seemed so silly, yet so real in the dark of night. I resolved to do better when the sun set.

I made some coffee and sat at my computer for hours while struggling to write a paragraph. I could not concentrate. I felt distracted. This felt like something other than writer's block. Instead, it felt like there was static interference in my thinking process, much like poor radio reception. Finally, I gave up for the day and chose to have some fun kayaking. Maybe I was tired from the lack of sleep.

I found a place to rent a kayak, something I had always wanted to do. I paddled all over the lake, taking in the picturesque views of the mountain. It was so quiet and peaceful. I could hear the water lapping against the boat when I stopped. There was no one around; it was past the tourist season. Later that afternoon, I lay on the dock, enjoying my dinner and tea as the sun set again. Was I ready to write now? I went inside and sat in front of the computer. I was blank. I felt anxious. When I entered the cabin moments ago, I noticed the energy had changed, and I felt unfocused and uneasy again. I then sat down in a big chair in the living room and tried meditating. As hard as I tried, I could not still my mind.

Evening came, and I repeated the same routine. Again, I had the distinct feeling I was being watched. I felt uncomfortable turning out the lights. I felt uneasy, and the chill bumps would appear on my arm when I walked by the second bedroom. I eventually passed out, exhausted from being the watchman on my bedroom's second and third-night shifts.

The following day, I had the same difficulty sitting in front of the computer—no focus. I struggled but could not get my writer's flow going. Finally, after several hours, I turned off the laptop in defeat. I couldn't remember having this problem when I sat down to write in the past.

To take a break, I drove to Bell Mountain Overlook. The top of Bell Mountain is 3,424 feet high and is known for offering a 360-degree view of the surrounding lakes and mountains. I stopped by the sandwich shop on my way. "Have you been to Bell Mountain?" I asked the woman behind the counter.

"Yes, but once was enough. The drive up is rugged and a bit scary," she warned.

I thanked her for the sandwich and hardly noticed what she said.

As I drove up the mountain, I found the road was wide enough to accommodate only one vehicle. There were small areas to pull off in case two cars rode in opposite directions. I drove slowly and, fortunately, did not encounter another car on its descent down the mountain. As I neared the summit, the narrow road became extremely steep. I shifted into low gear slowly and had to resist thinking about the car sliding backward. I gripped the wheel tightly when I saw a pull-off and drove in. I feared heights and was now driving on the steepest incline ever. Instead of worrying about why I couldn't write or how spooky the cabin was, I was trying to figure out how to turn around and get off the mountain.

Like my writing, I was stuck, afraid to go forward, and unable to go backward. I tried to relax and talk myself out of my fear. I heard the views were sensational here and worth the ride to the top. I took another deep breath. I can do this . . .

I pulled back onto the narrow road and focused straight ahead. Stay in the middle of the channel, I told myself. I kept driving until

THE HAUNTED CABIN

only a short distance ahead, and around one more curve, the road opened onto a flat parking area. I had almost given up with so little distance to go. I made it. I walked to the overlook and took in one of the most beautiful mountain views I had ever seen. It was a clear day, and I could see for miles in every direction.

As I drove down the mountain, I felt newfound gratitude for besting my momentary fear and just being alive. Maybe now I can write.

Once again, when I returned to the cabin and sat at my computer with some tea, I felt distracted. By nightfall, I felt an eerie presence invade the cabin.

This routine lasted for days, which then turned into weeks. I tried to do things that would lift my spirit and break the intense foreboding I felt in the cabin. I took long walks around the lake, shopped at the thrift store, went fishing, and even ate a few ice cream cones. But at night, I still wrestled with my fears of the unknown and slept with one eye open. I was tired, unfocused, and concerned with what was happening to me in this cabin. From all outside appearances, it looked lovely and ideal to write in, yet I was anxious and could not accomplish anything.

Then, one night, what I had been afraid of showed itself. It was midnight, and I was sitting on the couch in the living room, trying to read. Suddenly, I felt this dark presence enter the room and hover over me. It was tangible, and I felt it press against me and stay there. I could physically feel it. Paralyzed with fear, I had the initial impulse to get off the couch, run outside, and get far away. My next thought was, what if I ran into a big bear in the dark? Which would be worse, I asked myself. It was too late to call anyone.

This dark presence continued to press into and over me. Was this a spiritual attack? Then, the scripture 2 Timothy 1:7 came to mind, "*I have not given you a spirit of fear but peace, love, and a sound mind.*" I had to fight the fear with faith, or it would win. I had read that there is power in speaking the name of Jesus. So, I began saying, "Jesus, Jesus, Jesus . . ." Within moments, it left.

I wrapped myself in a blanket and stayed on the couch. I stayed awake as long as I could, focusing on positive thoughts and checking for any residual thoughts and feelings of fear. I wanted to avoid having a return visit.

I knew I didn't want to stay there any longer, but what would I do? I had left my job and paid for the place. What would I tell people: that I picked a haunted cabin to write in?

The following day, my daughter called. "Mom, our anniversary is this weekend. Would you consider staying at our house and babysitting while we spend the weekend in your cabin?" I had not told her or anyone about what I was experiencing there. So, without hesitating, I agreed. I welcomed the opportunity to get a good night's sleep in their beautiful new home and see my grandchildren. Besides, I could also find out if she detected anything here since she was sensitive to the spirit, too.

After we made the switch, she called me on the second morning of their stay. "How are you staying in this place by yourself? Aren't you afraid?" she asked.

"There is barely any crime in that town," I answered.

"I'm not referring to humans. Something else is going on in this cabin!" She then explained that she felt cold and had goosebumps when entering the second bedroom. "I couldn't even look at that painting of the girl hanging in there," she continued. "I feel like someone was in the room watching me. This place is haunted!"

My daughter confirmed what I had finally pieced together during my three weeks in the cabin. After my daughter's stay, I returned

THE HAUNTED CABIN

to the cabin and spent the morning packing up my stuff. Once I loaded my car, I searched the cabin for forgotten items. Walking toward the front door to leave, I felt that dark presence surrounding me and pressing toward me again. This time, I was not afraid. "You need to go to the light, in Jesus' name!" I commanded. I felt the darkness withdraw immediately, and peace settled into the room.

As I closed the door behind me, I felt empowered and a little lighter, having released some lifelong fears of the dark and being alone with the unknown. I had accomplished a lot, even though I had not written one word of the book. Instead, I had experienced something far more valuable and freeing for my soul: a truth. When you turn the light on darkness, it disappears.

So why couldn't I write? How would I start again? I sensed my life was a preparation for writing this book about finding my identity, truth, and healing. My life had become a tapestry woven of threads, creating love and family out of secrets and betrayal. My story had been unfolding for decades, with a clue, an encounter, and one adventure after another. Yet something was still missing, and maybe that was blocking me from writing. Was there one more missing piece to my story?

I needed to go home, but first, I decided to hike up Prayer Mountain in Moravian Falls. Why there? In 1752, the Moravian missionaries, who practiced a devoted and evangelical Christian way of life, migrated from Georgia to North Carolina, where they purchased a tract of land of almost 100,000 acres, known today as Moravian Falls. The Moravians dedicated themselves to continuous prayer, two people praying every hour, every day, every year for one hundred years. Many believe this opened Heavenly portals in the Moravian Falls area.

Such portals can allow spirit to pass through to the physical plane, much like *Jacob's Ladder* in Genesis 28:10-19, where Jacob saw angels ascending and descending on a ladder to and from Heaven. People have traveled from around the world to visit Prayer Mountain, located in the Brushy Mountain Range near the Blueridge Mountains. It is considered the second most active portal in the world, after the Mount of Olives in Jerusalem.

Numerous visitors have cited different accounts of their supernatural experiences, such as seeing unusual lights and orbs glowing at night, hearing celestial music, having angelic encounters, healings, insights, and revelations, and experiencing the peace and serenity of the land. After my stay in the haunted cabin, it would be an excellent place to clear my head and seek direction. If I were to have a Heavenly encounter, it would be there.

41

Entertaining Angels Unaware

It was a four-hour drive from Hiawassee, Georgia, to Prayer Mountain, North Carolina. The route took me through the Smoky Mountains, Pisgah National Forest, and the Blue Ridge Mountains. There were beautiful sights and outlooks, and I stopped at a few pull-offs to take in the picturesque views of the valleys nestled between these mountains. I arrived and followed the red dirt trail up the mountain. It was quiet and peaceful. I had not seen anyone along the way. Close to the top was a wooden prayer deck that some people had constructed. It was a spot known to attract spiritual seekers. There were a few black plastic chairs left there for visitors. I picked out a chair and faced it toward the valley. I put down my backpack and took out my water bottle. I was a little winded since the highest elevation above sea level on St. Simons Island is ten feet.

I drank some water, and then I sat quietly and prayed. I had visited Prayer Mountain before with expectations, but nothing unusual had happened then. This time, I was just grateful to be in such a holy place. I focused my meditation on the peace and beauty of the mountains. I kept trying to empty my mind of thoughts, but flashes of memory kept surfacing. I decided to let them flow through.

During my spiritual search, I studied different religions and philosophies. I learned about the supernatural, visited churches and temples, traveled to Stonehenge in England, the Great Pyramid in Egypt, the energy vortexes in Sedona, Arizona, and the Wailing Wall in Jerusalem. I was even baptized in the Jordan River in Israel. I hiked the Andes Mountains in Peru, explored the Mayan site of Chichen Itza in Yucatan, Mexico, and climbed the Temple of Kukulcan there. I even visited the Third Mesa to meet the Hopi elders. I remember waiting outside the kiva for them. But they were too sleepy to talk when they finally emerged after smoking a peace pipe in the kiva.

I had studied mystical Eastern Philosophies. I worked with New Age Spiritual teachers, ranging from Shirley MacLaine to those at Edgar Cayce Foundation, from Bob Monroe to Christian leaders like Joyce Meyer, Reinhard Bunnke, and Rick Joyner, and I had meetings with Rabbi Rachel and attended Torah classes.

I've lived in the Eastern, Western, Northern, and Southern regions of our country, in the cities, suburbs, mountains, and the desert. I've held an array of jobs, from cleaning houses for a living to working for legendary spiritual teachers.

My search for God led me worldwide, traveling to holy places, sacred spots, and ancient ruins. People from all walks of life crossed my path at divinely orchestrated moments. Each added to a greater understanding of my life and the unknown, yet there was still a missing piece. Why else would I sit alone on Prayer Mountain all day, still searching for answers? I let go of wanting God to talk with me, but I still wanted to hear from Him.

Two hours passed in meditation when I heard footsteps approaching on the trail. I turned and saw a young woman with long dark hair walking toward me. She smiled. I noticed she was barefoot and wearing a white, sleeveless, scoop-neck linen dress, even though the temperature was fairly cool.

"Would you like some company?" she asked, stopping at the trailhead.

"Sure," I said, pointing to an empty chair on the deck. "Aren't you cold?"

"No, it feels perfectly fine," she said.

I introduced myself. She looked at me and smiled. "What is your name?" I asked, feeling a little awkward. She looked like she was studying me, but she was still smiling.

"Eliana," she said. There was something different about her, but I couldn't pinpoint it. She seemed genuinely joyful.

"Where are you from?" I asked.

"The North," Eliana answered, tilting her head and smiling again. "What brings you here?"

"It's the last stop of a long journey I have been on," I resignedly said. "I was hoping to hear from God. I mean, it is Prayer Mountain, but I'm not expecting it." It was strange how comfortable I felt sharing this notion with her. Maybe it was because I didn't know her and figured I would never see her again.

"Have you gone to the Secret Place?" Eliana asked.

"What secret place?" I responded curiously.

"The place where you can spend time with God," she explained.

"Well, I thought that was here."

"Yes, this is a sacred place, but it is not the *Secret Place*," Eliana added.

I had to wonder about that distinction. "Have you been there, Eliana?" I asked, even more curious about this Secret Place.

"Yes, I go there often," she said.

"I guess it isn't far from where you live *in the North*," I said, thinking this was about geography. She smiled a bit mysteriously. "I'm from New York City, which is in the North. Is it near there?"

"No, the Secret Place is found where *you* live."

"How do you know where I live?" I asked, feeling she was talking in riddles.

She pointed at my heart. "That's where the Secret Place is," Eliana said excitedly. "It's within you. It will help your writing to go there."

"How did you know I am a writer?"

"I listen, and He told me," Eliana answered, smiling as she looked up at the sky.

Now I understood. She was talking about God. "Why won't He talk to me?" I asked, finally getting the drift of this conversation, but still feeling frustrated.

"He does," she said, smiling again.

"I don't feel like I'm hearing Him like you do."

"He talks to you all the time through people, circumstances, nature, dreams, intuitions, thoughts, and whispers," Eliana said, speaking with depth and light-heartedness at the same time.

"Why won't He just talk to me like the conversation we're having right now? He has appeared and talked to people in the Bible, you know! Why can't He grant me one visitation?" I asked, unsure of why I was confiding my heartache to a stranger.

"Wouldn't that take the fun and the mystery out of the journey?" Eliana asked. I felt a strange familiarity with her as if we had conversed before. She seemed eccentric, yet her joyfulness was mesmerizing and made me feel comfortable.

"I'm trying to figure out what's next. I had writer's block in a haunted cabin," I admitted. "Whatever is next, I hope I can do it. I am 0 for 2 with therapy and writing right now," I said dispiritedly.

Eliana looked out over the valley we were facing. The foliage was full, but you could see the leaves in the trees beginning to change color along the upper ridge of the mountains. She looked to be deep in thought. Eliana nodded slightly as though she were listening to someone talking with her and agreeing with them. I was having a hard time getting a read on her.

"There is something you were told that started in your mother's womb. It's not true. You are wonderfully and perfectly made. God knows you, created you, and has preserved you. Let go and pull the past out of your heart," Eliana said rather authoritatively.

I nodded my head. "Wow! You're right. It did start in the womb. I was not wanted. I've spent the last few years investigating and living in my parents and everyone's past." I said, amazed at her insight.

"Maybe you need to stop letting the past haunt you," Eliana said, referring to the haunted cabin. "If you had a physical encounter today, what would you ask of Him?" Eliana asked.

"I would ask Him to tell me what I was created to be. I don't seem to fit anywhere," I answered.

"Go to the Secret Place. Spend time there, and you will find Him. As you draw closer to Him, you will let go of the fears that have stuck with you. Keep going straight down the *center of the channel*, and you will step into your destiny. You have a story to tell, but you need to spend time with your Heavenly Father first. What you need will come as you go," Eliana explained.

"How do you know that?" I asked, thinking she was rather presumptuous, yet I wanted to believe her. She knew nothing about my struggles, my past, or my questions about the future. Yet she even referred to the maritime term that Cap and I use regularly.

"It's how He works. Have faith. He doesn't need to converse in words for you to know Him. You already do," Eliana said as she stood up, smiling at me. "I have to go, but it was sweet talking to you, Catherine."

I was too shocked to halt her retreat. I thanked her and watched her walk down the trail until the trail veered off to the right, and Eliana was no longer in view. I was stunned at the depth of our conversation and the clarity of resolution I felt from her prophetic words and supernatural insight into my life. I needed to thank her again, so I ran down the trail, leaving my backpack behind. She couldn't have gotten too far on the rough ground barefoot.

My attempt to chase down Eliana was futile. I looked down the trail, and she was nowhere to be found. Did Eliana just disappear? Had she been an Angel? Was Eliana a messenger of God? Or was she just a regular person with spiritual insight and a little leftover hippie in her? But I had to wonder if she had traveled through the Heavenly portal that Prayer Mountain is known for to visit me.

In my thoughts, I heard: *We entertain angels unaware.*

"Eliana, I don't know who you are, but thank you," I said softly, wondering whether I was alone on that mountaintop. I looked down at the ground and saw a gray rock about the size of my fist. It glistened as the sun's rays hit it through an opening in the tree cover. I picked it up and saw little bits of quartz crystal in it. I kept it and took it home as a reminder of my new direction toward the Secret Place and my encounter with Eliana.

That evening, I got a hotel room in Charlotte, North Carolina. I was still intrigued and curious about Eliana's identity. I considered the signs: Her name was Eliana. I Googled the spiritual meaning of the name Eliana. I gasped. It is of Hebrew origin, meaning *"God has answered."*

How could that be a coincidence? She knew nothing about my struggles, my past, or my questions about the future, and yet she addressed them all. Was Eliana a messenger sent by my spiritual Father, just like I received my biological father's ring when I needed it?

The following day, I drove back to St. Simons Island. Cap and I sat at the dining room table that evening for dinner. We had gotten Chinese takeout since he had been on the water guiding tours all day, and I had been driving home. From our phone conversations, Cap knew about the haunted cabin, but I was eager to tell him about my encounter with Eliana on Prayer Mountain.

"Eliana told me twice she was from the North. What do you think that means?" I asked Cap, as I was still looking for signs.

"Well, there is True North," Cap suggested.

I picked up my phone and Googled the spiritual significance of True North.

"*True north* is associated spiritually with *discovering your authentic self* and is a combination of our purpose and beliefs. It can be an inner compass that guides people through life, giving them an awareness of direction," I said aloud, impressed with the connection between visiting Prayer Mountain and meeting Eliana.

"Sounds like the direction you are going," he observed.

"Doesn't true north point to a star?" I asked Cap.

"The North Star. It's the one star that is fixed and immovable, making it a constant guide for mariners to keep them on their navigational course," Cap explained. He loved to share seafaring terms with me.

I looked up the *North Star*: "In many indigenous cultures, it is considered a symbol of the *Great Spirit*, guiding the people on their journey through life. It reminds us to stay true to ourselves and follow our own path," I shared with Cap.

"Now that you have your *North Star* to follow, you can take more chances. If you lose your way, you've got a sea captain who can help you get back to the *center of the channel*," Cap said encouragingly.

Cap and I were good teammates, helping each other along the way. Cap always told me that if he had to be in a foxhole with someone, he would want it to be me.

I went up to Prayer Mountain, seeking direction on my journey. It made sense to meet a young woman from *the North* who had a supernatural understanding of what I was seeking. I wanted to let go of my fears and find the Secret Place that Eliana had directed me to.

42

The Secret Place

I returned home to explore the Secret Place, wanting a deeper relationship with God. The following day, my friend Rochelle called. I was surprised to hear from her.

"I have had you on my heart a lot. Do you want to meet for coffee?" Rochelle asked.

"Sure. That's good timing. I just got back into town after being gone a month," I said, looking forward to seeing Rochelle.

"Are you still counseling?" she asked.

"No, not right now. Are you?"

"Same, I'll catch you up over coffee," Rochelle said. We decided to meet at a local café.

Rochelle was a counselor I met at the center where I worked last. The first week I started working there was her last week of interning. We met briefly and had a few conversations. We knew each other but not well. Rochelle was newly divorced and a single mom of twin teenage boys. She was in her forties, caring, and sweet-spirited. She was very intuitive. I felt she would be a gifted counselor. She was finishing her degree, so we lost touch when she left the center.

I arrived at the coffee shop first, got my coffee, and sat at a little table in the corner. Rochelle walked in a few minutes later. I waved at her. She returned a bright smile and came over to the table, and we hugged each other. She put her carry bag down and went to the counter for her coffee.

"What's happening for you, my friend?" Rochelle asked after sitting down.

"I just spent the last month in the mountains on a spiritual search. How about you?" I asked, noticing she looked surprised.

"I just returned from spending time in the North Georgia Mountains, too. I visited different churches, met numerous spiritual seekers, and even got baptized in one church," Rochelle said.

"So, what ended your trip?"

"I need to do some personal studying. I've come across something exciting on my mountain travels. I think it is what I have been looking for," Rochelle said excitedly, pulling a book out of her bag.

My jaw dropped. Rochelle handed me a small, light-brown book, *100 Days in the Secret Place*, by Gene Edwards. I told her about Prayer Mountain, Eliana, and being directed to the Secret Place. We were both stunned. Then she pulled a second book out of her bag.

"I just got this one; it looks good, too," Rochelle said as she handed me a black book titled *Secrets of the Secret Place* by Bob Sorge.

"We are living parallel lives," I said, still amazed at the timing and content of our divinely orchestrated meeting.

"I guess that's why you have been in my heart," Rochelle said.

We shared what led us to take a few months off from counseling and head to the mountains. It felt good to tell the whole truth to someone who was understanding, compassionate, and a seeker. As I listened to her story, it was obvious she was also on a healing spiritual journey to know God the Father.

That morning over coffee, we named ourselves *spiritual sisters* since we were looking for and being guided by the same Father. We also agreed to share insights and progress made with each other as we journeyed to the Secret Place.

So, how do we enter the Secret Place? The following scripture suggests we enter by faith. Psalm 119:114, *"You are my hiding place (or secret place) and my shield; I hope in your word."* (NIV) The key is to silence our thoughts and desires. We start with outward silence that leads us to inner silence. It is a practice of continually turning away from distractions and random thoughts and back to focusing on the Creator at the center of my being.

This is what time spent in the Secret Place with God can look like. He knows we are there, and He chooses how to meet us. All we need to do is present ourselves to Him consistently. This modality differed from meditation, where I directed my mind with an intended goal, and from prayer, where I sought an outcome.

In this practice, I was making myself receptive and available to sit with and experience the presence of God. This was how many found true intimacy and awareness of a loving Father who was unseen but a real spiritual presence in our lives.

So, where is the Secret Place? I discovered that the Secret Place was not a physical but a spiritual location, a state of receptivity and peace that God gave/gives in that place of waiting on Him and His presence. It is the place inside us where we meet God. It is a place where we commune with God—a place where we sit in His presence and receive His refuge, safety, and peace. It is a spiritual resting place where we can hear His voice, feel His presence, and be with Him. It is a Holy place of meeting that is within all of us. It is the inward way to center our whole being in the Divine Presence.

What are we promised when we spend time in the Secret Place with Him? Matthew 6:6-7 says:

"But you, when you pray, go into your room, and when you have shut your door, pray to your Father who is in the secret place and your Father who sees in secret will reward you openly." (NIV)

We can find safety in the Secret Place. On Earth, we call 911 for help and protection from danger. Psalm 91:1-2 tells us:

"He who dwells in the secret place of the Most High shall abide under the shadow of the Almighty. I will say of the LORD, "He is my refuge and my fortress; My God, in Him I will trust." (NKJV) Psalm 27:5, *"For in the day of trouble He shall hide me in His pavilion; In the Secret Place of His tabernacle, He shall hide me; He will set me high upon a rock,"* and Psalm 32:7, *"You are my hiding place; you shall preserve me from trouble; You shall surround me with songs of deliverance."* (NKJV)

So, how do we dwell in the Secret Place? In Psalm 91:1, God invites us to dwell in the Secret Place with Him. I felt I had dwelled in the peace of God numerous times but had not done a practice of intentionally seeking it.

Since *to dwell* there means to *live there*, I went to the Secret Place often. Regularly, I would spend moments or minutes throughout the day, as I carried out other tasks, focusing on being in the presence of God.

I became more aware of the difference between my will and God's will. I wanted my will to align with God's. In the past, I had experienced how following personal desires and choices not in alignment with my Higher Power had, at times, led me aground. I had to practice a deeper level of detachment and letting go, which is the way of surrender and acceptance. In recovery, we learn that you will lose what you put before your allegiance to God.

Over 100 days, just like the book title, I spent many early-morning hours seeking God's presence daily. I was learning how to experience real intimacy with God in the Secret Place. The Creator made us, so we are born with the desire for union with Him. The 100 days gave me structure and routine to start, but this was a practice I would continue indefinitely.

Waiting in the Secret Place was how many found true intimacy and awareness of a loving Father who was unseen but a real spiritual presence in our lives. I began the practice of spending time in the Secret Place with Him. The more time I spent in solitude with uninterrupted time with God, the more I would feel that tingling, sweet peace of His presence running in and through me. I was there to learn about Him. It changed from my seeking what God could do for me to what God would like from me.

Initially, I resisted seeing God as my Heavenly Father. The term father had meant pain, rejection, abandonment, and loss. Intellectually, I had learned to relate to Him as a God who loved me, but I wanted to experience His love, the love of a Father, the way other people had experienced their father's love in healthy childhoods.

I was no longer seeking a father who had passed and never knew me. I was seeking an ever-present Father who created me. I practiced and learned to address Him as Father, getting past previous notations of the term. I allowed myself to feel what I had always wanted father to mean in my life—unconditional, eternal love. I wanted to feel protected and safe and in a place where I would be cherished. Sometimes when I spent time in the Secret Place, I imagined I was a little girl sitting on my loving Father's lap. I reframed the lens through which I saw my spiritual Father. I imagined Him there with me; through faith, I received and felt His love and protection.

When Rochelle and I finished our first 100 days in the Secret Place, we met for breakfast at our local coffee shop. We each got a blueberry muffin and a coffee. That's what people living parallel lives do; they order the same thing! We saluted each other with our coffee cups.

"What are your thoughts now on the Secret Place?" Rochelle asked.

"I'm glad it is not a secret anymore," I said as we laughed. "It has given me clarity and insight, and I love the tingling feeling I get when I spend time there."

"The more I go there, the closer I feel to God. They say you find your identity vertically, not horizontally," Rochelle shared.

"It makes sense. This vertical search is bringing me closer to my True Self than I have ever been," I shared. "All I have ever wanted was to feel good enough and to know my Father."

"Same," Rochelle said, nodding in agreement.

I thanked Rochelle for following her intuition and calling me that day. Between Eliana and Rochelle, I found the Secret Place and a pathway home.

43

The Summit

It was time to go live my life as me. It was time to share my story. My two daughters and their husbands kept up with me along the way. Although I have chosen not to share my daughters' stories in this book to honor their privacy and keep the emphasis on my own spiritual journey, they are a vital part of my life, filling it with love, joy, and the beauty of family.

Out of the four grandchildren, two of them were too young to understand. My oldest granddaughter often visited or traveled with me when I discovered or met my biological family. My oldest grandson, Chandler, who was in his twenties, did not know the whole story. We had always been close, but over the last few years, he was busy creating his adult life, working, training at the gym, and dating. Hanging out with Grammy isn't usually a top priority for a young man starting out in life.

I sensed I needed to take him to New York City and show/tell him the truth about our family. God had often spoken to me subtly through thoughts and impressions. Early morning was the most common time of delivery. Then, throughout the day, I would step back and observe the people, conversations, and events that unfolded. When they matched up with the message, I would act on it.

Cap and I spent Thanksgiving with my children and grandchildren at my daughter's home. After dinner, I had a few moments alone with Chandler.

"If you could take a short trip anywhere in this country, where would you want to go?" I asked impulsively.

"New York City," Chandler said without hesitation. "I keep feeling drawn to go there."

Hearing his answer affirmed my intuition that it was time to tell Chandler about his ancestors and heritage. "Do you want to go to New York for a long weekend with me?" I asked.

"Yes!" Chandler answered enthusiastically. He had such a sweet and caring disposition.

So, I didn't imagine *my message.* "Well, let's go soon!" I said, knowing my intuition was on target.

It would be a great opportunity for me to have heart-to-heart talks. I wanted to set the record straight to dispel any secrets in my family and for the succeeding generations. I wanted to show him where his mother's side of the family came from and who his biological grandfather was.

I wanted my grandson to know his grandmother's story and his great-grandparent's name. There had been a cover-up in my family, and I was the secret that created a hole in the pattern of its fabric. Now, I would be the patch that covered it and brought continuity to our family line. By telling him my story, I could dispel some of the shame and stigma I had unknowingly carried throughout my life and in my relationships.

"What would you like to do in New York?" I asked, observing the synchronicity. I thought Chandler might say the Empire State Building, Times Square, Broadway, Central Park, or Fifth Avenue. I knew all these places well, having grown up there.

"The Summit," he answered.

I had yet to learn about The Summit.

"It's a new building, now the tallest skyscraper in Manhattan," Chandler said, responding to my silent pause.

"I'm impressed you have been following the building of skyscrapers in New York."

"It is very futuristic," Chandler passionately said as he pulled it up on his phone. "The top twenty floors are made of glass, and a glass elevator outside the building takes you up to the top, 1200 feet up."

Suddenly, my fear of heights and being closed in flooded my mind. Some things that continued to prevent me from feeling entirely free were part of his desired activity. Since COVID, anxiety and panic attacks have increased for me. I often skipped an elevator ride and climbed the stairs because of claustrophobia. Panic attacks increased when I was in crowded places and couldn't leave quickly. I desperately wanted to say, "No!"

Instead, I heard myself say in my Grammy voice, "Of course, we will go to New York and the Summit!"

Over the next few days, I felt New York calling to me. It was the place of my conception, birth, and youth. When I left, I was my grandson's age.

The following day, Cap and I returned home. That evening, I sat at my computer, just one click away from purchasing the tickets, to face my ultimate fear of climbing The Summit. *Could I wait in the lobby while Chandler went up? Did I want to quit now and show defeat to this next generation? Where was the hope in that? Did I want to be free once and for all? Could I leave a legacy of faith and not fear?* I pushed the button, booking our tickets for the glass skyscraper ride. We would reach The Summit together!

THE FATHER NOBODY KNOWS

Our flight was beautiful and smooth. We stayed in a hotel near Times Square. Over the next few days, we took a marathon ride through the city, exploring 5th Avenue, the Statue of Liberty, Freedom Tower, the 911 Memorial Museum, Wall Street, and Rockefeller Center. We went to a Broadway show and had dinner afterward at Sardi's. I had grown up in the city, so I took so much of it for granted, but seeing the city for the first time through Chandler's eyes was fun.

Over lunch and after visiting the Empire State Building, where my father used to have an office, I told Chandler about discovering my biological father and family. I showed him where his great-grandfather had a law office and where his great-grandparents would rendezvous at Lindy's for lunch. I told him my father and his wife frequented Broadway, my brother won a Tony Award, and my "would have been" stepmother performed there.

On our last morning, we got up early and ate breakfast. We returned to our hotel room, finished packing, and rolled our suitcases to the elevator. Each time the doors opened to go down, the elevator was full.

There were over 50 floors in the hotel, and we were on the 23rd. I usually avoided elevators and only entered one when it was half full. I knew I couldn't get on one of these elevator cars as full as they were. I didn't want my grandson to know I was starting to panic.

I suggested we walk down the stairs with our luggage. Chandler offered to carry it. He was a muscular bodybuilder, so I agreed with relief.

The stairwell was painted gray and had cement steps. After going down a few floors, I began to feel claustrophobic. I needed some air and didn't want a full-blown panic attack. On the 19th floor, we tried to open the exit door, but it was locked. I could feel my panic impulses rise another notch. We tried again on the 18th floor with the same results. Adrenaline pumped through my veins as we descended the stairs to the 17th floor. The exit door opened onto a hallway that matched the stairwell. I breathed a sigh of relief. I had to get out of the stairs.

As we walked down the 17th-floor hall, we tried each exit door, and they were locked. I was on my way to having a full-blown panic attack. I sat down on the cold cement floor. I was in a freeze mode and felt immobilized.

I took a few deep breaths and pulled my phone out. I quickly typed a post on Facebook and asked for prayers. I was used to praying for people who asked on that site, but I was not used to asking. I just needed help now.

After another moment, I got up, and we went back to the stairwell. We continued down to the 4th floor, and the exit door opened onto a carpeted hallway with rooms and a seating area. I sat down and breathed deeply. After a few minutes, the panic attack washed off me. I didn't want my grandson to see my weaknesses, but I couldn't help it.

We retreated to the stairwell and went down the last few stairs to the lobby. I was so relieved.

"Thank you, Chandler," I said, grateful for his strength, calm demeanor, and helping heart. I told him about the panic and anxiety I struggled with most of my life and how I was working to heal it and function better with it.

"It's okay to need help. You don't always have to be so strong," Chandler said, opening up to me. We discussed letting go of your fears and following your dreams and passions.

I realized how much I tried to project confidence and hide my weaknesses. Maybe the PTSD, the panic attacks, and the claustrophobia might not completely go away, but I was learning how to function better and minimize their occurrences. Mostly, I was learning how to ask for help and be kinder to myself. Getting down the stairwell with Chandler's help reminded me that being vulnerable and needing help at any age is okay.

We checked out and had the hotel hold our luggage while we went to the trip's main event. The Summit was only a ten-minute walk from the hotel. We waited in the line that started outside the building and were then escorted inside.

Next, we were taken to the entrance of a dark hallway, which led to the elevators.

"Once the elevator door shuts, there is no getting out until we reach the top floor," the guide said, not knowing those words made me feel trapped and panicky. I felt my heart pounding and worked to contain the fear.

"It's going to be okay, Grammy. We got this," Chandler said reassuringly. Hearing him helped calm me enough to stay put. I could do this for Chandler.

"This elevator ride will be about five minutes," I said.

"That's a long ride. How do you know?" Chandler asked.

"I called the front desk last week," I said, trying to remember to breathe.

"Wow! You must be worried," Chandler said as the hallway lights brightened, and we were guided into the elevator.

It would be a long five minutes up to the 93rd floor. Afterward, I would have to walk out onto the glass ledge outside the building—*the things we do for love*. Then, I remembered Eliana, on Prayer Mountain, telling me I needed to let go of my fear.

The elevator had wall-to-wall mirrors, which felt more open to me. It also had nightclub lights, which I found calming. The doors shut. I felt butterflies in my stomach from the movement of the elevator. I didn't look outside. The lights flickered on and off, and suddenly, we came to a stop. The doors opened.

That's when I discovered the front desk clerk had kidded me about it being a five-minute ride. It only took 45 seconds as the elevator traveled at supersonic speed. It was the nicest, fastest elevator I had ever ridden.

We walked around with its three levels of glass, including the floors and ceiling, offering a panoramic 365-degree view of the Manhattan skyline. It was the most breathtaking view of the skyline I had ever seen. There were numerous immersive experiences of three-dimensional art. Surprisingly, with all the openness, I did not experience any claustrophobia.

Then there was the glass ledge. It was fully enclosed, but even the floor was glass and was on the side of the building. It triggered my fear of heights, but I persevered and walked out with my grandson. I wanted faith, not fear, to be passed on to the next generation. I wanted to pass down a legacy of following your dreams. Recovery taught me to do it while afraid. That is what courage is.

We stood in front of the entrance to the glass ledge for a few minutes, taking in the views.

"Your life is now just beginning," I said, recognizing how much Chandler had going for him.

"And so is yours, Grammy," Chandler reminded me. We were generations apart, yet we stood on the same precipice of change.

We stepped out onto the glass ledge, Chandler first extending his hand so I would feel safe. The photographer captured a special moment between my grandson and me, standing 1100 feet up on a glass floor overlooking the skyscrapers of New York City. It was a life-changing memory for both of us. Chandler realized his dream of going to The Summit, and I released my fears.

"We did it," Chandler said, looking over the city.

"Yes, we did!" I said proudly, giving my grandson a fist bump and a wink.

For forty years, I had wrestled with finding my identity and freedom from fear, always seeking to uncover what I didn't know. All the pieces were coming together. So many hidden things in my life had been revealed, like the glass floors and see-through walls of the top 20 floors of this skyscraper. Mirrors are everywhere, magnifying everything within us. No longer could secrets hide inside me or from others. It would be the place to mark the beginning of my new life of authenticity, integration, and healing. I was finding and reminding myself of the truth:

You are not alone.
You are not lost.
You are not hopeless.
You matter.
You are loved.
You are safe.
There is a way.

Going to The Summit with Chandler was more than just a climb to the top of a building. The term *summit* refers to a mountain peak experience. Going to the summit of The Summit symbolized and marked my inner climb, which required a long hike to overcome the obstacles in my life. Only by going through them did I reach my inner and outer summit.

I felt exhilarated when we left The Summit. Facing and walking through a fear felt like doing a gym class, where you want to quit exercising in the first five minutes, but you stick it out.

To celebrate, we walked through Times Square and went to Junior's to have bagels, cream cheese, and lox before picking up our luggage and going to the airport.

When we got on the plane to go home, I noticed I was much calmer than usual. I looked at my phone and saw over 100 prayers had been sent in response to my earlier Facebook post asking for help. Was I feeling the effects of prayer? Maybe being honest, authentic, and vulnerable with each other is how we let go of fear and find our way home together.

I had my story. I felt complete with my journey to find my Father. I knew who I was. It was time to write, but could I break through my writer's block? Eliana said that as I released my fears and spent time in the Secret Place, I would be given what I needed as I went. So what did I need, or who did I need to break through to write?

Epilogue

Sometimes, what we are called to be is what we are most afraid of becoming. When I returned from New York City with my grandson, I was ready to write my story. It had been two years since I set out to write this memoir. I had sat at my computer day after day and still had yet to write one page. I felt overwhelmed by the complexity of my story and did not know where to begin. I was frustrated but kept returning to the Secret Place to meet and be renewed by my Father.

How did I finally get past my writer's block and write this book? It was through a God-orchestrated minor random act that seemed inconsequential at the time and became a life-changing moment of major significance.

On New Year's Eve, I was scrolling through Facebook. I came across a video of a beachfront walkway in Wailea, Maui, that I had visited years ago. It was beautiful, and I put a "like" on it. John Nelson had posted it. He was an old friend who had helped me start writing thirty-six years earlier and edited my first book, *Linking Up*. We had not spoken in thirty years.

He noticed my response to his Maui video and invited me to catch up with him on a Zoom call on New Year's Day. I remembered how our conversations in the past left me energized and motivated. He had a brilliant mind with an endless flow of new and fresh ideas and perspectives. There was a six-hour difference, so we set our call for 4 p.m. my time and 10 a.m. Maui time.

When the Zoom call started, I noticed he had hardly aged. As we spoke about incidentals, his same inspiring energy came through. He shared that he had edited over 100 books and authored twelve. He specialized in editing Spiritual, Psychological, and culturally based nonfiction, memoirs, and personal journey stories, as well as fiction of all genres. I was impressed. He had been busy!

"Are you still writing?" he asked.

"I have a book I've been trying to write for years," I answered.

"What's the story?" John asked. It was a complicated answer, so I told him it was about finding my biological father through DNA searches. Then he asked me one question after another until he brought the whole story out, including my abusive upbringing by my Greek stepfather.

"This is complex, and I need to help you get this done," John said. "Let me be your editor." Without a moment's hesitation, I agreed. I knew his talents, and I trusted him. He would understand the depth and breadth of this story. So, we signed a contract that day, January 1st.

The following morning, under John's direction, I sat at my computer with an assignment he had given me. It was to outline both timelines: my personal history and then my DNA search for my father. That took me three months. From that material, John outlined a 5-part approach, and I started writing my story. It was the first time in years that I could write again. John was the perfect person to help me overcome my writer's block and my feeling of being overwhelmed with telling my whole story. His encouragement and insights helped me at different junctures, including realizing who my true Father was.

EPILOGUE

From my first day working with John, I continued writing until the book was done. The entire project took nine months, a full-term pregnancy. How does that happen? What are the chances? I thought about Eliana and her directing me to the Secret Place. She said I would find it helpful in my writing endeavor. Did meeting with my Father in the Secret Place for two years cause a Divine alignment that brought John and me to work together? He told me that some writers were looking him up and asking, "Are you the John Nelson my angels told me to find?" I had to laugh at that one.

Parting Thoughts:

The other day, I saw a documentary about a young man who was a sperm donor. He was nice-looking and attracted numerous requests from infertile couples to use his sperm. He apparently donated sperm to sperm banks all over the world. Eventually, the couples discovered that he had lied about how many times he had donated his sperm and did not respect the suggested limits.

During an extensive investigation, it was estimated that he fathered nearly 1000 children, but the number could be higher. He was brought to court to stop his "donations" because of the potential harm they could cause. The concern was that these half-siblings could meet as young adults and not know they were related but be attracted to each other. This is called Genetic Sexual Attraction (GSA) and can result due to genetic similarities. But the union between two close blood relatives can create inbreeding, increasing the frequency of hereditary abnormalities.

Many parents organized a gathering of their families so these children could meet and identify each other. The parents noticed that most of the half-siblings had an instant connection, becoming friends and playing well together upon meeting.

But, since we were all created from the same source, a spiritual Father—the Creator—and were related in this unseen, intangible way, wouldn't we all be spiritual brothers and sisters?

What if awareness of our true spiritual connection was covered or hidden by our environmental identity adopted in childhood? Also, what if our genetically inherited tendencies made us unaware of our spiritual identity? If our adopted thoughts and beliefs stopped us from perceiving this spiritual connection to others, would it mean it did not exist?

I never met Irving, and I hadn't known he was my father for most of my life. That doesn't change the fact that he is my biological father. So, not physically seeing our spiritual Creator doesn't mean He is not there. If we all have the same spiritual Father, we are connected as one race, humanity, through our spiritual DNA.

I've come to believe that genetic and environmental influences play a part in shaping our identity while on Earth, but ultimately, it is our spiritual identity, from whence we originated and will return when our human journey is over, that is eternal and unchanging.

I am no longer the secret nobody knew, and neither is my Father. My life is no longer shrouded with betrayals, lies, and confusion. I am very human, and I am reminded of my shortcomings daily. Still, I choose to see myself as a spiritual being created by a loving Heavenly Father, which connects me spiritually to all life and all people.

For most of my journey and writing career, I tried to find a formula for living. I wanted a happy ending to tie a bow on it and use it to provide hope for others. Instead, I discovered that hope comes from riding the waves together and making it through a bit wiser.

So, what determines our destiny: Is it the adopted beliefs we gather from childhood, or the potential good or bad genetic tendencies inherited in our DNA? I believe it is not these influences that define us; it is what we do with them that shapes us. Ultimately, it's the choices we make, and the most significant choice is to choose Love. Love is the goal in everything I do every day I am here. I fall short a lot, but it doesn't change what I aim for. I leave you with my favorite quote about journeying through life:

> *"Life is amazing. And then it's awful. And then it's amazing again. And in between the amazing and awful it's ordinary and mundane and routine. Breathe in the amazing, hold on through the awful, and relax and exhale during the ordinary. That's just living heartbreaking, soul-healing, amazing, awful, ordinary life. And it's breathtakingly beautiful."*
> —L.R. Knost

I send you love on your quest to discover who you really are! It is a beautiful journey . . .

About the Author

Catherine Fendig holds a master's degree in Clinical Mental Health Counseling and brings both personal and professional insight to the powerful journey told in *The Father Nobody Knows*. Fendig is an award-winning motivational memoir writer and an inspirational conversationalist. She has written five books and had her first book published thirty-five years ago. Catherine has worked as a therapist and a life coach. With 30 years in recovery, she has mentored hundreds of women on alcoholism, addiction, and relationships. Through her writing, Catherine invites readers into a path of emotional recovery, spiritual awakening, and the enduring hope of being truly known and loved. She lives with her family in St. Simons Island, GA.

Catherine Fendig is available for select speaking engagements. To inquire about a possible speaking appearance, please get in touch with catherine@catherinefendig.com or visit www.catherinefendig.com.